LINA BO BARDI

THE THEORY OF ARCHITECTURAL PRACTICE

CATHRINE VEIKOS

Routledge
Taylor & Francis Group

LONDON AND NEW YORK

First edition published 2014
by Routledge
2 Park Square, Milton Park, Abingdon, Oxon OX14 4RN

and by Routledge
711 Third Avenue, New York, NY 10017

Routledge is an imprint of the Taylor & Francis Group, an informa business

© 2014 Cathrine Veikos

Lina Bo Bardi, Contribuição Propedêutica as Ensino da Teoria da
Arquitetura (São Paolo: Impresso na Habitat Editôra Ltda., 1957)
was translated by Cathrine Veikos.

British Library Cataloguing in Publication Data
A catalogue record for this book is available from the British Library

Library of Congress Cataloging in Publication Data
Veikos, Cathrine.
  Lina Bo Bardi: the theory of architectural practice/translated by
  Cathrine Veikos. – First edition.
    pages cm
  Includes bibliographical references and index.
  1. Architecture – Philosophy.   2. Bardi, Lina Bo, 1914–1992 –
  Written works.   I. Bardi, Lina Bo, 1914–1992. Contribuição
  propedeutica ao ensino da teoria da arquitetura. English.   II. Title.
  NA2500.V44 2013
  720.1 – dc23
  2012023432

ISBN: 978-0-415-68912-0 (hbk)
ISBN: 978-0-415-68913-7 (pbk)

Typeset in Garamond 3 and DIN
by Florence Production Ltd, Stoodleigh, Devon, UK

Cover: "Uma cadeira de grumixama e tabôa é mais moral do que um divã de babados" [A chair of
Grumichama [Brazilian cherry wood] and reeds is more moral than a frilly sofa]. A photo of architect
Lina Bo at the drawing board.
    Source: *Diário de São Paulo* [newspaper]. The caption is the title of an article published in *Diário
de São Paulo*, November 13, 1949, and based on an interview with Lina Bo Bardi by Quirino da Silva.
    Courtesy of the Library and Center of Documentation of the Museu de Arte de São Paulo Assis
Chateaubriand-MASP.

To Alexander

CONTENTS

ACKNOWLEDGEMENTS

My foremost thanks are due to the dedicated team at the Institute Lina Bo and P.M. Bardi, whose efforts first introduced me to the work of Lina Bo Bardi, and to Renato Anelli, Anna Carboncini and the other members of the Board of the Institute today, for granting permission to translate this text and to reproduce many images from it. I am grateful for the catalog of the international retrospective, *Lina Bo Bardi*, compiled by Marcelo Ferraz and the beautiful 1986 film, *Lina Bo Bardi*, by Aurélio Michiles and Isa Grinspum Ferraz for bringing the architect and her words together with her work. I benefited greatly from the publications by Olivia Fernandes de Oliveira, which made images of Bo Bardi's drawings from the archive accessible to the public. An excellent essay by Esther da Costa Meyer inspired my research. I appreciate the generosity of the friends and former colleagues of Lina Bo Bardi, who took the time to talk to me, especially Joaquim Guedes, Marcelo Suzuki, Renato Anelli and Paolo Bruna. Thanks are overdue for the many discussions and insights of friends and colleagues who share an interest in Lina Bo Bardi, especially Zeuler Lima, Marina Grinover, Fernando Moreira, Fernando Atique and Gabriella Campagnol. A special thanks to Maria de Fátima de Mello Barreto Campeio, who generously shared her unpublished dissertation with me and scanned valuable material from her records for the Appendices of this book. I am indebted to Annette Fierro, David Leatherbarrow, John Dixon Hunt, Mary McLeod, Rebecca Williamson, K. Michael Hays, Kenneth Frampton, Ruth verde Zein and other readers of the book proposal and early drafts of the Introduction. I was fortunate to have the invaluable assistance of Constance Mood at the Anne and Jerome Fisher Fine Arts Library Image Collection at the University of Pennsylvania. Ivani Di Grazia Costa was extremely helpful and welcoming at the Library and Documentation Center of the Museu de Arte de São Paulo Assis Chateaubriand-MASP, as were the librarians at the Faculdade de Arquitetura e Urbanismo da Universidade de São Paulo. I could not have done the translation without the help of doctoral and graduate students, both at the University of Pennsylvania and elsewhere: Tania Calovi Pereira, Adriana Vasconcelos, Mariana Carlos, Eduardo Duarte and Ana Gisele Ozaki. I appreciate the discussions, editing and research support from Stephen Anderson. I owe special debt to Franca Trubiano for her carefully considered advice, contributions and unwavering encouragement for this project. She and Fulvia Serra helped me through the Italian parts of the text: conversations with Jeanne Scandura and Michelle Fornabai provided enormous support to me at critical moments. I would like to acknowledge the following for providing reproductions of images: The Anne & Jerome Fisher Fine Arts Library, University of Pennsylvania, The Lina Bo and P.M. Bardi Institute, the Lina Bo and P.M. Bardi Collection at the Library and Documentation Center of the Museu de Arte de São Paulo Assis Chateaubriand-MASP, the Environmental Design Library Rare Books Collection, University of California, Berkeley, Avery Library, Columbia University, Les Documents Cinématographiques, Paris, and the Museum of Modern Art, New York. Many thanks to the team at Routledge, Taylor & Francis: Francesca Ford, Laura Williamson, Jennifer Birtill, Judith Oppenheimer and Samantha Freeman. Several institutions supported my work over the last six years, including the California College of the Arts, the Rotch Traveling Studio Scholarship funded by the Boston Society of Architects, the University of Pennsylvania Research Foundation, the Alice Paul Summer Research Fellowship from the University of Pennsylvania Trustees' Council of Penn Women Faculty. I would like to acknowledge the following for providing reproductions of images: Avery Library, Columbia University, The Anne & Jerome Fisher Fine Arts Library, University of Pennsylvania, The Lina Bo and P.M. Bardi Institute, São Paulo, the Library and Documentation Center of the Museu de Arte de São Paulo Assis Chateaubriand, The Saul Steinberg Foundation, The Environmental Design Library Rare Books Collection, University of California, Berkeley, Les Documents Cinématographiques, Paris, and the Museum of Modern Art, New York. the International Archive of Women in Architecture at Virginia Polytechnic Institute and Faculty Research Grants from the University of Pennsylvania. Finally, the warmest thanks to Richard Stuverud, who kept the rhythm throughout, and to my parents, for whom my gratitude is beyond words.

INTRODUCTION

Yet, whoever it is that teaches "theory" cannot fail to be an architect . . .

Theory and practice

To teach is to construct. *Propaedeutic Contribution to the Teaching of the Theory of Architecture* [1] is a theory of architectural practice written by the architect Lina Bo Bardi (b. Rome, 1914, d. São Paulo, 1992) in 1957. It was constructed, as an architect constructs an edifice, and designed accordingly, in anticipation of its reception. Any reader who takes the time to educe its organization and details will be rewarded with a singular introduction to the theory of architecture. Cultivated from Italian, French, English and American sources, Bo Bardi intended it to stimulate students towards the development of a professional conscience. In her view, students of architecture needed to develop a philosophical view of their relationship to society: "This will give Architecture Theory significance for our times, for humanity . . ." and, she wrote, "provide for a stance that is critical and composed, devoid of utopian enthusiasms, but conscious of its own responsibilities." [2] Holding out Geoffrey Scott's *The Architecture of Humanism: A Study in the History of Taste* [3] as a herald of a new type of humanism, Bo Bardi posited the architect as no meek observer of the natural world, but someone who "may construct, within the world as it is, a pattern of the world as he would have it." [4] Bo Bardi's goal is to construct a new theory of Architecture, one which would match the pace of the technological and scientific developments of the post-war period: "maybe 'cold' or 'scientific,' but certainly conscious of its own 'humanity.'" [5] Lina Bo Bardi's proposition attempts to characterize art and history as concrete and vital to the present rather than as abstract and academic. How aesthetic interest, or "delight" can combine with accommodation or "commodity" and the science of structure, or "firmness," suggests Scott, is the practical problem of the architect. "To trace how this union has been achieved, and by what concessions, is the task of the historian." [6] Bo Bardi makes sure there is no mistake about her position. She is not a historian, but an architect, participating in the formulation of a theory of practice. Fundamentally at odds with the pervasive tenets of modern architecture's expression of industrialization and technological progress

1 Lina Bo Bardi, *Propaedeutic Contribution to the Teaching of the Theory of Architecture* (*Propaedeutic Contribution*), translated in this volume. Lina Bo Bardi, *Contribuição Propedêutica ao Ensino da Teoria da Arquitetura* (*Contribuição Propedêutica*), São Paulo: Impresso na Habitat Editôra Ltda., 1957.

2 *Propaedeutic Contribution*, p. 50/*Contribuição Propedêutica*, p. 6.

3 Geoffrey Scott, *The Architecture of Humanism: A Study in the History of Taste*, Garden City, NY, 1954 (first edition 1914).

4 *Propaedeutic Contribution*, p. 52/*Contribuição Propedêutica*, p. 7.

5 *Propaedeutic Contribution*, Preface, p. 50/*Contribuição Propedêutica*, p. 6.

6 Scott, *The Architecture of Humanism*, p. 178.

7 Vincenzo Scamozzi, *L'Idea della Architettura Universale/di Vincenzo Scamozzi*, Venezia, 1615.

8 Julien Guadet, *Eléments et Théorie de l'Architecture, Cours professé à l'École Nationale et Spéciale des Beaux-Arts*, Paris, 1909, 3rd edn, vol. 4.

9 Carlo Lodoli, as recorded by Andrea Memmo, Venetian ambassador at Rome, *Elementi dell'architettura Lodoliana o sia l'arte del fabbricare con solidità scientifica e con eleganza non capricciosa. Libri due. Vol. primo*, Roma, 1786.

10 Teofilo Gallaccini, pubblicato *Trattato di Teofilo Gallaccini sopra gli errori degli Architetti ora per prima volta*, la Venezia, 1767.

exclusively, Bo Bardi was nonetheless a modernist. Her "treatise" follows treatises she respects from her own architectural formation, *L'idea dell'Architettura universale di Vincenzo Scamozzi*, [7] *Eléments et Théorie de l'Architecture, Cours professé à l'École Nationale et Spéciale des Beaux-Arts*, [8] and the less obvious *Elementi dell'architettura Lodoliana o sia l'arte del fabbricare con solidità scientifica e con eleganza non capricciosa* [9] and *Trattato di Teofilo Gallaccini sopra gli errori degli Architetti*. [10] *Propaedeutic Contribution* offers several attempts at a definition of architecture, both in relation to other subjects and disciplines and through some examples of good practice. Somewhat surprisingly, in this category American work dominates, in particular, the trajectory of Louis Sullivan and Frank Lloyd Wright. Bo Bardi also presents the American work of Walter Gropius, Richard Neutra, Mies van der Rohe and Skidmore, Owings and Merrill as exemplary.

Lina Bo Bardi built her career over a span of fifty years, in Italy and Brazil. In both countries, she has long been considered amongst the most important modern architects of the twentieth century. She designed buildings, graphics, gardens, exhibitions, sets and costumes for theater, furniture and jewelry. Her modern chairs, counter-weighted glass shelving, transparent, double-sided display systems for art, and lighting and shading solutions for interiors constituted a new field of modern industrial design in Brazil. Several of her chair designs are still in production today. Her two major buildings in São Paulo, the iconic Museum of Art of São Paulo (MASP), completed in 1968 (Figure 1.1), and the bold Social Service for Commerce Building—Pompéia, São Paulo (1977–86) (Figure 1.2) have

FIGURE 1.1
Museum of Art of São Paulo (MASP) (1957–1968).

© Institute Lina Bo and P.M. Bardi, photo by Hans Günter Fleig/Instituto Moreira Salles Collection, 1969.

FIGURE 1.2
Social Service for Commerce Building—Pompéia, São Paulo (1977–86).
Photo by Aaron Ryba, 2006.

gained recognition in recent years and her Brazilian reputation is beginning to be acknowledged internationally. Bo Bardi followed opportunities into many areas of design, often creating her own commissions. Her first built work, a residence for herself and her husband, Pietro Maria Bardi [11] (P.M. Bardi), gained wide acclaim and appeared internationally in architectural periodicals, including *Domus: nella casa e nell'arredamento* (*Domus*), *Architecture d'Aujourd'hui*, *Contract Interiors* and *Architect and Building News* through 1953–54. [12] P.M. Bardi was a powerful cultural force for modernism in Italy under Mussolini and he found fertile ground in Brazil to continue his work as an art critic and connoisseur. [13] The ambition of the self-made Brazilian newspaper man Assis Chateaubriand [14] (Chatô) to have a major art gallery in São Paulo made it all possible. In 1947 he named P.M. Bardi the director of this first gallery, and Lina Bo Bardi its architect. The Bardis moved from Rio de Janeiro to São Paulo in June, and within the year installed the São Paulo Museum of Art on the second floor of Chatô's new headquarters, the *Diários Associados* building

11 The Institute Lina Bo and P.M. Bardi (ILBPMB), which houses the archive of Lina Bo Bardi, documents the marriage of Pietro Maria Bardi (b. La Spezia, Italy 1900, d. São Paulo, 1999) and Lina Bo in a photo dated August 1946. The photo shows them standing together outside a church in Genoa. One month later, on September 24, 1946, they boarded the ship *Almirante Jaceguay* and traveled from Naples to Rio de Janeiro, Brazil. Several sketches and watercolors by Lina Bo Bardi document the voyage. They arrived on October 17, 1946.

12 Publications of the residence, nicknamed the "Glass House" include: *Casa e Jardim*, no. 1 (1953): 8; *Habitat*, no. 10, São Paulo (January–March 1953): 31; Gio Ponti, "La 'Casa de Vidro,'" *Domus*, no. 279, Milan (February 1953): 19–30; "Built in Brazil: a light glass casa in the air," *Contract Interiors* 112, no. 10, New York (May 1953): 74–83; *Architect and Building News*, no. 17, London (April 1953): 488–494; Guiseppina Pirro, ed. Renee Diamant-Berger, "Habitations," *Architecture d'Aujourd'hui* 24, no. 49, Paris (October 1953); "Habitation Près de São Paulo," *La Maison: Revue Mensuelle d'Architecture de Décoration et d'Art Ménager*, no. 4, Editions Art et Technique, Brussels (April 1954): n.p.

13 Francesco Tentori, *Pietro Maria Bardi: primo attore del razionalismo*, Torino: Testo & Immagine, 2002. Tentori's biography is based on a series of interviews with P.M. Bardi beginning in 1986; David Rifkind, "*Quadrante* and the Politicization of Architectural Discourse in Fascist Italy" (PhD. Diss, Columbia University, 2007) is an excellent and informative study of the magazine, *Quadrante* (co-founded by Bardi and playwright, Massimo Bontempelli in 1933) and P.M. Bardi's role as its editor and promoter of modern Architecture as the expression of the Fascist state.

14 Francisco de Assis Chateaubriand Bandeira de Melo (1892–1968), known as Assis Chateaubriand or "Chatô," wielded considerable political power in Brazil because he controlled a far-reaching media empire through his company, Diários Associados, including the major newspaper, *O Jornal*. Fernando Morais, *Chatô. O Rei do Brasil*, São Paulo: Companhia das Letras, 1994.

15 *Habitat*, no. 1, São Paulo
(October–December 1950):
17–51.

16 *Habitat*, no. 1, São Paulo
(October–December 1950): 21.

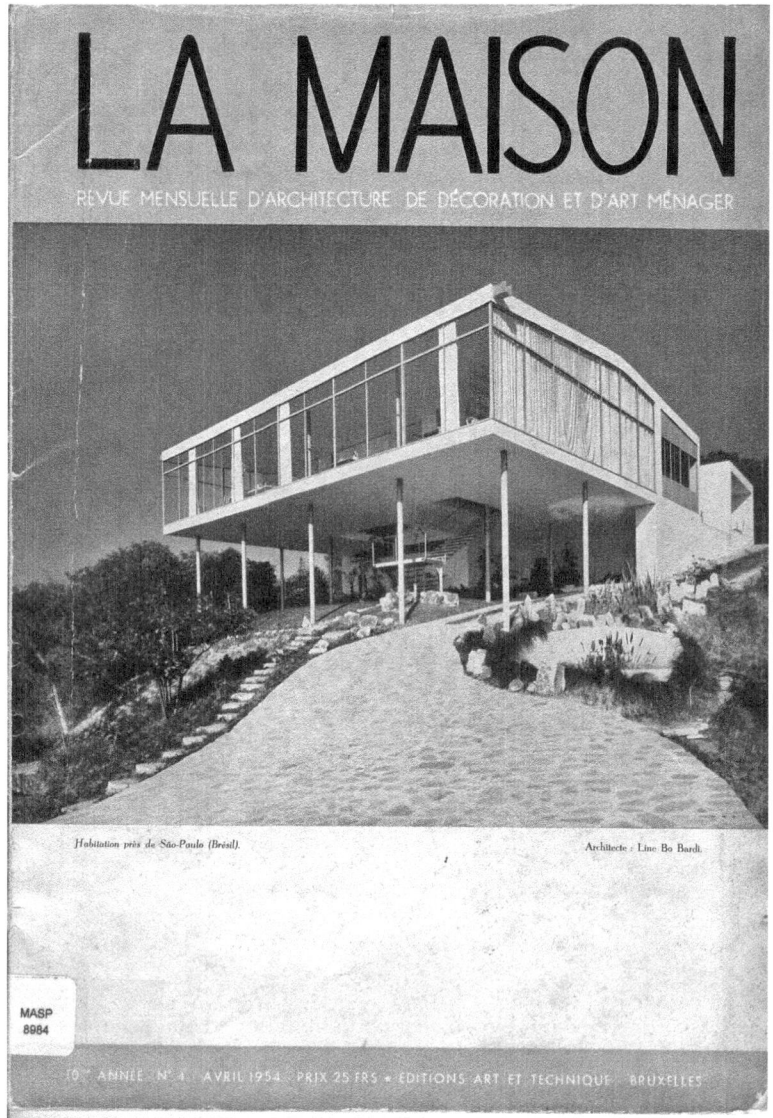

FIGURE 1.3
House for Mr. and Mrs. Bardi, "Glass House" (1949–51).
"Habitation Près de São Paulo," *La Maison: Revue Mensuelle d'Architecture de Décoration et d'Art Ménager, Editions Art et Technique,* Brussels, n. 4 (April 1954) : n.p.

at rua 7 de Abril in São Paulo. By 1950, the museum had expanded to include the quickly growing collection of ancient and modern art and the progressive pedagogical program of the museum. Bo Bardi designed the interiors, including several auditoria, classrooms, a library and a Picture Gallery for temporary exhibitions. [15] She designed the so-called "Casa de Vidro" [Glass House] (Figure 1.3) soon after. Originally, it was to be one of several planned "studios in Morumbi," [16] (conceived in the same

17 Henrique E. Mindlin, *Modern Architecture in Brazil*, London: Architectural Press, 1956, pp. 42 and 182.

FIGURE 1.4
Cover image of Museum at São Vicente (1951, unbuilt).
Lina Bo Bardi, *Habitat*, no. 8 (July–September 1952).

spirit as the Bauhaus' *Meisterhauser*), a school annex for the museum in the Morumbi area of São Paulo. Brazilian architect and author Henrique E. Mindlin included the interior architecture for the São Paulo Museum of Art (1947) and the 1951 "House for Mr. and Mrs. Bardi" in his influential book *Modern Architecture in Brazil*, where it was presented alongside the work of Oscar Niemeyer, Lucia Costa, Gregori Warchavchik, J. Vilanova Artigas and Rino Levi, among others. [17] An unbuilt work, "Museum by the Sea" (Figure 1.4), was part of the exhibition of Contemporary Brazilian Architecture at the Building Centre in London and appeared in *The Architectural Review*'s "Brazilian Preview" with Affonso

18 "Brazilian Preview," *The Architectural Review* 114, no. 679 (July 1953): 11–17.

19 The first project for the Museum of Art of São Paulo was featured in the following publications: "Architetti e Critici d'Arte Italiani in Brasile: Un Museo Dell 'Architetto Lina Bo," *Metron* 30 (December 1948): 34–35; "Museum of Art, Sao Paulo, Brazil," *Architectural Review* 112, no. 669 (September 1952): 160–163; "Introduzione al Museo de Arte de San Paolo," *Domus*, no. 284, Milan, Italy (July 1953); "Brazilian Preview," *Architectural Review* 114, no. 679 (July 1953): 10–15; P. M. Bardi, "Zeitgenössische Kunst in Brasilien," *Werk* 40 (February 1953): 261–268. After its completion in 1968, the new building was also published widely: "Museu de Arte di Sao Paolo del Brasile," *L'Architettura* no. 210, Roma (April 1973); "Museo De Arte De São Paulo," *A + U: Architecture and Urbanism*, no. 6 (1975): 51–66 ; and figured prominently in all commemorations of Bo Bardi's work after her death in 1992: "Musée en Péril: Un Espace Trop Libre (MASP, Musée d'Art De São Paulo De Lina Bo Bardi)," *Architecture d'Aujourd'hui*, no. 320 (January 1999): 134–139; Lina Bo Bardi, [1914–1992] "São Paulo Art Museum: São Paulo, Brazil 1957–1968," *A + U: Architecture and Urbanism* (February 1999): 18–33.

20 "Free Tilting Cuddle-Bowl," *Contract Interiors* 113 (November 1953): 98–99; "Bardi's Bowl," *Domus*, no. 282 (May 1953): 4–7. Letter referring to the failed patent application found in the folder, "American Correspondence," ILBPMB.

FIGURE 1.5
"Free Tilting Cuddle-Bowl," *Contract Interiors* 113 (November 1953): 98–99.

Eduardo Reidy's School in Paraguay, Niemeyer's sinuous Flats at Rio de Janeiro and Petropolis and the enormous serpentine block, Hotel at São Paulo. [18] Both the museum and the house were featured in the Italian architectural magazines *Domus* and *L'Architettura* as well. [19] "Bardi's Bowl" (Figure 1.5), a chair design for which Bo Bardi unsuccessfully sought an American patent, appeared in *Domus* and on the cover of *Interiors*. [20]

Beginning in the late 1950s and in the period which coincided roughly with the years of the right-wing military dictatorship of the country (1964–79), Bo Bardi did major architectural projects elsewhere in Brazil, which are less known, but equally significant. They include the House of Chame-Chame, (1958, destroyed, c.1984), the Solar do Unhão (Figure 1.6), the Bahia Museum of Modern Art and the Museum of Popular Art (1959–63) in Salvador de Bahia, and the powerful yet modest brick and concrete church, Espirito Santo do Cerrado, in Uberlandia, Minas Gerais (1976–82). When the historic district of Salvador was registered through UNESCO as a World Heritage Site in 1986, Bo Bardi was invited back to the Brazilian northeast. Her master plan for Salvador de Bahia shows infra-structural and building interventions that strengthen the definition of public spaces and programs throughout the district. In collaboration with the young architects André Vainer, Marcelo Carvalho Ferraz and Marcelo Suzuki, Bo Bardi designed nine renovation projects in the historic center of Salvador between 1986 and 1990 (Figure 1.7). Unfortunately, just five were realized. Between 1990 and the time of her death in 1992, Bo Bardi presented a bold competition design for the Brazilian Pavilion at the Universal Exposition of Seville (Expo 1992) and again worked on important

21 Bo Bardi worked with collaborators André Vainer and Marcelo Carvalho Ferraz on the Cerrado Church, the Santa Maria dos Anjos Chapel, in Vargem Grande Paulista (São Paulo State, 1978) and the SESC–Pompéia. Another young architect, Marcelo Suzuki, joined Bo Bardi's team on the building renovation projects in Bahia and the later projects in São Paulo, Oficina Theater (also with Edson Elito, 1991) and the new City Hall (1990–92).

FIGURE 1.6
Solar do Unhão, Museum of Modern Art of Bahia (MAMB) and Museum of Popular Art Salvador de Bahia (1959–63).
Photo by C. Veikos, 2006.

projects in São Paulo, including the transformation of the Oficina Theater and renovations to the new City Hall. [21]

In the last twelve years, retrospectives of her design work, created by the Institute Lina Bo and P.M. Bardi (ILBPMB) in São Paulo, have toured architecture schools, museums and galleries around the world. Recently, the Japanese architect Kazujo Sejima, in her role as director of the Architecture sector at the 2010 Venice Biennale, mounted a retrospective of Bo Bardi's buildings and drawings, thus assuring a newly expanding audience for her work. Contemporary architects across the globe, including Sejima and Fumihiko Maki, American Steven Holl, and Aldo Van Eyck of the Netherlands (d. 1999), have praised Bo Bardi in print and her name has been included in recent anthologies of modern architecture by Kenneth Frampton, Herman Hertzberger and Andrea

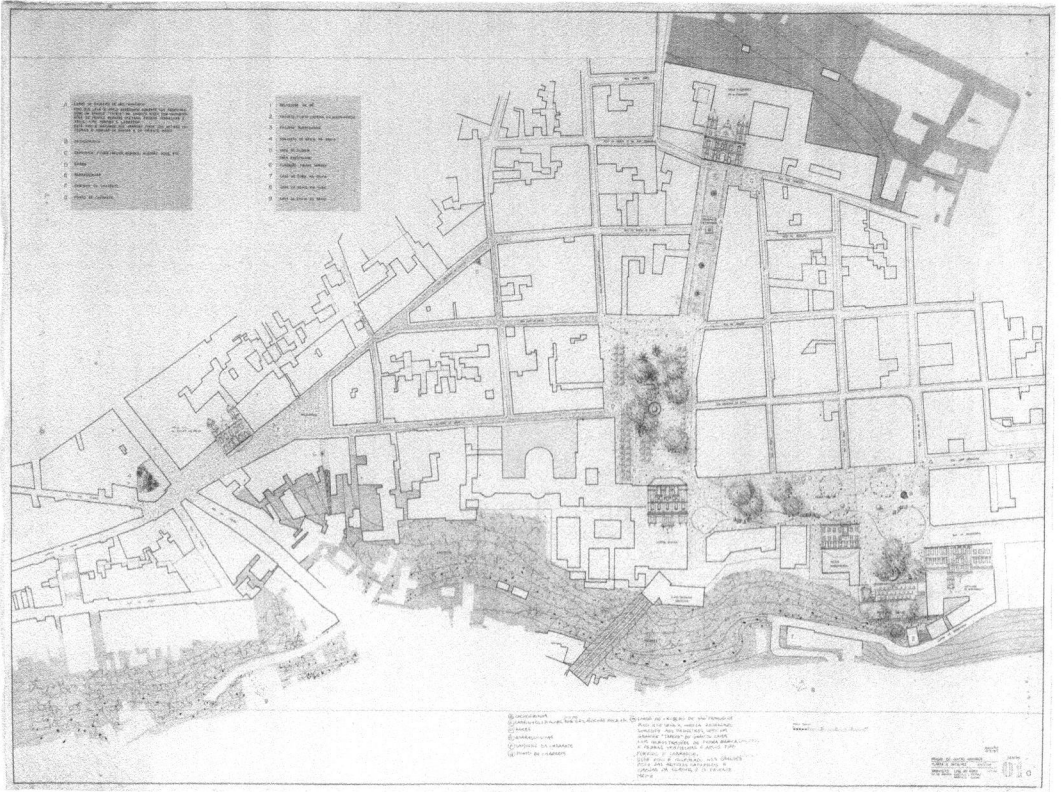

FIGURE 1.7
Master plan of the historic district of Salvador (1986).
© Institute Lina Bo and P.M. Bardi.

22 Kenneth Frampton, *The Evolution of Twentieth Century Architecture: A Synoptic Account*, Springer, 2007; Herman Hertzberger, *Space and the Architect: Lessons in Architecture 2*, Netherlands: 010 Publishers, 2000; *Space and Learning: Lessons in Architecture 3*, Netherlands: 010 Publishers, 2008; and Andrea Deplazes, *Constructing Architecture: Materials Processes Structures—A Handbook*, Basel: Birkhauser, 2006.

23 Sylvia Rubino and Marina Grinover (eds), *Lina Por Ecrito: Textos Escolhidos de Lina Bo Bardi*, COSACNAIFY, 2009.

Deplazes. [22]A book published recently in Brazil, *Lina Por Ecrito: Textos Escolhidos de Lina Bo Bardi*, [23] features articles written by Bo Bardi in Portuguese as well as Portuguese translations of three early Italian texts, one from the magazine *Lo Stile* and two from *Domus*. Bo Bardi's major writing on architecture, *Propaedeutic Contribution to the Teaching of Architecture Theory* (*Propaedeutic Contribution*) has not been translated up until now, and is not well known or understood.

Lina Bo Bardi wrote the text in response to a national competition for a newly formed teaching position in Architecture Theory at the Federal University of São Paulo School of Architecture and Urbanism (FAU/USP). As such, it is a primary example of an attempt to construct a theory of architecture that would be instrumental for the construction of a new kind of practice. Bo Bardi reviewed architectural treatises, evaluated alternative definitions of architecture and reflected on the state of the discipline and the way it was taught in schools. She included comparisons to other important architectural pedagogies and theoretical texts of the period,

FIGURE 1.8
Cover, *Propaedeutic Contribution to the Teaching of Architecture Theory.*
São Paulo: Habitat Ltd., 1957.

including those that comprised her own formation in 1930s Italy. It is not only a key to her formation as an architect, but an important inquiry into the nature of architecture theory, its role in education and its relation to practice and to the history of architecture.

Propaedeutic Contribution (Figure 1.8) was originally published in Portuguese by Habitat Ltd., São Paulo, the publisher of the Bardis' magazine of the same name. ILBPMB printed a facsimile on the tenth anniversary of her death (2002), subtitling it "An Unedited Lina Bo Bardi." Bo Bardi enriched her text with a spectacularly diverse collection of images. These constitute an autonomous visual narrative, assembled in a compelling didactic montage. Bo Bardi built a critical and constructive theory of architecture from this collection of textual and visual artifacts. The aim of *Lina Bo Bardi: The Theory of Architectural Practice*, is to translate her text into English and to contextualize it theoretically, taking into account the specific historical sources and contemporaneous discourses

24 *Propaedeutic Contribution*, p. 144/*Contribuição Propedêutica*, p. 53.

25 *Propaedeutic Contribution*, p. 48/*Contribuição Propedêutica*, p. 5.

26 Svetlana Alpers makes this distinction in her excellent interpretation of the geographically and technologically motivated "impulse to map" on the part of Dutch painters, as opposed to the prevailing perspectival visual constructs emanating from Italy and France, in *The Art of Describing: Dutch Art in the Seventeenth Century*, Chicago: University of Chicago Press, 1983.

27 *Propaedeutic Contribution*, p. 74/*Contribuição Propedêutica*, p. 19.

from which it draws. Because Bo Bardi wrote as a practicing architect, rather than a historian or theoretician, her text is perhaps most interesting for the way in which she attempts to synthesize architectural theory and practice. Regarding the relationship, Bo Bardi regrets that,

> To this day, a sort of professional distinction between theory and practice still exists, and the architecture of Wright, Le Corbusier and Mies van der Rohe has not been interpreted in its real sense, even by the most modern manuals of theory, criticism and history. [24]

Although her text does not quite achieve the synthesis she proposed, it is clear that in *Propaedeutic Contribution* Bo Bardi began to articulate a way towards an authentically Brazilian expression, liberated from European theories. Potentially empowering for an already modern Brazil, whose economy continued to boom into the late 1950s, it is an important basis from which to understand both her own formation and her ambitions for Brazilian design.

The purpose of *Propaedeutic Contribution*, she begins, is to "create an impassioned student, a student with an incentive to think, a motivation towards research . . .". [25] Though Bo Bardi did not state it explicitly, the experience of reading and looking carefully at the images, of following the footnotes to the original sources, and the family of thoughts they represent, makes this goal palpable. The work seeks to engage the reader, to make her complicit in the construction of its meaning. Bo Bardi's arguments may seem far flung; they are not linear, nor do they serve to elucidate a central point. One moves from one area of intense detail to another, mapping a territory rather than creating the illusion of depth. [26] The point is not to position an omniscient reader, but to guide her through the terrain of the subject matter. In addition, the method for constructing the work, the words and images together, puts the reader into the space of the subject being discussed and prepares her for a role in defining it. "In school, it is not sufficient to merely teach Architecture; it is necessary to transmit the enthusiasm of predecessors and masters to students." [27] Bo Bardi did this by positing an equivalence between the teaching of architecture theory and the construction of the building. Like the surface of a building, the surface of a text constitutes its perceptual reality; the surface creates the effects that the building produces. The effect of Lina Bo Bardi's text, written in Portuguese, using Italian syntax and references in French, German and English, is, like some building surfaces, impenetrable at first glance. To read the surface, it is important to perceive it creatively, to be open to associations between themes, to construct new themes between the images and the text while understanding the unstated impact of certain accumulations and juxtapositions, even taking into account some obvious omissions. To read the surface is to encounter the text and images with a kind of distracted scrutiny. The method by which the text and its intentions are elucidated is based on mapping the details of the terrain and understanding that its boundaries are always moving away from you, revealing new, uncharted territories. Citing the "Lodolian principle of 'not confining' architecture," [28] Bo Bardi makes this point many times in the text, enlarging the definition of Architecture to extremes; for example,

> What is meant by the term, Architecture? At first, it might seem safe to limit it to the art of construction and, in a narrower sense, to the construction of buildings; but architecture is almost implicitly every type of structure and representation, from the structure of rocks, the skeleton, the infinitesimal figure of the atom, to the appearance of the spheres that compose the planetary system. [29]

But architecture achieves its effects not only through the design of its surfaces, but in the way that surfaces define and give atmosphere to space. Bo Bardi highlights a long passage from Geoffrey Scott's *Architecture of Humanism*:

> But besides spaces which have merely length and breadth—surfaces, that is to say, at which we look—architecture gives us spaces of three dimensions in which we stand. And here is the very centre of architectural art . . . Architecture alone of the arts can give space its full value . . . it uses space as a material and sets us in the midst. . . . The architect models in space as a sculptor in clay. He designs his space as a work of art; that is, he attempts through its means to create a certain mood in those who enter it. [30]

In *Propaedeutic Contribution*, Bo Bardi extended Scott's analogy, spatializing word and image. She anticipated that the book could also be a space, a work of art to enter, capable of exciting the reader to action, or perhaps encouraging her to pause and reflect. The book provokes us to reflect on architectural education today, on the relevance of theory, the advantages of history, and ultimately on the caliber and constitution of future professionals in the discipline and the work that they will be prepared to contribute to the built environment. Bo Bardi's *Propaedeutic Contribution* reminds us that theory and practice form a strange loop: "the elaboration of theory," she wrote, "may originate from practice and be its consequence." [31]

Reading the surface

It is quite clear that from the start of her career Lina Bo Bardi engaged architecture primarily in the context of its representation, particularly in its role in the political and social sphere of the architectural magazine. [32]

28 *Propaedeutic Contribution*, p. 54/*Contribuição Propedêutica*, p. 9.

29 *Propaedeutic Contribution*, p. 58/*Contribuição Propedêutica*, p. 10–11.

30 *Propaedeutic Contribution*, p. 130/*Contribuição Propedêutica*, p. 45. I have edited the passage here.

31 *Propaedeutic Contribution*, p. 96/*Contribuição Propedêutica*, p. 29.

32 Beatriz Colomina, "Introduction: On Architecture, Production and Reproduction," *Architecture-production*, Princeton: Princeton Architectural Press, 1988, pp. 7–23, points to the fact that the changes engendered in literature with the advent of mechanical reproduction are well known, while the same claims cannot be made about the changes to architecture brought about by mechanical processes. Of course, her later books, including *Privacy and Publicity: Modern Architecture as Mass Media*, MIT Press, 1994, and her recent *Clip, Stamp, Fold: The Radical Architecture of Little Magazines 196 –197X*, Actar-D, 2009, make substantial strides towards achieving parity; Rifkind, "*Quadrante*" provides a case study of the transformation of architectural practice in Italy engendered by the magazine in its relatively short run, 1933–36; Brian McLaren, "Under the Sign of the Reproduction," *Journal of Architectural Education* 45, no. 2 (February 1992): 98–106, looks specifically at *Casabella* and *Architettura*, during the inter-war period in Italy as a case for how publications have conditioned our understanding of architecture and, consequently, "exacted profound changes within the very art that it reproduced."

33 Marcello Piacentini, *Architettura d'oggi*, Roma: Cremonese, 1930.

34 Giovanni Giovannoni, *Vecchi città ed edilizia nuova*, Torino: Unione Tipografico-Editrice Torinese, 1931.

35 Gaetano Ciocca, "La Casa Rurale" [The Rural House], Quadrante n. 22, Feb. 1935.

36 Guido Marangoni founded *La Casabella* in 1928. The editorial direction was taken on by architects Giuseppe Pagano and Edoardo Persico (1900–36) in 1933.

37 Giuseppe Pagano, and G. Daniel, *Architettura rurale Italiana*, Milano: Ulrico Hoepli Editore, 1936.

38 Michelangelo Sabatino, "Back to the Drawing Board? Re-visiting the Vernacular Tradition in Italian Modern Architecture," *Annali di architettura: Revista de Centro internazionale di Studi di Architettura Andrea Palladio di Vicenza*, v.16 (2004): 169–185.

Lina Bo became an architect in the difficult years surrounding the Second World War in Italy, during the Fascist regime of Benito Mussolini. She was educated at the Scuola superiore di architettura di Roma [Architecture College of Rome University of Engineering], attending between 1933/34 and 1939/40. As the academic home of Marcello Piacentini (1881–1960), Gustavo Giovannoni (1873–1947) and Luigi Piccinato (1899–1983), neo-classical and *Novecento* tenets prevailed at the school, with "ambientismo," the context or environment of Italian cities, seen as a primary cultural value. Piacentini's book, *Architettura d'oggi*, [33] argued for modernization on Italian terms, following the requirements of Italian tradition, history and climate. Giovannoni's important book, *Vecchie città ed edilizia nuova*, [34] proposed the city as a "palimpsest" of old and new, and the idea of urban form as transitional, making manifest its previous iterations, rather than absolute. This complementarity between old and new, the importance of the physical attributes of landscapes and regional materials, colors and workmanship, in the formulation of an architectural language had a strong influence on Bo Bardi, and she regarded Giovannoni as one of her most important teachers. Piacentini and Giovannoni referred to the Italian vernacular, as "architettura minore" (minor architecture). *Architettura,* the magazine of the Fascist syndicate of Architects, led by Piacentini, promoted this as a kind of historical eclecticism. The first and most potent critique of Piacentini came from P.M. Bardi, author of the polemical *Tavola degli Orrori* which ridiculed the Neo-Classicism and Eclecticism of the "Official Style." He advocated for the reconciliation of functionalism and the natural forms of *Mediterraneità*, calling for a new morality in architecture that would represent the patriarchal benevolence of the Fascist State. In *Quadrante,* (1933–1936) the cultural journal he founded with Massimo Bontempelli, he extolled the virtues of the rural house and promoted the schemes for rural housing by engineer and inventor, Gaetano Ciocca (1882–1966). [35] The architect and professor Giuseppe Pagano (1896–1945) ran the Milan-based architectural magazine, *Casabella,* [36] which provided a modern counterpoint to the traditionalism of the Roman school. Pagano studied Italian rural architecture and its construction process as a model for Rationalism (Italian modernism). [37] The logical construction of form derived from the constraints of materials, climate and labor in rural, "spontaneous" construction produced an implicit continuity between tradition and innovation that was captured not in style but in the more abstract terms of aesthetics and function. Pagano was also critical of Piacentini, calling him "historicist." Pagano's polemical rebuttal to "archi-tettura minore" was "architettura rurale" (rural architecture), interpreted as practical and pure. [38]

Not long after finishing her degree in Rome, Lina Bo moved to Milan. While she would later regret that work was not available in the Milanese architectural circle she preferred, namely, the offices of Pagano, Lina Bo bragged that she was able to support herself well in Milan. She shared a studio at 12 via Gésu with Carlo Pagani, a Milanese classmate from the Scuola Superiore di architettura di Roma, and the architecture firm of recent graduates Olivieri, Angeli, and De Carli, all of the Milan Polytechnic. [39] Starting in 1941, she and Pagani did exhibition design and competition drawings together and for the office of architect, designer and editor Gio Ponti (1891–1979). Ponti was the founding editor of the magazine *Domus* [40] and director of the IVth (1930) and Vth (1933) Milan Triennale, "Decorative Industrial and Modern arts and Modern architecture." The work in his office reflects the broad spectrum and scale of the Triennale: Sempione Station, 1937–48, an urban development scheme, a competition for the Foreign Ministry in Rome, 1939, "An Ideal Small House" for *Domus*, the competition for A Palace of Water and Light for the Exhibition, "E-42," 1939, as well as paintings, books, theater sets and costumes. This multivalent environment proved to be a significant model for Bo Bardi's later practice.

Late in 1941, an internal reorganization of *Domus* severely reduced Ponti's role at the magazine. Instead of staying in the directorial position, Ponti joined with the powerful Italian entrepreneurs, Sante Astaldi, Pier Luigi Gomez and publisher Aldo Garzanti to constitute CEIM, the Centro Edizioni Italiane Moda, with the goal of launching a new magazine, *Linea*, with the same subtitle as *Domus*: "Style in the house and furnishing." The name was changed later, to *Belleza*, and another magazine, *Lo Stile*, [41] acquired the *Domus* subtitle, *nella casa e nell'arredamento*. Lina Bo called herself "a technical journalist" and got work through Ponti's extensive network, writing and drawing for several magazines, newspapers and women's journals under the Garanti Company umbrella, including *Domus*, *Belleza*, *Vetrina*, *L'Illustrazione Italiana*, *Rima*, *Grazia*, *Tempo*, *Milano Sera* and *Carriere della sera Magazine*.

Documents reveal that just four days after Ponti resigned from *Domus*, P.M. Bardi wrote to Ponti, "If sometimes I have criticized you, it was because I held you in high esteem; and, now, as the times have matured, I will participate in the 'cameleonisme' that the times demand, you have the task to dictate various laws in the Italian taste . . .". [42] With Bardi's counsel, Ponti's ambition for *Lo Stile* was to seize the moment. He wrote to Giuseppe Bottai, Minister of National Education:

This, Excellence, is our moment—France prostrate, no art of creative value either in England, America, Sweden, or Spain: but we have prominence over Germany with regard to painting, sculpture, architecture, productions of art, schools of art . . . *Stile* will target all this propaganda, and will also have translations in German and Spanish; it must penetrate abroad, profiting from the lack of equivalent German reviews, and from the passing of *Architectural Review* and *Architecture d'Aujourd'hui*. [43]

39 The resumé of the firm of Luigi Claudio Olivieri, Renato Angeli and Carlo De Carli shows associations with architect and pioneer in industrial design Luigi Caccio Dominioni (1913–) and his design partners at the time, Livio and Pier Giacomo Castiglioni. The young firm had been active in the VIth (1936) and VIIth (1940) Milan Triennales, exhibitions of Modern Art, Architecture and Design, in which Pagani had also participated. The works in progress included furniture for the new headquarters for Montecatini, the largest Italian industrial company at the time, for the offices of *Popolo d'Italia*, the newspaper founded by Mussolini in 1914, as well as for the "Istituto nazionale fascista assicurazioni infortuni sul lavoro" (INFAIL). They were mentored by Ponti, whose commissions at the time included the Villa Donegani at Bordighera (1937–40) for Guido Donegani, the CEO of Montecatini. The Villa is pictured on the cover of *Lo Stile*, no. 7, 1941.

40 Gio Ponti founded the magazine in Milan in 1928.

41 Between January 1942 and August 1943, Bo and Pagani's shared studio space at 12 via Gésu was the address of record for *Lo Stile*.

42 Letter from P.M. Bardi, 20 November 1941, quoted in Massimo Martignoni, *Gio Ponti: gli anni di stile: 1941–1947* Milano, Abitare Segesta, 2002, p. 105.

43 "Questo, Eccellenza, è il nostro momento. La Francia prostrata, nessun'arte di valore creative né in Inghilterra, né in America, né in Svezia, né in Spagna: ma preminenza di valori nostri sulla Germania in fatto di pittura, scultura, Architettura, produzioni d'arte, scuole d'arte . . . 'Stile' sarà tutto teso a questa propaganda, ed avrà anche traduzioni in tedesco e spagnuolo; esso deve penetrare all'estero, approfittando della mancanza di equivalenti riviste tedesche, e della scomparsa di 'Architectural Review' e di 'Architecture d'Aujourd'hui.'" Letter from Gio Ponti, 28 December, quoted in Martignoni, *Gio Ponti*, p. 105. Ponti solicits Ugo Ojetti, Enrico Fulchignoni and Guilio Carlo Argan to write for the new magazine as well.

44 Lina Bo and Carlo Pagani, "
3 Arredamenti," *Lo Stile*, no. 1
(January, 1941): 88–104.

45 *Lo Stile* no. 3 (March 1941)
(in collaboration with Ponti); no. 4
(April 1941) (with Pagani) no. 10–no.
24 (October, 1941–December 1942)
are signed, GIENLICA, an acronym
for Gio Ponti, Enrico Bo (Lina's
father)/Enrico Ciuti, Lina Bo and
Carlo Pagani.

46 "Terrazze in città," *Lo Stile*,
no. 4, Milan (April 1941): 70–71;
"L'acquario in casa," *Lo Stile*, no. 10,
Milan (October 1941): 24–25;
"Serre," *Lo Stile*, no. 5–6 Milan
(May–June 1941): 113; "Architettura
e natura: la casa nel paesaggio"
Domus, no. 191, Milan (November
1943): 464–471 (Melchiorre Bega,
Director; Pagani, Bo, co-editors).

47 The exhibition, "Western Living:
5 Modern Houses under $7500" ran
from April 4–27, 1942 at the San
Francisco Museum of Art and later
went to the Museum of Modern Art
in NY, as "Five California Houses"
from March 17–April 18, 1943. It
was sponsored by the magazine
California Arts and Architecture. The
article reporting on the exhibition,
by Dr. Grace L. McCann Morley,
appeared in v. 59, 1942. p. 23–25.

48 Talbot Hamlin, "The Trend of
American architecture." *Harper's
Magazine* (Jan. 1942): 164–171.

49 Gio Ponti, "Case semplici per
la vita sana" *Lo Stile* n. 4 (April
1941): 2.

50 Martignoni, *Gio Ponti*, p. 134.

51 *Lo Stile*, no. 10 (October 1941):
65; *Lo Stile*, no. 12 (December): 67.

52 Via Gesù 12, via
Montenapoleone, Garzanti
headquarters in via Palermo 10,
and Ponti's studio in Piazzale Giulio
Cesare 14, where the magazine was
edited after no. 21, in September
1942, were also destroyed in the
Allied bombing of August 13, 1943.

53 *Quaderni di Domus* direzione
della collana Lina Bo and Carlo
Pagani: Latis, Vito, 1 *Libri nella casa*,
Milano: Editoriale Domus, 1945;
Gandolfi, Vittorio. 2 *Gli Studi nella
Casa*, Milano: Editoriale Domus,
1945; Tevarotto, Mario,
3 *Camini*, Milano: Editoriale Domus,
1945; Zanuso, Marco, 4 *La Cucina*.
Milano: Editoriale Domus, 1945;
Olivieri, Luigi Claudio, 5
L'Illuminazione della Casa, Milano:
Editoriale Domus, 1946. There were
eleven volumes in the series
(1945–1954).

Essays by Ponti and Bottai inaugurated the first issue of *Lo Stile*, in January 1941. Glossy advertisements promoting the Italian publishing company, the Montecatini Group, and the industrial titan, Saint-Gobain Glass, supported the venture in the opening pages. Almost twenty pages of photos and drawings of custom-designed furniture, murals and iron-work followed, signed "Bo and Pagani." [44] (Figure 1.9) Lina Bo signed articles, projects and drawings in sixteen issues, and in the following year contributed to all the cover images except one. [45] Traces of her articles in *Lo Stile*, about garden terraces in the city, aquariums and greenhouses, and "Architecture and Nature: The House within the Landscape" in *Domus*, are evident in *Propaedeutic Contribution*. [46] In the *Domus* article Bo transposed Pagano's arguments about rural Italian architecture to examples in India, Egypt and the American southwest. She used Pagano's term, "architettura rurale" rather than the prevailing "architettura minore" of Piacentini. Among the projects featured, the house for actress Greta Granstedt by Harwell Hamilton Harris can be identified by its plan and by photographs that also appeared in an exhibition of the San Francisco Museum of Art, called "Western Living" in 1942. [47] Inspired by an article titled, "The Trend in American Architecture" by the architectural historian, Talbot Hamlin, [48] the exhibition also featured work by Wright, Neutra, Harris, William Wilson Wurster, Hervey Parke Clarke and John Ekin Dinwiddle.

Lina Bo's collages of furniture, interiors and gardens *in Lo Stile* underscored its recurring themes: mixing ancient and modern motifs, integrating nature and architecture, building simply and efficiently. In an article called "Simple House for Healthy Living," which introduced a house by the architect Andrea Busiri-Vici, Ponti posited the "desire to live" expressed by "the simple and primordial joy of green, air and sun" [49] against the "desire to be seen" communicated by the use of decorative excess. Images of a simple, sun-bleached open terrace surrounded by old trees and greenery and inhabited by happy babies and children made the point abundantly clear. A project by "L. Bo" appeared in September, no. 9 (64), an issue of *Lo Stile* in which the "support of Le Corbusier continues." [50] Later issues in that year featured an international selection of modern projects by Brazilian architect Oscar Niemeyer and American émigrés R.M. Schindler, Walter Gropius and Marcel Breuer. [51]

It is no surprise that, in the final stages of the war, the attention of architects and architecture magazines would turn to housing and to the pressing issues of reconstruction. In the chaotic last months of 1943, after the office was destroyed by the Allied bombings, Pagani resigned from *Lo Stile* and ran *Domus* from Bergamo, with Lina Bo as the deputy editor. [52] During this time of limited means, she managed to edit a series of five small volumes on the house, called *Quaderni di Domus*, with Pagani. [53] Her documented contribution to the first Italian Reconstruction

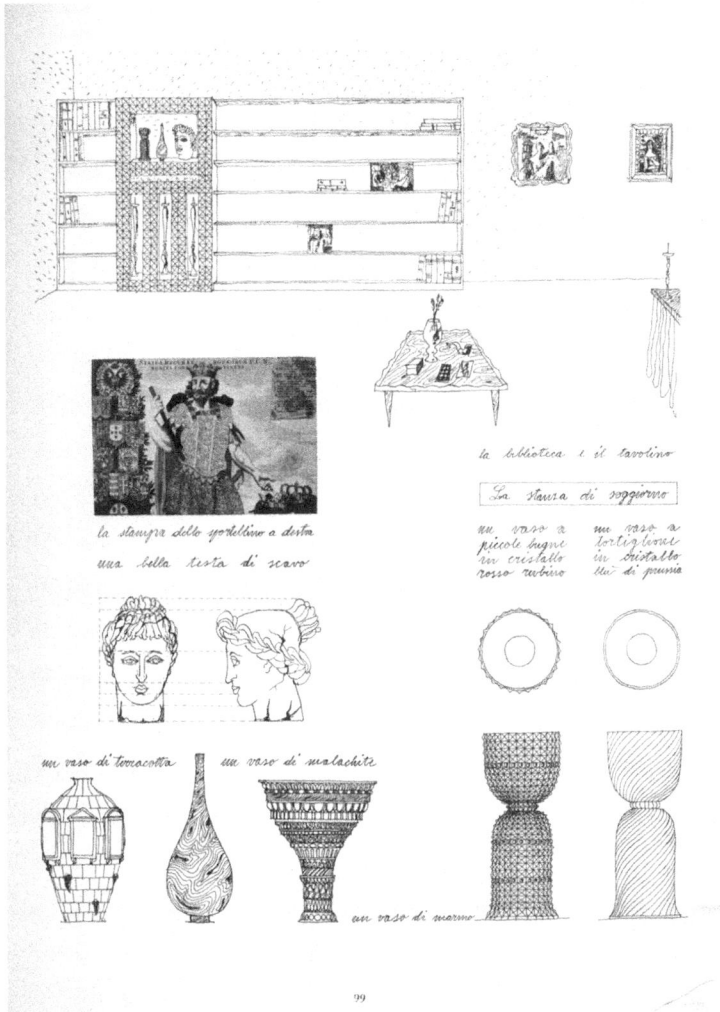

54 Lina Bo, "La Propaganda Per La Ricostruzione," in Fabrizio Brunetti, *L'Architettura in Italia Negli Anni della Ricostruzione*; *Le vicende e le immagini*, Maria Coli Brunetti, ed., Appendice: Interventi dal Primo convegno nazionale per la ricostruzione edilizia, Paola Signori, ed., Firenze, Italy: Alinea (1986): 239–241.

55 *"A" – Cultura della Vita* ran for 7 weekly and 2 bi-weekly issues, from Feb. 15, 1946–June 8, 1946. Gianni Mazzochi-Bastoni of *Domus* discontinued publication with material for 5 additional issues already prepared. A provocative article by Zevi on birth control seems to have perpetuated the cancellation.

FIGURE 1.9
"3 Arredamenti degli architetti Lina Bo e Carlo Pagani," *Lo Stile*, Milan, no. 1 (January 1941): 99.

Congress, in Milan, December 14–15, 1945, which included presentations by architects Mario Ridofi, Ernesto Rogers, Bruno Zevi, Pier Luigi Nervi, Piero Bottoni and others, made an appeal for the use of propaganda for the Reconstruction, as a method to involve the populace in the decision making. [54] The fact that she was planning a radical weekly magazine of architecture, "stemming from the Resistance," called *"A" —Cultura della Vita* ["A"—Culture of Life"] [55] is noted by the editors of the conference proceedings. *"A,"* founded by Lina Bo with Pagani and art critic Raffaele Carrieri, addressed architecture as an instrument of change. The subtitles all began with the letter *"A"* in Italian, "News—

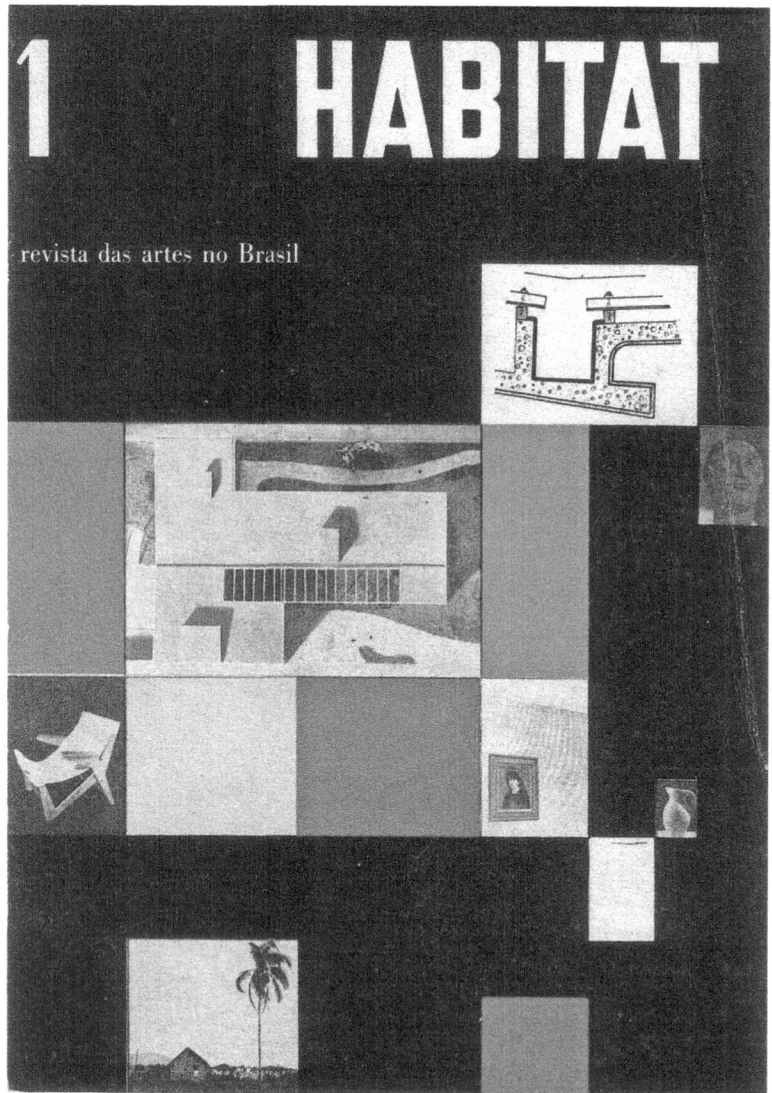

FIGURE 1.10
Cover, *Habitat* no. 1 (October–December 1951).

56 "A" (1946) reprinted in *Arbitrare*, no. 393 (March 2000): 135–137.

Architecture—Housing—Art", the theme was to address other topical *"A"* issues, like anxiety, love, alliance, boldness, warning, harshness, association, absurdity and the somewhat forced anti-meanness. On every cover, was the question, "Why do we live so badly?" With issue number 7, Bruno Zevi joined the directorial team and the question changed to a declaration, "We can live better." [56] This preoccupation, evident also at CIAM (Congrès Inter-nationale d'Architecture Moderne) IX and X on the theme of Habitat, no doubt inspired the name of her Brazilian architectural magazine of the same name.

Lina Bo wrote copiously and edited several architectural magazines, including the wartime editions of *Domus*. [57] She drafted, drew in ink and watercolor, did page layout of image and text, and designed covers and layouts for *Lo Stile*, *Bellezza* and *Domus*, using collage and photographic montage. As she perfected her graphic and compositional skills, her direct experience with publication only enhanced her belief in the persuasive power of the image. Her experience in the Italian milieu under Fascism was not unique in this regard. These groundbreaking techniques of communication were evidenced in many other architectural magazines of this prolific period, especially *Spazio* magazine, edited by Luigi Moretti (1907–73), an architect based in Rome, as well as *Architettura e arti decorativi*, *Domus* and *Casabella*. In *Quadrante*, Bontempelli heralded the transformation: "The polemic within architecture," he wrote, "is a profoundly political polemic." [58] Their purpose with *Quadrante* was to promote Rationalism as the official expression of Mussolini's fascist regime. Moreover, they meant to make modern architecture the "art of the state."

Habitat, the magazine Bo Bardi founded with P.M. Bardi in Brazil in 1950, showcased her design work and promoted the exhibitions and events of the São Paulo Museum of Art (Figure 1.10). In the inaugural editorial, P.M. Bardi and Lina Bo Bardi explained that they chose the word "habitat" because it was closely related to Architecture, and therefore gave value not only to artistic interpretations, but also to those that had a social function as well. As director of the Museum, P.M. Bardi was largely responsible for its stunning international success. The magazine and the museum operated together, to create and to display, to represent and to propagate a new way of thinking. This was the legacy of P.M. Bardi's Italian experience as director of several galleries in Milan and Rome, including Galleria Bardi (1927) and Galleria d'Arte Moderna (1930), and as editor of the magazines of art and culture *Belvedere*, *L'Ambrosiano* and, perhaps most notably, *Quadrante*. His goal was political: he intended to cultivate a thoroughly modern expression of living, making and thinking. It is not an overstatement to consider *Habitat* and the museum as a direct import to Brazil of the cultural and political representational strategies P.M. Bardi practiced to such great effect in Italy in the 1930s. Lina Bo Bardi's exceptional skills, honed roughly ten years later in the same Italian climate, in her case at *Lo Stile*, proved to be indispensable to their combined project. Lina Bo Bardi was careful to distinguish her work from work she did with her husband. In *Habitat* it is quite subtle; whenever images or text of the house or museum appear, they are signed "Lina Bo Bardi," suggesting that P.M. Bardi played a collaborative role in these projects. However, when *Habitat* published the Taba Guaianases Project in São Paulo, the byline read: "Lina Bo, Eng. Pier Luigi Nervi." Likewise, "Lina Bo" was credited for all furniture,

57 Lina Bo and Carlo Pagani, *Domus*, nos. 195–204 (March–December 1944).

58 Massimo Bontempelli, cited and translated in Rifkind, "*Quadrante*," p. 16.

59 Giancarlo Palanti (1906–77), Italian architect and professor at the Milan Polytechnic, directed the magazine *Domus* (1932–33), *Casabella* (1933) and *Casabella Costruzioni* (1946) with Franco Albini, with whom he also collaborated architecturally. He immigrated to Brazil in 1946 and worked in partnership with Daniele Calabi, among others, until 1952 when he partnered with Henrique E. Mindlin.

60 Giuseppe Pagano, *Architetture e scritti/Giuseppe Pagano Pogatschnig (1896–1945)*, Milan: Domus, 1947.

61 The book is in the personal library that the Bardis donated to the MASP. Several concepts and headings from Pagano's notes appear and are reinforced in *Propaedeutic Contribution*; for example, about the moral and social condition as an explanation of novel aesthetics, not only technical honesty, but sincerity and clarity of thought; the client and the importance of knowing how to choose an architect; the value of criticism; the relationship between students and professors; methods of teaching, especially to instill a love of nature, a critical sensibility and an ethical sensibility.

62 The exhibition traveled from the ICA Boston, and opened on July 5, 1950 at MASP. It was coordinated by Lina Bo Bardi and reviewed in "Una Exposición de Le Corbusier en Brazil," *Arquitectura Mexico*, no. 37 (March, 1952): 115–116. A catalog accompanied the exhibition, P.M. Bardi, *A Critical Review of Le Corbusier: Leitura crítica de Le Corbusier*, São Paulo, Brazil: Habitat Editora Museu de Arte de São Paulo, 1951.

63 P.M. Bardi, *Neutra: residências/residences*, 2nd edn. (1st edition, October 1950 for exhibition at Diários Associados Building, MASP).

64 "Built in Brazil; A light glass casa in the air," *Contract Interiors* 112, no. 10, New York (May 1953): 74.

65 The mosaic is by Enrico Gallassi, an artist in Rome, who was featured, with this and other original works, in the pages of *Lo Stile*.

collages or jewelry. When applied to the articles and editorials in *Habitat*, this subtle insistence on her identity apart from "Bardi" is a very revealing marker for when they worked autonomously or when and how they might have disagreed. Lina Bo Bardi drew substantially from her years of writing and directing *Habitat* (1950–54), and continued to do so after she and P.M. Bardi resigned as editors of the magazine (after issue no. 15, March–April 1954). *Habitat* was an important filter through which Bo Bardi both assimilated and provoked the prevailing intellectual and academic environment of Brazil.

Publications, competitions, displays and exhibitions focused architects' attention on representational, didactic and narrative goals in Italy during the early years of Bo Bardi's career, 1939–46. She was engaged in precisely this kind of work, in both Italy and Brazil, in the years before setting her thoughts down on architectural theory, its definition, and its usefulness for the education of the future architects of Brazil. With her husband and fellow Italian émigré Giancarlo Palanti, [59] she inaugurated an architecture and design office named after P.M. Bardi's Italian "Studio de Arte Palma," dedicated to Industrial Design, particularly modern furniture. Before he left Italy, Palanti, together with architect Anna Castelli and architect Franco Albini, curated a collection in homage to Giuseppe Pagano, called *Architetture e scritti/Giuseppe Pagano Pogatschnig*. [60] The book contained architectural work, projects and sketches by Pagano and reproduced some notes he had made for lectures about architectural education. If Bo Bardi did not have access to Pagano in Italy, she did, posthumously, in Brazil, through the writings that Palanti transcribed. [61] P.M. Bardi continued to initiate cultural activities through the Studio d'Arte Palma, as he had done in Rome and Milan before the war; he mounted exhibitions of modern and ancient art, industrial art, and cultural exhibitions from other countries, musical concerts, avant-garde theater plays, conferences and publications, and was responsible for the evaluation, conservation and commercialization of works of art. Many of these events were design opportunities for Bo Bardi and Palanti. The first exhibitions at the newly founded São Paulo Museum of Art included Le Corbusier's "New World of Space," [62] the sculpture the Swiss architect Max Bill, and houses by the architect Richard Neutra. [63] Bo Bardi participated in the production of the catalogs published by the museum and was in charge of designing the exhibitions. It was during this period, between 1951 and 1952, that she completed the "Glass House." "The point," she expressed, "was to have a place physically sheltered from rains and winds, but sharing the poetry and ethics to be found even in a storm—disregarding the usual protections." [64] A dialog on the relationship between architecture and nature, the house welcomed the visitor with an enigmatic mural, a replica in mosaic of a work by de Chirico, titled *A Metaphysical Interior* (Figure 1.11). [65] This visual

FIGURE 1.11
Mosaic by Enrico Gallassi. *Lo Stile*, Milan, no. 17 (May, 1942): 51.

moniker, and the fact that publications of the house were often accompanied by advertisements for the materials and systems employed, is another example of the predominance of strategies of display, representation and narrative in Bo Bardi's activities. In *Habitat*, and elsewhere, the spreads included extensive documentation of each product name and manufacturer, from roof insulation to mosaic tile, from lighting and mirrors to plumbing. Photos of the house accompany advertisements in the same issue of the magazine; for example, in the ad for the vinyl "Plavonil," which was used as a curtain on the house's glazed northeast elevation at the library to "insulate and absorb the sun's rays." The same exterior photo of the house appeared in an advertisement for "Natal Electrica, S.A.," the company credited for providing all the modern household appliances, including a garbage disposal, washer and dryer, mixer, radio-phonograph, air-conditioner, refrigerator and television. The museum and the magazine were a forum for Bo Bardi's work and interests, her collaborations with others, her praise for artists whom she admired in all disciplines and her scathing critiques of bourgeois tastes and values, administered under the pseudonym "ALENCASTRO."

The importance of her tutelage under Ponti, however, cannot be underestimated. Ponti traveled to Latin America in 1952. He initiated

66 These are published in *Domus*, no. 283 (1953), no. 379 (1961), and no. 284 (1953), respectively. The Faculty of Theoretical Nuclear Physics project was conceived as a gift from the Italian immigrants in São Paulo to the city. It was never built.

67 *Habitat*, no. 12 (July 1953).

68 ILBPMB Archive, folder: "Misc. Correspondence."

69 *Propaedeutic Contribution*, p. 48/*Contribuição Propedêutica*, p. 5.

70 *Propaedeutic Contribution*, p. 54/*Contribuição Propedêutica*, p. 9.

71 *Propaedeutic Contribution*, p. 47/*Contribuição Propedêutica*, title page, verso.

several projects in São Paulo, the Taglianetti House, the Predio Italia (Italo-Brazilian center) and the Project for a Faculty of Theoretical Nuclear Physics at the University of São Paulo, all in 1953. [66] After his visit he published Bo Bardi's "Glass House" in *Domus* in February, 1953 and the armchair, "Bardi's Bowl," in May. In turn, *Habitat* published Ponti's project for the Faculty of Theoretical Nuclear Physics. [67] He sent Bo Bardi colorful "painted letters" from Milan, inquiring as to how she was getting along. [68] Ponti published his joyous, effervescent and rambling collection, entitled *Amate L'Architettura* [*In Praise of Architecture*] in 1957, contemporaneously with *Propaedeutic Contribution*. Ponti wrote in the preface: "This book [is for] lovers of architecture, for those that dream about an architecture that is itself a civilization . . .," and "written not to lay down laws but rather to encourage debate." In *Propaedeutic Contribution* Bo Bardi reiterated Ponti's message in her opening lines: "Architecture is the product, or better still, the projection, of civilized man in the world." [69] Regarding the architectural treatise, she wrote, "We should discuss [it] with the purpose of finding its true meaning, substituting the method 'treatise or theory to be officially followed' with the method 'treatise to be discussed.'" [70]

A visual narrative

In its use of rhetorical flourish and erudition to impress and persuade, *Propaedeutic Contribution* demonstrates some of the valuable lessons Lina Bo Bardi learned from "the chameleons," Ponti and P.M. Bardi. Her published writing before *Propaedeutic Contribution* was limited to short essays, articles and reviews. Regardless of its intended academic venue, the text of *Propaedeutic Contribution* retains an expository and polemical tone. The use of illustrations complements the journalistic style, suggesting the presentation of evidence to be examined. After the title page Bo Bardi noted: "The illustrations that accompany this work form a basis for the discussion of Architecture Theory and attempt to show the amplitude of possibilities for its exemplification." [71] Sometimes the visual evidence supports the argument, but often the images point to alternative sources and arguments that counter and question the arguments made in words. In the case of Moretti, Camillo Boito and Emil Kaufman, among others, the illustrations give clues to a whole range of sources which provide important counterpoint to Bo Bardi's arguments, but which she did not address explicitly in the text.

Propaedeutic Contribution is a text of just over 27,000 words, accompanied by 227 images drawn from chronologically and geographically diverse sources and media. The use of image and text is central, as it set the basis for Bo Bardi's approach to the subject. The text was certainly up to date, including images and references from as late as June 1957, just months before the deadline for the text in September. Bo Bardi's arguments promote modern architecture and are critical of Beaux-Arts "academicism." She exalts Frank Lloyd Wright, Mies van de Rohe, Le Corbusier and Walter Gropius as exemplary practitioners. It is therefore somewhat curious that the twentieth-century sources for texts and images are juxtaposed by an almost equal number of classical texts, some quite obscure, and images and texts from the eighteenth and nineteenth centuries. For example, the treatise Bo Bardi considers "the most serious" is *Éléments et Théorie de l'Architecture, Cours professé à l'École Nationale et Spéciale des Beaux-arts*, by Julien Guadet. She ends the chapter "Regarding a Few Treatises" with this citation from Guadet's text: "S'affranchir de la servitude du passé, de tous les passés, c'est libérer l'avenir." [To free oneself from the servitude of the past, of all pasts, is to liberate oneself to the future.] "Naturally," she adds, "to free oneself from the servitude of the past does not mean to ignore the past. This is evidenced by his treatise, which is full of examples, interpretations and discussions about the history of Architecture." [72] Her sensibility on this topic may belie her reading of Kaufmann and her understanding of the continuity he posited between neo-classicism and modernism. [73] Certainly, the arguments for historical continuity with reference to the enigmatic Italian theorist, Father Lodoli, are consistent with this idea as well, as is the resurgence of Scott's 1914 text during the 1950s.

Along with her promotion of modern architecture, Bo Bardi is also critical of modernists because they resist a concept that envisions architecture as part of a larger realm, or "as a simple component of urbanism or even of a vast geography." Perhaps, she says, modernists are "influenced by the old habit of sub-dividing and separating the parts of the world into things and thoughts." [74] This was not the case for Bo Bardi. In *Propaedeutic Contribution*, as I have discussed, she uses visual techniques like montage, juxtaposing thoughts from different disciplines or different time frames to create a field of associations. Conversely, her juxtapositions are sometimes contradictory and prompt inquiry on the part of the reader. The images also make their own argument; they constitute a visual narrative that provokes new and multiple understandings of the text. Like allegories, they suggest concepts visually. "Things" and "thoughts" are not separated.

Another example of this is in the Preface, where Bo Bardi chose six images to introduce her initial set of themes. A seventh image illustrates the first endnote, demonstrating an equivalence between the text and the references to the text. In fact, the images, references and texts, as Bo Bardi states on the first page, work together to "form a basis for the discussion of Architecture Theory . . ." On the first page *Cataclysm* by Leonardo da Vinci (*Propaedeutic Contribution*: Figure 1) is followed by images of three allegories, Theory, Practice and Design, from the 1625 *Iconologia* by Ripa (*Propaedeutic Contribution*: Figures 2, 3, 4). The unstated visual argument,

72 *Propaedeutic Contribution*, p. 58/*Contribuição Propedêutica*, p. 10.

73 In the caption to Figure 40, Bo Bardi cites Kaufmann's "Three Revolutionary Architects: Boullée, Ledoux and Lequeu," *Transactions of the American Philosophical Society*, vol. 42, Part 3 of Transactions, Philadelphia, 1952.

74 *Propaedeutic Contribution*, p. 112/*Contribuição Propedêutica*, p. 37.

75 It is likely that Bo Bardi took the Ripa images from the source she cites for the Scamozzi frontispiece, where they also appear, in the article by D.J. Gordon, "Poet and Architect: The Intellectual Setting of the Quarrel between Ben Johnson and Inigo Jones," *Journal of the Warburg & Courtauld Institutes* 12 (1949): 152–178.

76 Cesare Ripa, *Iconologia*, Padua, 1625, pp. 255ff, 666ff., cited in Gordon, "Poet and Architect," p. 167.

77 I examine Bo Bardi's built work in a forthcoming book, titled *Sense of Surface.*

78 Gordon, "Poet and Architect," p. 164.

79 *Propaedeutic Contribution*, p. 184, note 6/*Contribuição Propedêutica*, p. 72, note 6.

a supplement rather than an illustration of the text, comes quite lucidly into view: there is a crisis in the schools of Architecture. To begin to clear the "Cataclysm," we must understand the nature of theory, practice and design, and their interrelation. Theory, *concetto*, is young and looks towards the sky. A compass on her head indicates that the function of the intellect is the measure and proportion of things. Practice, *magistero*, looks down, supported by a compass and a rule. She is concerned only with sensible experience, working from the particular to the universal, rooted to the earth and to change and corruption. [75] Those readers familiar with *Iconologia* will recall the allegories as Ripa describes them:

> Theory is concerned with reason and the operations of the intellect; Practice with the operations and movements of the senses . . . the former contemplates the highest causes, the latter investigates the lowest effects. So that one is the summit and the other is the foundation of the whole fabric of human discourse. [76]

That the creation and investigation of effects would be the foundation of a theory of architecture is the stimulus to an interpretation of Bo Bardi's text which reconceptualizes surface as constitutive. Such an interpretation is supported by the text itself and by similar themes which Bo Bardi elaborates in her lectures and notes, and even in her built work, whose restrained formal character highlights its expressive material surfaces. [77] The third figure, Design, *effetto*, is a young man, holding a compass pointing upwards and a mirror: "Design is based on measures, which are beautiful insofar as they correspond to right proportions, and a mirror, to show that Design is the act of an interior faculty of the soul." [78]

On the next page, the frontispiece from Scamozzi's 1615 Treatise, *L'Idea dell'Architettura* (*Propaedeutic Contribution*: Figure 5), is paired with the frontispiece from an eighteenth-century German book dedicated to the ornament of windows and doors (*Propaedeutic Contribution*: Figure 6). Further evidence of Bo Bardi's textual and visual strategy is discernible here as she begins to describe her own contribution to a theory of a "technical humanism." She selected Scamozzi's treatise because of its articulation of the architectural discipline as both art and science. Scamozzi's text is a paradigmatic example of the fifteenth- and sixteenth-century Italian humanism that Bo Bardi tried to champion. She distinguished it from what she referred to as the pseudo-humanist "transcendentals" of the Counter-Reformation. [79] Scamozzi has been described as "equally at home with *literati* and scientists," a scholar who "display[ed] a tour de force of humanistic culture within his analytical method." Additionally, his is the first architectural treatise to provide an exhaustive index which, with other writings, "literally offers a genealogy of his thinking, often deliberately displayed to the reader as a *demonstratio* about making theory . . . Scamozzi prints his thought process." [80] By selecting Scamozzi's treatise for the Preface, Bo Bardi leaves no doubt about the historical precedent on which she builds. The meaning of Scamozzi's design for the frontispiece is given in the article from which Bo Bardi draws these images, "Poet and Architect: The Intellectual Setting of the Quarrel between Ben Johnson and Inigo Jones." Its author, D.J. Gordon, points to Ripa as the source of the figures on the proscenium pictured on Scamozzi's frontispiece: "by these two, all works of Architecture and Ingining have their perfection." [81] The figures, Gordon tells us, represent the union of theory and practice as "the basis for these marvels of the architect's art." [82] The portico carries the inscription "Nemo huc liberalium artium expers ingrediatur" [Let no one ignorant of the liberal arts enter here], and Bo Bardi appropriates and re-presents the warning with good cause. The sheer number and scope of the scholarly references in Bo Bardi's text often seem overwrought and superfluous, displays of erudition rather than of meaningful content for the argument put forward. Likewise, the images often make sense only when they are interpreted in relation to one another. Like Scamozzi, she too "prints her thought process." In fact, this is one of the main reasons why this collage-like assemblage of citations and images, impossibly juxtaposed textual sources from Aristotle to Zevi, and image sources from twelfth-century France to 1957 New York, has been almost entirely neglected, with only passing reference to it by contemporary Brazilian scholars writing on Lina Bo Bardi. It appears superficial; it resists a focused, linear reading and easy synopsis. Another interpretive methodology is needed to make sense of it—one that takes account of what is stated, pictured and cited, and what is not, and why.

Lina Bo Bardi's *Propaedeutic Contribution* begins with an affirmation that she characterizes at the onset as "romantic": There is not a single piece of stone laid down by man at the center of any of our cities that does not express an idea, that does not represent a letter in the alphabet of our civilization. [83] With arguably the most impressive personal library of art and architecture in Brazil at her disposal, [84] including *Il Quattro Libri dell'Architettura di Andrea Palladio* (1570), the anonymously published *Elementi dell'architettura Lodoliana ossia L'arte del Fabbricarecon solidità scientifica e con eleganza non capricciosa* (1786), Vol. I, [85] as well as a copy of the 1833 Cosimo Bartoli edition of Alberti's *Della Architettura, Libre Dieci*, [86] it is significant that Bo Bardi begins the book by referring to a Brazilian text. She does cite significant Italian and French sources later, as they contribute directly to the themes she professes throughout. As her only Brazilian textual source, however, her selection cannot be seen as incidental. Besides the explicit proposition put forward, that Architecture is an art expressive of its cultural condition, a "projection of civilized man in the world," the reasons for the observation of this principle, Bo Bardi explains, provide the criteria for the "excursion through the ample theme of Architectural Theory" which follows. First, materials express ideas, and

80 Alina Payne, *The Architectural Treatise in the Italian Renaissance: Architectural Invention, Ornament, and Literary Culture*, Cambridge: Cambridge University Press, 1999, pp. 217–218.

81 Gordon, "Poet and Architect," p. 170.

82 Gordon, "Poet and Architect," p. 164.

83 *Propaedeutic Contribution*, Preface, p. 48/*Contribuição Propedêutica*, p. 3.

84 P.M. Bardi's library, which he donated to form the library of the Museum of Art in São Paulo (MASP), is now accessible to the public.

85 The later edition, published by the author's daughter and including the second volume, *Elementi dell'architettura Lodoliana ossia L'arte del Fabbricare con solidità scientifica e con eleganza non capricciosa, dall'autore Andrea Memmo, etc.* Zara, 1834 is also part of the collection.

86 This is a reprint of the 1565 edition.

87 P.M. Bardi, *Quadrante 22* (February 1935): 24, cited and translated in Rifkind, "*Quadrante*," p. 1.

88 Bo Bardi was born in Rome in 1914 and emigrated in 1946. She became a Brazilian citizen in 1951.

89 G.P. Ricci and Antonio Jannuzzi, *Irmão e Cia. na Exposição Nacional*, Rio de Janeiro, 1908, p. 35; Marie Robinson Wright, *The Brazilian National Exposition of 1908 in celebration of the centenary of the opening of Brazilian ports to the commerce of the world by the Prince Regent Dom João of Portugal in 1808*, Philadelphia, G. Barrie & Sons, 1908.

90 Antonio Jannuzzi, Irmão e Cia., Rio de Janeiro, was responsible for the obelisk and many of the palaces on the Avenida Central at the National Exposition, as well as the Comercio Building and the Santos Dock Building.

second, Architecture, like art and literature, is a *projection* of civilized man in the world, an artifact of human intelligence. P.M. Bardi defined it much the same way, roughly twenty years earlier, when he wrote "Libro verde della polemica dell'architettura italiana" in *Quadrante:* "For us architecture is the principal art, director, co-director of man's activities, the predominant note of his living expression, the most certain sign which he leaves during his passage on the earth." [87]

The documentary photos, sketches and drawings by Bo Bardi, engravings and etchings from Renaissance treatises, paintings, cartoons, newspapers and magazines, in *Propaedeutic Contribution* trace a wide circle of activities which are unified in the figure of the statement's author, Manuel de Araujo Porto-alegre (1806–79), an architect trained at the École des Beaux-Arts, who was also a poet and playwright, as well as a painter, cartoonist, journalist, critic and art historian, design professor and diplomat. Besides the association with a figure whose activities Bo Bardi's career had already begun to parallel, the identification of Araujo Porto-alegre as her interlocutor also accomplished two other important things: First, it introduced Bo Bardi to the University Committee through the vehicle of an esteemed Brazilian man of letters, known and remembered in Brazil for his contributions to the modernization of Brazilian institutions. In his role as the director of the *Academia Imperial de Belas Artes (AIBA)*, the Imperial Academy of Fine Arts in Rio, he reformed the curriculum to include industrial design, applied mathematics and perspective theory, and advocated the social and aesthetic role of the artist. Second, the selection of this particular citation served to deflect rebuttals against Bo Bardi arising from prejudices against foreigners, particularly bourgeois Europeans such as herself. Furthermore, by beginning her thesis with a statement drawn from a catalog of the National Centennial Exposition in Rio, which was inaugurated on August 11, 1908 to celebrate the centenary of the opening of Brazilian ports to global trade, she identified herself as someone who was aware and appreciative of Brazil's long history as a cosmopolitan nation. Notwithstanding her status as a naturalized and not native Brazilian, [88] she presented herself as nothing like the European émigré often caricatured in Brazil as elitist and presumptuous. Her opening demonstrated her understanding and respect for Brazil's abundant resources, its historical development and growing industries, and the accomplishments of its illustrious and forward-thinking business leaders, facts which were documented and appreciated internationally more than fifty years earlier. [89] That she cited this text, which is primarily a review of the work of the successful construction company Antonio Jannuzzi, Brothers and Co., [90] also signaled that she was an architect interested both in the construction of buildings and in the attempt to understand them as statements of architectural theory and, ultimately, as artifacts of a particular time and place.

Bo Bardi's dialogical use of the visual narrative alongside the text is related to the contemporaneous emergence of the field of visual criticism in modern art, particularly as evidenced in the work emerging from Italy. A prodigious circle of Italian art historians met in Rome in the early 1930s: Carlo Ludovico Ragghianti, Guilio Carlo Argan and Bruno Zevi. [91] Ragghianti was a student of professor of Art History at Pisa, Matteo Marangoni, whose important work, *Saper Vedere* [Knowing how to see] (1933), was central to the younger Italian critics. Ragghianti's project, in broad terms, was to establish a language of vision within the limits of vision itself. From 1952 to 1962 he ran the review *seleArte* in Florence. He founded the magazine with the help of the principal Italian industrialist of the period, Adriano Olivetti, whose participation assured widespread distribution of the magazine in its role as a marketing instrument of the company. Ragghianti's famous "critofilms on art," produced between 1948 and 1964, are also part of this collaboration, a primary example of the intertwining of educational and "cultural value" for the public, and image building or "publicity" for Olivetti. Contemporaneously with Bo Bardi's *Habitat*, *seleArte* featured work and essays on Max Bill (1952), Alexander Calder (1952, 1956), Lazlo Moholy Nagy, Le Corbusier and the painter Giorgio Morandi (1953). After the war, this group began to focus their attention on architecture. Ragghianti pioneered studies in the temporal nature of vision, considering the museum as its foremost expression, an "archive of points of view," "criticism in action." Bo Bardi cites his 1956 publication, *Il Pungolo dell'Arte* [The Sting of Art], in her argument to consider architecture and urbanism as part of the same discipline.

Bruno Zevi published his seminal *Towards an Organic Architecture* in 1945, and followed it with *Saper Vedere l'Architettura* [Knowing how to see Architecture] in 1948. [92] Bo Bardi drew heavily on Zevi's work in *Propaedeutic Contribution*, citing a long passage from *Saper Vedere l'Architettura*, and dedicating a good part of the second chapter to addressing his "Theory of Internal Space." Both share the pervasive desire to link modernism to a cultural order as a way to establish an architectural tradition. Zevi's annotated bibliography is clearly a starting-point for Bo Bardi. In all, Bo Bardi's text shares sixteen books with Zevi's bibliography from *Architecture as Space*. [93] She introduced his "Theory of Internal Space" early on, as a way to clarify the meaning of architecture theory, and noted that it seems "to be far from clear and definite." [94] Through Zevi, Bo Bardi also highlights many themes treated by Ragghianti, particularly notions drawn from the little-known German philosopher Conrad Fiedler and the art historian Heinrich Wölfflin regarding "the visual" as a form of knowledge distinct from the scientific. [95] The ability to "read" the visual necessarily conditions the possibility of a true understanding of Architecture. Zevi advocates the application of Fiedler's "pure visibility" to architecture, though he acknowledges that it clearly has its limitations,

91 Carlo Ludovico Ragghianti (1910–87), Giulio Carlo Argan (1909–92) and Bruno Zevi (1918–2000).

92 It is reviewed in Giulio Carlo Argan, "A Proposito di spazio interno" [About Internal Space], *Metron*, no. 28 (October 1948). See Bruno Zevi, *Architecture as Space*, trans. Milton Gendel, New York: Horizon Press, 1957.

93 These include reference texts on theories of art and architecture, such as: Miloutine Borissavliévitch, *Les theories de l'architecture*, Paris, 1951; Julius Schlosser-Magnino, *De Kunstliteratur*, Vienna: Schroll & Col, 1924; Lionello Venturi, *History of Art Criticism*, New York: E.F. Dutton & Co., 1924; and Scott, *The Architecture of Humanism*; as well as Fasola, Ragghianti, Argan, Bettini, Collingwood, Gutton and Hamlin.

94 *Propaedeutic Contribution*, p. 64/*Contribuição Propedêutica*, p. 13.

95 See especially, "Architecture and Science," Chapter 1, and "Theory of Architecture and Caractère of Buildings," Chapter 2.

96 Zevi, *Architecture as Space*, p. 213.

97 *Propaedeutic Contribution*, p. 79/*Contribuição Propedêutica*, pp. 21–22.

98 *De Prospectiva Pingendi*, edizione critica a cura di G. Nicco Fasola, Raccolta di Fonti per la Storia dell'Arte, Firenze, G. C. Sansoni, 1942. A new edition was published in 1984. Nicco Fasola taught treatises and Aesthetics from 1944 to 1947 at the School of Architecture in Florence. Beginning in 1948, she taught Art History at the University of Genoa. The architectural theorist Giulio Carlo Argan was an early student. Other works include *L'Arte nella Vita dell'Uomo*, 1956; chapter 11 in *Ragionamenti sull'Architettura* [*Discourse on Architecture*], 1949 (new edition, 2005), titled "Fattori sociali nell'architettura" ["Social Factors in Architecture"] was translated into English by Creighton Gilbert and published in *The Journal of Aesthetics and Art Criticism* (June 1950). She wrote several articles on Frank Lloyd Wright and commented on organic architecture for the magazine *Citta Nuova*.

citing that Fiedler's notions "were born of [Wölfflin's] critical rehabilitation of Baroque architecture." He makes the analogy that "to pass from vague concepts of symmetry, contrast, variety, emphasis . . . to modern architectural criticism is like going from the simple categories of a critic like [Anton Raphael] Mengs . . . to the penetrating schemas of a Fiedler and a Wölfflin." [96]

Although Bo Bardi cites Fiedler to support the distinctions between subjects, particularly art (in which she includes architecture) and science, in her chapter "Architecture and Science" she ultimately tries to synthesize his dialectic, prefacing her conclusion with the optimistic assurances that "it is apparent that the fusion of art and science has increasingly characterized the development of Architecture," and, "The eventual fusion of art and science shall certainly be realized . . ."

> But the reconciliation between a concern for external appearances, sometimes regarded to be of superfluous, aesthetic interest, and an accommodation of the interior, may, at the very least, afford something inevitably of interest—a hedonistic-utilitarian. The architect (Fiedler was writing about the artist and the scientist in a broad manner) will one day reconcile these two human activities, and be the mediator of approaches that exceed their disciplinary boundaries, because it is said that, despite growing warnings about the prevalence of scientific progress, there is nothing approaching a reaction in art, throughout its continued presence. [97]

Science, for Bo Bardi, alternatively referred to industry, mathematics, medicine, the machine, technological progress in material and structure (stadia, skyscrapers, bridges, prefabrication), ecology and Norbert Wiener's cybernetics. Only one painting, Mondrian's *New York City* (1942) (Figure 62) stands as exemplary of modern art in *Propaedeutic Contribution*. By deduction, Bo Bardi indicates that Architecture would be the venue for the anticipated "reaction in art."

The 1957 publication of *Propaedeutic Contribution* constitutes the first of the genre by a practicing female architect. An indication that Bo Bardi was not only conscious of the status of her contribution to the subject of architecture theory, but preoccupied with pointing it out, is the opportunity she makes in the early part of the text to mention a female contemporary in the field of art history, Giusta Nicco Fasola (1901–60). Fasola often signed her name "G. Nicco Fasola," so her gender is sometimes incorrectly identified. She was an art historian whose extensive writings on art and artists range from the Medieval to the Mannerist and include the critical edition of Piero della Francesca's *De Prospectiva Pingendi*. [98] Bo Bardi made reference to this important text several times in *Propaedeutic Contribution*. She recorded a peculiar exchange between Fasola and the Italian art historian, Sergio Bettini (1905–86) in a note in the opening pages of the text. The note concerns issues related to Nicco Fasola's 1949 book, *Ragionamenti sull'Architettura* [*Discourse on Architecture*]. Bo Bardi sides with the critical and patronizing remarks made by Bettini on Nicco Fasola's use of "outdated philosophies in recent Architectural Theory." This served to explicitly distinguish Bo Bardi from Nicco Fasola and from the discipline of architectural history, which Bo Bardi saw as having to do with philosophy rather than science. [100]

Bo Bardi's pointed reference in her text to Giusta Nicco Fasola, particularly to her work on Piero della Francesca, prompts an interesting thesis which further supports the interpretive methodology of "reading the surface." In her introduction to the treatise, Nicco Fasola begins directly with a discussion of Part Three of *De Prospectiva Pingendi*. [101] It is here that Piero describes his "altro modo" ["other method"] of perspective construction; it is a method that has no vanishing points. [102] He explains in the preface that he introduces the other method for two reasons, "one is because things will be easier to demonstrate and to understand; the other is because of the great multitude of lines that would be necessary to make these bodies following the first [Alberti's] method, so that the eye and the mind would be confused by these lines . . ." [103] And so it is with Bo Bardi's *Propaedeutic Contribution*. This visual analogy to Bo Bardi's text is a way of accepting its superficiality, a way to read and understand the surface, and find meaning by looking at the relations she draws between things, rather than by looking for an ordered construction that converges towards a single point. As Nicco Fasola points out, one's perspective does indeed become the center of one's thinking:

> When Piero della Francesca wants to exhaust the entire sense of painting in perspective, such that painting would be nothing but the exposition of surfaces and objects as they decrease or increase relatively, he dictates that this notion become the central focus of all our thoughts. [104]

The main difference, in theoretical terms, between the "Other Method" of perspective and Alberti's, as described by Robin Evans in his treatment, is that Piero "concentrates on local relations among eye, picture plane, and object." [105] Evans' point is that Piero painstakingly constructed each object using locally related points, and shifted these to address the points of view of multiple viewers, or to signify temporal dislocations within the picture plane. Bo Bardi constructed her text similarly. It is evident that she was keenly aware of her audience, the faculty members and critics who she knew would be judging her; the students, to whom she felt responsible; and, perhaps, the larger field of her European contemporaries and posterity. She assured the committee that her approach "avoids, from the onset, any interference from other disciplines in the

100 *Propaedeutic Contribution*, p. 186, note 16/ *Contribuição Propedêutica*, p. 74, note 16.

101 "Nel proemio della parte III del suo trattato Piero della Francesca dice per quei pittori che per diffidenza o per incapacità non le vogliono prestar fede, che la prospettiva è *necessaria alla pittura*; e anche più vivacemente aveva già parlato contro quelli *che stanno in dubitatone la prospectiva non essere vera scientia giudicando il falso per ignoranza*." De Prospectiva Pingendi, p. 3.

102 Robin Evans, *The Projective Cast: Architecture and its Three Geometries*, Cambridge, MA: MIT Press, 1995, ch. 4, "Piero's Heads," pp. 123–179.

103 Piero della Francesca, cited and translated in Evans, *The Projective Cast*, p. 150.

104 "Quando Piero della Francesca viene quasi ad assorbire nella prospettiva *la funzione della pittura: la pittura non è se non dimostrazioni de superficie et de corpi degradati o accresciuti nel termine*, c'impone che tale convinzione divenga centro del nostro pensiero." De Prospectiva Pingendi, p. 4.

105 Evans, *The Projective Cast*, p. 148.

106 *Propaedeutic Contribution*, p. 48/*Contribuição Propedêutica*, p. 5.

107 Several professors with whom I spoke about the text concurred about the reasons for its historically negative evaluations.

108 The May 21, 1957 lecture was recorded as "The Case for a Theory of Modern Architecture," *RIBA Journal* (June 1957): 307–313.

109 Bruno Zevi, "John Summerson: una teoria per l'architettura moderna," *Architettura: cronache e storia* 3, no. 25 (November, 1957): 436–437.

curriculum . . . the great multitude of lines" that may "confuse" the eye and mind) "and provides the student with an accurate idea of the unity and spirit, in other words, the *lineamenta*, the 'cosa grande e divina' of Architecture" ("easier to demonstrate and understand"). Bo Bardi ends the thought by citing Alberti, as if to suggest the counterpoint to which she alludes. [106]

Furthermore, Evans' speculation about how the "Other Method" might affect the composition of paintings is also instructive here. He described how objects "would tend to tumble into pictorial space," how they might "look as if they were stuck to the surface of the picture" because of the way the method was conducive to the mapping of discrete objects in the absence of a preordained metrical framework that would relate them to each other. This is certainly reminiscent of critics' estimations of the composition of Bo Bardi's text, and the way that topics appear to be disconnected from each other, and lacking in depth. [107] In order to be able to read the work both synthetically and analytically, an understanding of the "otherness" of its construction is required. We must see the surface as an assemblage and understand its juxtapositions, as in a collage. Meanings are not given on the surface, but must be constructed, not only from the elements in view, but from their differences, from the way they are joined together, and for whom. It is clear from the text that Bo Bardi was not only aware of the mixed group she was addressing, and their concerns, but of the importance of the pedagogical position that the course in architecture theory would play amongst the interlocking disciplines of art, architecture and engineering.

Constructing a theory of practice

In a presentation to the Royal Institute of British Architects (RIBA) on May 21, 1957 John Summerson expressed "a practical need for . . . a theoretical formula as a means of introducing students to the principles of modern design." [108] In his review of the talk, Bruno Zevi suggested that, after a review of the three most important theories of modern architecture, namely Le Corbusier's *Towards a New Architecture*, Moholy-Nagy's *The New Vision*, and the theory he promoted in his own, *Towards an Organic Architecture*, Summerson "accepted the organic theory" that Architecture was based on a social, not a formal idea, and its principles needed to include sociological, psychological, figurative and semantic points of view. [109]

On the same date, a competition was launched in Brazil for a Chaired position in Architecture Theory at the Faculty of Architecture and Urbanism, Federal University of São Paulo University (FAU/USP). Submissions were due just four months later. In her response, Bo Bardi highlighted similar themes and made reference to many of the same sources as Summerson when addressing the question of the relations between theory, practice and history. In his argument for architecture theory as "statements of root principle," as opposed to discursive studies of types and elements of architecture, Summerson ventured that principles of architecture theory could be much more closely related to each other than to the architectural production of their time. He reasoned that this was because they evolved following their own dialectic. He warned that the actual relationship of architecture theory to architectural production at any given time is problematic, and concluded: "There is no question either of principles being abstracted wholly from practice or of practice being necessarily a reflection of theory." [110] Bo Bardi differed. She was very careful, from the first pages of her text, to establish the terms for the relation between architecture theory and history:

> I would like to emphasize that "theory," precisely because of its development in a broad sense, is just as infinite as the historical process through which its development occurs. It is therefore wrong to treat any of its historical moments as absolute and, consequently, to speak of a theory (in our case, "theory of Architecture") that is valid in and of itself. In this sense, an absolutely valid formal and abstract "theory" of Architecture does not exist. It is its history that gives the "theory" its character and that, at the same time, surpasses it. [111]

If we forego the unity of antique forms as the source of architectural unity, wondered Summerson, on what can we base modern principles? He considered "program," calling it "a local fragment of a social pattern" to distinguish it from "function," and deemed it the "one new principle involved in modern architecture." Bo Bardi, along with Zevi and Summerson, argued that the source of unity lies in the social sphere, in the architect's program. With Gropius, she added the importance of methodology.

In 1957, FAU/USP was a relatively young school, founded fewer than ten years earlier, in 1948, by a group of professors from the Polytechnic School at the University of São Paulo. The curriculum was based largely on the engineering program already in place at the school, with some elements from the standard curriculum of the National School of Fine Arts in Rio (ENBA/UFRJ). The art and architecture program at ENBA/UFRJ was famously radicalized with Bauhaus pedagogy and Modern architectural ideas by its director from 1930 to 1931, the architect Lucio Costa (1902–98). [112] Professor Luiz Ignacio Romeiro de Anhaia Mello (1891–1974) was one of the founders and the first Director of FAU/USP and was responsible for inviting ENBA/UFRJ graduates and São Paulo partners Alberto de Souza and Hélio Queiroz Duarte, as well as several other graduates from the post-Costa years at the school (1932–34), to faculty positions at FAU/USP. [113] This mix of engineer-

110 Zevi, Summerson, p. 307.

111 *Propaedeutic Contribution*, p. 184, note 8/*Contribuição Propedêutica*, p. 73, note 8.

112 The fact that he was forced to resign after only one year attests to the dominance of French Neo-classicism in Brazil and the Beaux-Arts pedagogy.

113 Silvia Ficher, *Os Arquitetos da Poli: ensino e profissão em São Paulo*, São Paulo, Brazil: Edusp., 2005, pp. 150–151.

114 Architect Carlos Millan, quoted in the 2005 informational materials for FAU/USP. In the early 1950s Millan shared an office with architects Sidney Fonseca and Luiz Roberto Carvalho Franco in the Diários Associados Building, the first home of the Museum of Art of São Paulo (MASP) and the *Habitat* offices.

115 "Renovation in Architectural Education," *Habitat*, no. 37 (December 1956): p. 1.

116 Abelardo de Souza, "Teaching Architecture," *Habitat*, no. 18 (September–October 1954): 1.

117 *Habitat*, no. 26 (1956): 5.

118 A period marked by technological revolutions.

119 Geraldo Ferraz, "Teaching architecture in F.A.U. University of São Paulo," *Habitat*, no. 38 (January 1957): 59.

120 Geraldo Ferraz, "Habitat initiates a survey on the conditions of university education in statements made by leaders of different chairs FAU," *Habitat*, no. 26 (1956): 5. Professor and architect Rino Levi (1901–65) was highlighted next, but the series seems to have ended there, replaced by "Personalities in the history of the current architecture in Brazil," a series of appreciations by Ferraz.

121 See Appendix 2 for the syllabus of this course and Bo Bardi's evaluation.

122 *Habitat*, no. 26 (1956): 5.

architects and artist-architects was seen by critics as creating a "didactic and programmatic asymmetry" at FAU/USP, "between the technical training provided by engineers, and that provided by the so-called artists." [114] In 1953, as a sign of the necessity for a "Theory of Architecture" course, and also, perhaps, to redress this asymmetry, Anhaia Mello changed the name of his fourth-year course from "Architect-engineer" to "Notions of Architecture."

Following student strikes at several Brazilian universities, *Habitat* reported on the "preoccupation of youth with the need for reform in the teaching of architecture" and "the positive implications of the crisis that would lead to a higher level of education, participation and responsibility" for those who study architecture and urbanism. It was clear, the article concluded, that "the teaching of architecture is going through a deep transformation." [115] Brazilian architects had already expressed their concerns in the pages of *Habitat* as early as September 1954, complaining that "our schools, their teaching methods and their programs have not evolved as necessary to teach architecture as it presents itself today or where it is headed in the future." [116] The classic examples of Brazilian modern architecture, starting in the 1930s, had not been based in schools, "but were isolated cases—Warchavchik, Reidy and Marcelo Roberto, who worked with Corbusier in the Ministry of Education building." [117] Paraphrasing the popular thesis of anthropologist and politician Darcy Ribeiro (1922–97), that Brazil was in a "civilizatory process," [118] educators called for a "civilizing stage" in Brazilian architecture, "a school of architecture to focus on a new architecture, Brazilian and contemporary, national and international, regional and functional—a new time demands a new architecture." [119] *Habitat* again resonated with *Quadrante*, promoting a message very close to Mussolini's well-known challenge to artists to produce "a new art, an art for our time, a fascist art . . ."

To promote exemplary endeavors in this area, the magazine began a series on university education, with presentations made by leaders of the different chairs of FAU/USP. Lina Bo Bardi was the first to be highlighted. [120] The article praised the innovative ideas that she brought to the school, comparing her approach to the Bauhaus pedagogy of Walter Gropius. Because she considered the title of her fifth-year course, "Composição Decorativa," [121] inadequate, Bo Bardi added the subtitle "Architectural Interiors, Industrial Design." In the article, she argued that there should be no distinction between the design of a chair and the design of a building because they had the same compositional basis. Similarly, the design of a contemporary structure as well as the architecture of interiors should both be based on a technical study of the needs of man, needs that are part of our immediate context, but also our spiritual and cultural realities: "The architect needs both moral and technical education." [122] The course included one hour of "theory" and two hours of "practice" each week. The schedule included a project to design an exhibition of materials, for example, chairs, ceramics, glasses, and vintage fabrics borrowed "from the architect, Lina Bardi," and visits to furniture factories and studios to acquire direct knowledge from industry of different methods of production.

To a certain extent, the volatility of the academic architectural climate in Brazil is paradoxical. Concern over post-war European issues like housing and themes of reconstruction seems uncalled for in a country that had escaped the destruction of the Second World War. Though it remained neutral until 1941, Brazil became the "most conspicuous" Latin-American partner of the United States, by providing access to its coastline for strategic air and sea bases, and valuable raw materials. In return, the United States supported the basic industrialization of Brazil, for example, financing a Brazilian steel mill at Volta Redonda; the Pan American Airways Project, which modernized airports; and perpetuating a Hollywood "takeover" of the Brazilian film industry, all part of what has been termed by Latin-American scholar and Brazilian authority Thomas Skidmore a US "cultural" and "economic offensive". [123] US influence in Brazil, arguably in play since the Rockefeller Foundation's health campaigns of the 1920s had successfully curbed the rise of epidemic diseases, had paid off, especially for US companies. New markets and new immigrants made the years 1945–60 an especially optimistic period for the political and economic elite in Brazil. However, during this time the Brazilian urban population exploded, putting a strain on existing housing, schools and healthcare facilities. [124] The socio-economic inequalities multiplied precipitously. Thus, the problems related to building the Third World and re-building Europe produced strangely parallel calls for academic reform in Brazil's architecture schools.

Ultimately, change did come to the curriculum, including, ironically, the cancellation of Bo Bardi's course. By November 1956, a Federal law, n. 2.938, convened an "Egrégio Conselho Universitário" [Distinguished University Council] to prepare the competition program for a newly formed position, "Professor Catedrático de cadeira [Chaired Professor] n.14 in Architecture Theory" for the second-year Architecture course at the school. The "Notice of Contest" was delivered by order of a Professor who was regularly criticized in *Habitat*, Pedro Gravina. [125] The only way Bo Bardi would be able to continue to teach at FAU/USP would be to win the competition. The competition program presented the "Theory of Architecture" in five categories. Candidates were expected to choose one to develop in response to the competition. [126] The categories were

A. *Elements of Architecture*
B. *Elements of Aesthetics*
C. *Concepts of Architecture*
D. *Aesthetics of Architecture*
E. *"Caraterologia" of Buildings*.

123 Thomas Skidmore, *Brazil: Five Centuries of Change*, New York and London: Oxford University Press, 1999, pp. 120–121.

124 Skidmore, *Brazil*, pp. 138–139.

125 Ferraz, "Teaching of architecture," p. 59. Ferraz, a regular contributor on architecture to *Habitat*, argued that, as a specialist in hydraulics, Gravina completely ignored architecture and urbanism, and was not suited for the leadership of an architecture school.

126 The five-page document with a hand-written note on the first page is translated and included here as Appendix 1.

127 *Propaedeutic Contribution*, p. 140/*Contribuição Propedêutica*, p. 51.

128 Her handwritten comments on the document, in Italian, describe its written style as "unctuous."

129 Walter Gropius, "In Search of a Better Architectural Education," transcribed in *A Decade of New Architecture*, ed. Sigfried Giedion, Zurich, 1951, pp. 41–46.

130 *Propaedeutic Contribution*, Preface, p. 48/*Contribuição Propedêutica*, p. 5.

131 *Propaedeutic Contribution*, Preface, p. 48/*Contribuição Propedêutica*, p. 5.

132 Auguste Perret, *Une Contribution à une théorie de l'architecture*, Paris: A. Wahl, 1952.

A, B and C were concerned with defining architecture: (A) in terms of construction and related professions, (B) in terms of Philosophy, Psychology and Sociology, and (C) according to ten points of relation: to urbanism, complexity, atmospheric elements, comfort, metabolic equations, salubrity, construction systems, materials, economy, and democracy and habitation. (D), "*Aesthetics of Architecture*" began with the statement "Architecture —Material expression of the soul of the people," and ended with a phrase that recalls Bruno Zevi, "Space—protagonist of Architecture." (E) "*'Caraterologia' of Buildings*," belied the reform intended by the competition, by giving place to "caractère," arguably the most entrenched Beaux-Arts notion in Brazilian schools. Bo Bardi was not silent about her disapproval: "Although no longer appropriate . . . the so-called 'Caractère' of Buildings," . . . a criterion from the educational system of the second half of the nineteenth century continues to be used . . ." [127]

In the text of *Propaedeutic Contribution*, Bo Bardi complied with these "general principles [as] outlined by the committee," but she was implicitly critical of the competition program, and of the faculty that produced it. [128] Remarking that architecture theory is a "complex discipline [to teach] in just a single academic year," she proposed to outline a methodology for teaching it. The members of the Distinguished University Council did not mention methodology in the competition statement, in apparent disregard of Gropius' July 1949 speech at CIAM VII, where he began with a very straightforward declaration: "In architectural education the teaching of a method of approach is more important than the teaching of skills." [129] Accordingly, Bo Bardi pointed out, "Rather than choose one of the topics offered by the competition program and develop it in detail in a limited, technical sense, I thought it more appropriate to interpret the spirit of this program," and announced her plan to "make a contemporary contribution to the expression of a subject that has only recently been defined as Architecture Theory." So, in defiance of the competition guidelines, rather than select a single topic, she proposed to "integrate each item" into an overall theory, "reworking it, without change, of course, to its composition or to the structure of each one of its items . . ." [130] Even with its appeasing qualifier, this subtle yet powerful gesture went directly against the pedagogy in place at FAU/USP. It is just one of several critiques Bo Bardi intimated in the text that followed.

Indeed, as a "propaedeutic," or introductory, text, her thesis is primarily concerned with delighting the aspiring student of architecture with the sheer amplitude of the topic, together with a clear sense of its "unity of spirit." [131] She presented her contribution as pedagogy; it is an architectural theory, together with a methodology for teaching it. Her title recalls Auguste Perret's *A Contribution to a Theory of Architecture* of 1952. [132] *Habitat* published a selection of maxims from Perret's book under the heading "From the book 'Contribuição à uma teoria da

arquitetura'—Auguste Perret, 1874–1954" alongside his obituary. [133]
The use of the uncommon word "Propaedeutic" in the title, and Bo Bardi's
ambition to "create an impassioned student, a student with an incentive
to think, a motivation towards research," recalls Jacob Burckhardt's remarks
in a letter to Nietzsche, February 25, 1874:

> . . . I have never taught history for the sake of what goes under the
> high-falutin' name of "world history," but essentially as a propaedeutic
> study: my task has been to put people into the possession of the
> scaffolding which is indispensable if their future studies of whatever
> kind were not to be aimless. I have done everything I possibly could
> to lead them on to acquire personal possession of the past. . .and at
> least not to sicken them of it; I wanted them to be capable of picking
> the fruits for themselves; I never dreamt of training scholars and
> disciples in the narrower sense, but only wanted to make every
> member of the audience feel and know that everyone may appropriate
> those aspects of the past which appeal to him and that there might
> be happiness in so doing . . . [134]

Bo Bardi positioned her text outside the parameters of the competition
requirements and offered a theory to guide the ambitious out of the crisis
of the schools, through its practical application. Following Burckhardt's
conception of "cultural history" evolving along a continuous tradition,
exemplified in his seminal *Civilization of the Renaissance in Italy* and *The
Cicerone*, Bo Bardi argued for a theory of architecture that was ultimately
a history of architectural culture. *Propaedeutic Contribution* has a simple
organization, with a preface and just two chapters. For the first chapter,
"Problems of Theory in Architecture" Bo Bardi selected elements from
the competition requirements as subheadings, but she did not treat them
independently, as suggested, but always put them in relation to history.
This definition of history is central to her treatment: "The task of every
professor should be to awaken a critical consciousness, to teach the student
a sense of history as a continuity, not as a cultural elegance, but as a vital
source of real contributions." [135] Every element from the brief, "Concepts
and Meanings," "The Measure of Man," "science," "materials," "society,"
"the client," and "Romanticism," is related to this notion of history.

> There is no difference between "modern" and history; the "modern"
> is itself a product of history, and only through it is it possible to avoid
> repeating obsolete experiences. This history is not seen as a "cosa da
> forbici e colla" [cut and paste] but as something alive and present, a
> history revived with fundamentals, endowed with the capacity to
> transmit fruitful lessons. It is clearly not the history of textbooks,
> monotonous and second hand, merely capable of suggesting that the

133 *Habitat*, no. 18 (September–
October 1954): 11. The obituary
is accompanied by a text by his
French rationalist contemporaries,
architects Paul Nelson and Bernard
Zehrfuss. The same issue begins
with an editorial by the architect
and FAU professor Abelardo de
Souza, "Ensino da arquitetura"
["Teaching architecture"]; see also
Julien Guadet, *Éléments et Théorie
de l'Architecture, Cours professé à
l'École Nationale et Spéciale des
Beaux-Arts* [*Rudiments and Theory of
Architecture, Course taught at l'École
Nationale et Spéciale des Beaux-Arts*]
Paris, 1909, 5th edn, vol. 4; and
Miloutine Borissavliévitch, *Les
théories de l'architecture* [*The
Theories of Architecture*], Paris:
Payot, 1926.
Bo Bardi cites the 1951 edition
and its introduction by Louis
Hautecoeur.

134 *The Letters of Jacob Burckhardt*,
selected, edited and translated by
Alexander Dru, New York: Pantheon
Books, 1955, p. 158.

135 *Propaedeutic Contribution*,
p. 116/*Contribuição Propedêutica*,
p. 39.

136 *Propaedeutic Contribution*, Preface, p. 50/*Contribuição Propedêutica*, p. 6.

137 *Propaedeutic Contribution*, p. 116/*Contribuição Propedêutica*, p. 39.

138 Joseph Hudnut (1887–1968) was the first Dean of the Harvard University Graduate School of Design (GSD), serving from 1936 to 1953. He was responsible for bringing Walter Gropius and Marcel Breuer to the GSD Faculty and working with them to bring Bauhaus pedagogy to the United States. Ultimately, he differed with Gropius on several pedagogical issues, including the importance of history.

139 *Journal of Architectural Education* 12, no. 2 (Summer 1957): 8.

"past" is past, and no longer valid, suggesting that the world began today, and man, alone, has the task of reconstructing a "paradise lost." It is a history that is not "History" as a mere abstraction, but, like life itself, concrete and fecund." [136]

Bo Bardi described it as "the historical present" or "the continuous present," borrowing from Sigfried Giedion's term "the eternal present." As such, she made the study of history inseparable from the study of architecture, at one point concluding that there should be "a consolidation of all relevant disciplines into a single course, under a single professor. It would not be a course about 'theory' or 'character' or even 'history of art'; it would be a course about History." [137] In this, Bo Bardi differs significantly from Gropius, to whom she was compared for her pedagogical contributions to FAU/USP. While his pedagogical formulae for "teamwork" and the emphasis on methodology were otherwise lauded in *Propaedeutic Contribution*, his attitude about history was remiss, according to Bo Bardi. In his contribution to a discussion on pedagogy, recorded in the *Journal of Architecture* in the summer of 1957, Joseph Hudnut, then at MIT (he was formerly Dean of the School of Design at Harvard University), [138] agreed, recommending that students study history from the very first day of architecture school. Like Hudnut, Bo Bardi reflected on the eagerness of students to have a sense of certainty, and argued for the autonomy of the professor regarding the selection of course materials. Professor of Architecture William Shellman of Princeton University also remarked that "a knowledge of history should make the student sense that he is not a separate entity but part of a continuing flow." Though he was more adamant about the issue in other venues, in his short contribution to the journal, Gropius dissented only slightly from the others, recommending a delay in historical studies, deferred to a more advanced stage of education:

> My experience has been that a student in architecture will learn more from architectural history in an advanced stage of his development . . . I have found that the very young student, who hasn't found his own ground to stand on, is sometimes rather discouraged when he faces the old masters. [139]

Bo Bardi reiterated Gropius' sense of the students' position, and wrote that they are "hanging by a thread, with no knowledge of where to find solid footing." She also supported Giedion's view of history as a "dynamic, ever-changing process" and his reference to Burckhardt's sense of the past as a "*continuum*, which forms part of our supreme spiritual heritage." She summarizes her position on history: "the problem of architecture . . . appears to us full of facts and anxious doubts; of assurances because of what has already been achieved, and, simultaneously, questions and fears. History is implicit in these thoughts," she ends, more reminiscent of William Morris than of Giedion or Gropius, "history, whose living presence is synthesized in our actions precisely because we are its result." [140]

"Methodological update," the last and longest essay of four in the second chapter, is the only one which is explicitly related to methodology. Theoretical issues are not neatly relegated to autonomous consideration, as suggested in the competition brief. Rather, theoretical questions deliberately spill over into the chapter on methodology; clearly, in Bo Bardi's view, the dominant problems of method are theoretical, and find expression in practice.

> . . . and here, just to exemplify the problems associated with this, I remind the readers of Benedetto Croce, for whom the totality or the spirit have two essential and distinct forms: the *theoretical* form and the *practical* form, or *knowledge* and *volition*, *contemplation* and *action*; and Giovanni Gentile, for whom there was an essential identity between *theory* and *practice*, conceiving that knowledge, as a spiritual act, is simultaneously volition and vice-versa. [141]

The preface to *Propaedeutic Contribution* makes reference to the long-standing unpopularity of the subject of architecture theory and the confusion in the nineteenth century surrounding its identity in the context of architectural education. Bo Bardi used an elaborate note to contextualize her own treatment of the subject. [142] In it, the reader is alerted to the philosophical lineage that underlies much of her thinking. The dominance of the Idealist philosopher Benedetto Croce [143] in Italy at the time does not portend any argument for his exclusive influence on Bo Bardi; rather, an understanding of some of the more pervasive tenets of his thinking serves to illuminate the framework she has constructed for the topic. For example, the "single piece of stone . . . in any of our cities" that "represents an idea" for Manuel de Araujo Porto-alegre can be understood as a trope for a primary Idealist concept, the "concrete universal," a concrete reality that is simultaneously an abstract idea and, importantly, one that is organic and dynamic rather than fixed and formal. Bo Bardi proved the relation to be transitive: a dynamic, unfixed abstract idea is also a dynamic, concrete reality. Ze Celso, a radical Brazilian theatrical director for whom Bo Bardi designed stage sets and costumes in the late 1960s and 1970s, said: "She made a strait-jacket into a sail— the physical strength of a dream; poetry into concrete, cement and wood." [144] If the "single stone" serves Araujo Porto-alegre's observation effectively, then *concrete*, the preferred building material of Bo Bardi (and Brazil), is an image and a reality still more apt.

An undated curriculum plan amongst Bo Bardi's papers at FAU/USP is entitled "University Extension Courses: Contribution to a Technical

---

140 William Morris famously said, "The past is not dead, it is living among us, and will be alive in the future which we are now helping to make."

141 *Propaedeutic Contribution*, p. 184, note 8/ *Contribuição Propedêutica*, p. 73, note 8.

142 The note references a letter from Franscesco de Sanctis (1817–83), an illustrious Italian literary critic, published in a book of letters collected and annotated by Benedetto Croce (1866–1952), one of his most accomplished students. The letter remarks on the lack of interest in Th. [*sic*] Vischer's course on theory and aesthetics at the Zurich Polytechnic in the 1850s.

143 That Croce was the author of the "Manifesto of the Anti-Fascist Intellectuals," published by the newspaper *Il Mondo* on May 1, 1925, also served to distance Bo Bardi from a prevailing assumption about the politics of post-war immigrants to Brazil.

144 His comments are from the film, *Lina Bo Bardi*, 1993 directed by Aurelio Michiles and Isa Grinspum Ferraz.

145 See Appendix 3 for facsimile and translation.

146 *Propaedeutic Contribution* p. 184, note 8/*Contribuição Propedêutica*, p. 73, note 8.

147 Andrea Memmo, *Elementi dell'Architettra Lodoliana*, Roma, 1786, 1834 and Francesco Algarotti, *Saggio sopra l'architettura e sulla Pittura*, Milano, 1756.

148 *Propaedeutic Contribution*, p. 150/*Contribuição Propedêutica*, p. 56.

149 Luigi Moretti, "Strutture e sequenze di spazi," *Spazio* 7 (December 1952–April 1953): 9–20, 107–08. Zevi, a life-time critic of the unrepentant Fascist, Moretti, discussed the theory in his *Architecture as Space* of 1948. In his review of Zevi's book, Argan also discussed the theory. See G.C. Argan, "A proposito di spazio interno," *Metron*, no. 28 (October 1948): 20–21.

150 *Propaedeutic Contribution*, caption for Figure 113.

Humanism." [145] It is a sequence intended not for "specialists, "but for students from various departments." It is an integrated, interdisciplinary approach to the History of Esthetics, Architecture and Industrial Design, and didactic exhibitions. She defined her terms in the first paragraphs, again, following Croce: "Technical," is adopted to characterize the courses, which deal with problems in the history of art as "vital and concrete" rather than "academic and abstract." Esthetics is not meant to be understood in the traditional way, as "philosophy of art," but as "a *synthesis of theory and practice . . .*" In fact, *Propaedeutic Contribution* consistently and intentionally resists defining theory. Bo Bardi explained that she would not define theory first, because to do so would create a "vicious cycle" whereby the definition would become "philosophical," staying uselessly within the sphere of theory, rather than becoming practical and "scientific." [146] She advocated a non-dogmatic approach throughout. As to the use of treatises, Bo Bardi thought that they should be evaluated for their usefulness to current practice, and studied not with the end of discovering their meaning, but rather, to revitalize inquiry. She traced a very particular historical stream, common to few but the most attentive scholars of Rationalism. She began by picturing the frontispiece of Scamozzi's treatise, alluding to his emphasis on the liberal arts, on ornament and appearances. Next, Geoffrey Scott, and the assurance that the act of architecture somehow lies between the act of the savage, who cowers before nature, and that of the scientist, who studies it impartially. Bo Bardi introduced Alberti, Serlio, Scamozzi, Lodoli (through both apologists, Algarotti and Memmo) [147] and even the little-known Gallaccini, before admitting that it would be irreverent to continue without mentioning Vitruvius. Like Zevi, she was critical of French Academicism, particularly the treatise of André Lurçat, who, she says, despite all his merits as an architect, has not come to terms with the issue of "didactic communication," which must be primary within the scope of education. She opted, rather, for the definition given by Viollet-le-Duc,

> Theory and practice; theory includes: the art itself, the rules inspired by taste, from tradition, and science which can prove itself with absolute invariable formulas. Practice is the application of theory to needs; it is practice which bends art and science to the nature of materials, to the climate, to the customs of an era, to the needs of the moment. [148]

Bo Bardi summarizes the article "Structures and Sequences of Spaces," [149] by Moretti, which sets out his main principles for the theory of internal space. In the caption for the illustration of Michelangelo's reconstruction project for the church of S. Giovanni de Fiorentini in Rome, [150] she says the theory can have severe consequences in the academy, and may lead to inhibitions on the part of the students and a fixation of "pseudo-scientific" definitions, like "pressure" and "energetic load" of space. She adds the authority of art critic and painter Gillo Dorfles (1910–) to refute the theory. Her alternative theory, "Space-total-Space," follows his statement that Architecture is an art of space that makes use of internal space, external space, and imaginary space. In *Propaedeutic Contribution*, however, it remains unclear what the grounds of Bo Bardi's disagreement with the theory are, and she does not elaborate sufficiently on her alternative. This, and the promising "Theory of a Technical Humanism" are merely in formation at the time of this writing, introduced, but never fully argued. Near the end of Chapter 2, Bo Bardi admits to "the difficulty that lies in the theoretical systematization of architecture." [151] Discouraged, she changes the subject.

Bo Bardi's "Theory of Technical Humanism" was perhaps a response to Zevi's proposition for a new Architectonic Humanism, which was possible, he said, "only through a fertile dialogue between architects and historians." Zevi had recently inaugurated the magazine *L'Architettura: Cronache e Storia* (1955), replacing his first post-war magazine, *Metron*. In his first editorial he also noted a crisis, that of the European intellectual, following Albert Camus' reflections. His writing elaborated on the "disquiet, anxious hope of universality" and "the integration of architectonic culture." The Dictatorship, the impetus of liberation, the war and the frenetic vitality of reconstruction, have passed and, having "won its technical language battle," the modern movement had begun to "stop and think . . . and realized that without cleaving to reality and without an intimate feeling for tradition, it is doomed to failure even with the theoretical perfection of form if this is to be void of meaning." The ambitious program of *L'Architettura* was political, artistic and technical. Zevi promised that it would "weld contemporary and traditional experience, which will integrate the feeling of the present day art with studies of the past, made with modern orientation." Bo Bardi's insistence on the technical over Zevi's historical (as differentiated from her own understanding of history as a "continuous present") is here more consistent with her indebtedness to Gropius and his program for the Bauhaus. It is also consistent (and contemporaneous) with the description Max Bill gave in his lecture "Beauty Generated by Function and as Function," delivered in São Paulo on the occasion of his first International Sculpture Prize at the São Paulo Biennale in 1951. In it, Bill discussed his extension of Bauhaus ideas for the pedagogy of the Hochschule für Gestaltung (HfG), or Ulm Institute for Design. [152] Bill's "Beauty" was rational design defined by the efficient use of material and technique; he aligned artistic production with engineering. Bill became infamous in Brazil because of his scathing, critical remarks against the architecture of Niemeyer, and Bo Bardi was careful to censor him entirely from *Propaedeutic Contribution*, in favor of Gropius.

151 *Propaedeutic Contribution*, p. 144/*Contribuição Propedêutica*, p. 53.

152 Max Bill, "Beleza Provida da Funcao e como Funcao," *Habitat*, no. 2 (January–March 1951): 61–65, English summary. For a discussion, see Rene Spitz, *HfG Ulm. The View Behind the Foreground, The Political History of the Ulm School of Design 1953-1968*, Stuttgart: Edition Axel Menges, 2002, pp. 64–65.

153 Max Bill, "Report on Brazil," *Architecture Review* 116, no. 694 (October 1954): 234–250. Kenneth Frampton points out that Bill is referring to Niemeyer's Palace of Industry, under construction in São Paulo, when he says, "modern architecture has sunk to the depths, a riot of anti-social waste, lacking any sense of responsibility toward either the business occupant or his customers." Quoted in Kenneth Frampton, *Modern Architecture, A Critical History*, New York: Oxford University Press, 1980, p. 257.

154 "Max Bill: The Iconoclast," *Habitat*, no. 12 (July–September 1953): 34.

155 Lina Bo, "A New Born Child," *Habitat*, no. 2 (January–March 1951): 3.

156 Max Bill, *Eine Bilanz über die Formentwicklung um die Mitte des XX Jahrhunderts* [*Form. A Balance Sheet of Mid-Twentieth Century Trends in Design*], Basel: Verlag Karl Werner A.G., 1952. Bill dedicated a copy to P.M. Bardi's library.

157 "Vitrinas das formas" *Habitat*, no.1 (October–December 1950): 35.

The Architecture Review "Report on Brazil" of 1954 delivered the critique from Bill, who condemned some of the expressive formalism he had seen in São Paulo as "born of a spirit devoid of all decency and of all responsibility towards human needs." [153] *Habitat* defended his remarks, [154] and published his lecture "The Architect, Architecture and Society" as a polemic, paired with Gropius' "The Architect within our Industrial Society." Diplomatically, Bo Bardi had previously published a view of the Ministry of Education in Rio, while simultaneously acknowledging that "certain free forms by Oscar are plastic complacencies, that their realization is not always satisfactory . . . (I agree in this point with my European friends)." She continued, echoing Pagano: "Architecture must . . . collect inspiration from the intimate poetry of the Brazilian land . . . this lack of politeness, this roughness . . . this continuous possession of the consciousness of technique and the spontaneity and zeal of the primitive." [155] Bo Bardi's "Vitrina das Formas," a glass display box she curated periodically at MASP, was an exercise in illustration of Bill's *Eine Bilanz über die Formentwicklung um die Mitte des XX Jahrhunderts.* [156] In the vitrines she displayed various forms created by different civilizations, celebrating human inventiveness. In *Habitat* she described them as having "a different sense in terms of the common meaning of a museum: they don't aim to be a presentation of 'ancient' objects, but an organic assemblage of variable forms, created for different civilizations or simply originated from casual circumstances." The hand-made and the machine-made were displayed side by side to show the "variability of human fantasy in the act of creation and transformation of materials within a constant and renewable impulse." [157]

In her attentiveness to the effects of European and North American influences in Latin America, Bo Bardi found particular resonance in the similarity of the post-war socio-economic conditions of Italy and Brazil, where a pre-industrial, craft-based and largely agrarian economy remained. Certainly, Bo Bardi's vantage as an Italian émigré to Brazil was a significant factor in this recognition. The poignant experience of watching as "the Popular Soul" of Italy and of its artisanal production was lost, "petrified by Fascism," gave her a Cassandra-like quality, particularly with regard to the popular culture of the northeast region of Brazil. In this context, the term Bo Bardi later coined to characterize her work, "Arquitetura Pobre" [Architecture of Poverty] was a challenge to the oppressive international economic and cultural system brought forth on the heels of rapid technological progress and the vapid consumerism she recognized in these two developing economies.

In her short elaboration of "Technical Humanism," Bo Bardi's definition of humanism draws not from Zevi's historical tradition but, as discussed, from the aestheticism of the early twentieth-century text by Geoffrey Scott, *The Architecture of Humanism—A Study in the History of Taste.* Scott is both foil and model for Bo Bardi's argument. Her allegiance to Scott was confirmed when, over thirty years later, on the occasion of a far-reaching exhibition of her architectural work, mounted at the very same School of Architecture and Urbanism in São Paulo, she had her vindication; in her lecture "Uma Aula de Arquitetura" [A Class in Architecture], she returned to Scott as a point of departure, proof of her continued commitment to this approach and, perhaps to a greater extent, of her persistence and headstrong character. [158]

Intending to write a clear statement of the principles of classical design, Scott concluded that it was not possible without first clearing up the confusion created by certain "architectural habits . . . caprices and prejudices" that made it impossible to escape the uncritical circumstances which fostered the entrenched eclecticism of the period. So, the problem of method became the problem of Scott's book, an identification of certain "Fallacies" he categorized as Romantic, Mechanical, Ethical and Academic. Again, in an expository, journalistic style, Bo Bardi recast Scott's fallacies as critical responses to the subject headings required by the competition guidelines. Resonances of Scott's words and references color Bo Bardi's text throughout. Bo Bardi's so-called "romantic" introductory overture, parallels Scott's: "The history of civilization thus leaves in architecture its truest, because its most unconscious record." [159] Both books begin with the basic understanding of architecture as an artifact of culture, a trace of the history of ideas, as opposed to the efficient accommodation of function. According to Scott, it is only through a critical consideration of architecture's aesthetic impulse ("delight"), as opposed to the evaluation of its constructional logic ("firmness") or even its ability to satisfy practical or societal ends ("commodity"), that architecture can be studied in the strict sense as an art. Notwithstanding Bo Bardi's occasional rejection of aestheticism in her later writings, "Technical Humanism" is meant to recuperate the art of architecture. With man as its main protagonist, architecture understood through technical humanism projects the image of his movements and functions into concrete forms. Architecture is a transcription of man. Bo Bardi cites the same lengthy passage from Scott, which Zevi cites in *Space as Architecture*, underlining Architecture's "monopoly on space" and the failure of criticism "to recognize this supremacy in architecture of spatial values." [160]

Simultaneously, Bo Bardi built her case for the role of industrialization and the machine. But she did so historically, and argued that the re-unification of architecture and engineering should be the plan for any reform of architectural pedagogy. She pointed out the books of Vitruvius' treatise which are dedicated to *Machinatio* [Machines] and to *Gnomonica* [Sundials], and that he includes topics related to hydraulics, "clocks and many other techniques, sciences and arts in his treatise." The treatise of painter Giovanni Paolo Lomazzo (1537–92) is brought to bear on the topic, particularly his argument that the perfection of the human body

158 "Uma Aula de Arquitetura" ["A Class in Architecture"], *Revisto Projeto* no. 133 (1990): 103–108, no. 149, reprinted, *Projeto* January/February 1992, edited and abridged, *Domus*, no. 753 (1993): 17–24.

159 Scott, *The Architecture of Humanism*, p. 16.

160 *Propaedeutic Contribution*, p. 130/*Contribuição Propedêutica*, p. 45.

161 *Propaedeutic Contribution,*
p. 76/*Contribuição Propedêutica,*
p. 19.

162 *Propaedeutic Contribution,*
p. 150/*Contribuição Propedêutica,*
p. 56.

163 *Propaedeutic Contribution,*
p. 142/*Contribuição Propedêutica,*
p. 52.

164 *Propaedeutic Contribution,*
p. 206, note 105/ *Contribuição
Propedêutica,* p. 86, note 105.

165 *Propaedeutic Contribution,*
p. 146/*Contribuição Propedêutica,*
p. 54.

166 *Propaedeutic Contribution,*
p. 62/*Contribuição Propedêutica,*
p. 12.

should be the criteria for all "the norms and measures to construct temples, theaters, and all the other buildings with all their parts, columns, capitals, channels, and so on; ships, cars, and all sorts of machines." [161] Quoting Nervi, she concluded:

> The existence of separate departments of civil engineering and architecture increases our uncertainties and clearly shows our lack of unified purpose. In fact, these departments do not differ so much in the subject matter they teach as in their viewpoints and the training methods they use, while both types of schools try to make designers and builders. [162]

Bo Bardi was not in favor of architecture being absorbed into schools of engineering, but she was critical of her professor, Giovannoni, for advocating a separation of "the whole of architectural knowledge into traditional, categorical, subdivisions: Architecture as theory and as 'caractère' . . . or Architecture and utilitarian Civil Engineering, for example." [163] She argued repeatedly for synthesis in pedagogy and was equally critical of curricula that offered separate courses in "Decoration" as complementary to "Architectural Design." She asserted that architecture should acknowledge both its technological and expressive opportunities; however, she warned against specialization, quoting again from the French theorist Guadet:

> Too often, we separate the study of construction from the study of decoration, and in our modern society where specializations dominate, we have created two novelties: so-called decorative art, and the profession of decorator . . . construction, decoration, it is all one thing, it is architecture. [164]

The expressive should never be conceived as an ornamental device, added *a posteriori*, but rather as an elaboration clearly anticipated by creative thought. Architecture should be rigorous, minimal and *not* without ornament, except that the ornament should be an "integral part of the fabric itself; so that whatever is represented must appear of service." [165] Here she echoed the maxims of Lodoli; "Devonsi unir e fabbrica e ragione e sia funzion la rappresentazione" [166] [Construction, reason, and function should be united in the representation]. Clearly, Bo Bardi was amongst the few in her time to understand that the rigor of functionalism, following Lodoli and the "rigorosi," did not mean that architecture had to be completely without ornament. When Bo Bardi criticized the "volubility" of decoration in her time, "characterized by the pleasure of display and of standing out, by boredom with things already seen, by the constant renewal of fashion launched by the decorative industry" she argued against her anti-dogmatic position: "It seems absolutely necessary to look with some distrust at an integration of decoration that corrupts an architectural unity . . . Absolute unity founded in the wisdom and the heart of a sole master, that is what translates into the teaching of the many disciplines that compose Architecture." [167]

It is significant that, in 1957, Bo Bardi eschewed Rudolph Wittkower's evaluation of Renaissance aesthetics, *Architectural Principles in the Age of Humanism* (1949), [168] especially since it is seen as a rebuttal to (or, as some view it, a negation of) Scott. This suggests that Bo Bardi's construction of the relationship between theory and history, art and "science," in the general terms in which she defined it, may represent another, less recognizable trajectory for modern architecture. Rather than the Wittkowerian alliances to modernism and classicism, Bo Bardi rejected the academic rules and proportioning systems of the Classical tradition and advocated for a "practical, common-sense" approach, emphasizing methodology and creative practice. Returning to Scamozzi, Bo Bardi's sense of the centrality of the human body does not rest on its proportions, but on bodily functions and organizations. Methodology, as Gropius held, is key. In the definition of theory, Bo Bardi includes art and science, tradition and taste. Practice, she defines as the application of theory to materials and climate, to the needs and the customs of the present. Needs are determined through direct investigation, and include both "practical" and "spiritual" ones. These are addressed by terraces, play areas for children, gardens, and panoramic views, for example. The architect cannot ignore these things; they are essential requirements to develop for the lives and activities of the inhabitants. They give a sense of *purpose* to an architectural work. Bo Bardi was interested in what she called "valid realities." For the architect, this meant solutions within the limits of *real* possibilities rather than "sterile desires based on ideological or literary suppositions": achievable structures, and plan organizations conceived according to a natural order.

Bo Bardi again reiterated the importance of representation and the necessity for students to learn all of the systems that are used to represent architecture, including drawing, film, photography and material models. "Architecture is brought to life through the art of Drawing," and students should learn to draw freehand, with lines that are clean, coarse and analytical, and display design clarity. She saw the different media of representation as different *ways of seeing*, and even noted that Brazilian photographers see in a manner that is "different" from that of the past and from that adopted by European photographers.

If there is an over-arching directive for the teaching of Architecture Theory, it is, perhaps, found among Bo Bardi's concluding remarks: "The ethical significance of the profession of architecture, in the context of its moral responsibility before society transcends the value of what, in the

167 *Propaedeutic Contribution,* p. 148/*Contribuição Propedêutica,* p. 55.

168 Although she draws on it as a source for her references to Manuzio, Lomazzo and Guadet in "The Measure of Man" section of *Propaedeutic Contribution.*

169 *Propaedeutic Contribution*, p. 172/*Contribuição Propedêutica*, p. 66.

170 Olivia de Oliveira, "Interview with Lina Bo Bardi," *2G: Lina Bo Bardi*, Olivia de Oliveira, ed., *Built Work*, no. 23/24 (2002): 249–250.

171 This is reported in Marcelo Ferraz, "Minha Experiência com Lina" (November 1991) published in *Urbanismo* 40 (January/February 1992): 39.

fine arts, has been called 'self-expression' . . .". [169] While she was a modernist, Bo Bardi believed that an abstract international language would not solve problems. The real problems of different countries, she said, must be solved through the use of *effective* means, and not with abstract criticism. Students must be made to understand that "beautiful plastic solutions" will not relieve us of the existence of sad country homes, favelas and shacks. The concept of "ethics," for Bo Bardi, began with artistic modesty, the elimination of the desire to "capture the limelight through frightening or surprising solutions, novelty or strangeness . . .". The moral responsibility to society is to base all work on the real needs of each country. It was important that the success of Brazilian Modernism on the international scene should not blind young students to the improvements they were responsible to make in their own country. Bo Bardi warned against the feeling of confidence that the success of Architecture during the "boom" had brought to Brazil. She saw one of the main problems of contemporary architecture, common to every country in the world, as the absence of "doubt." Ultimately, Architecture Theory should not be taught in a unilateral way, with the professor guiding the student through a determined path. Doubt should inspire curiosity, a desire to look in many and multiple directions, but in a focused and rigorous way. Rather than the professor leading the student, they should work side-by-side to explore the vast scope and richness of the subject of Architecture.

Coda

In a 1991 interview, Bo Bardi recounted that the committee at FAU/USP prevented her from entering the competition for the Chair of Architecture Theory because of her political stance and reputation. Despite the fact that she made an official complaint (which was decided in her favor) and supplied a writ from the capital ordering that she be admitted to the competition, the rebuttal from the committee was to suspend the competition entirely. [170] The fact that she was Italian, a woman, and married to the controversial former Italian Fascist P.M. Bardi should not be underestimated as reasons for her abjection. Arriving with him into the wealthy and powerful circle of Brazilian industrialist art collectors provided Lina Bo Bardi with both commissions and media coverage, but this clearly came at a price. Despite her repeated assertions about her role in the Italian resistance and her Communist partisanship in Brazil, it was not an easy dis-association from the taint of Fascism. Even through the late 1970s, students at FAU/USP were discouraged from studying her work or working with her. [171] The benefit of her liminal position, both as a woman and as a naturalized Brazilian, relative to the dominant discourses in Europe, Britain and the United States, makes the perspective she sets out in *Propaedeutic Contribution* especially illuminating in the context of architectural education and its effects on Modernism in the post-war period. Bo Bardi is remembered in Brazil as provocative, outspoken and beautiful. Her design work spanned across disciplines, from architecture to industrial design, exhibition design and "installation art" *avant la lettre.* [172] In the 1960s she engaged in film and theater design, including scenography and costume design, working with an unwavering commitment to the avant-garde project of the 1920s, and engendering a uniquely Brazilian modern project from the "savage" richness of the masses. [173] She was critical of academicism, romanticism and dogmatic theories. She promoted the study of history, but never as a model for imitation in practice: "l'Antico non deve servir de norma, esso deve essere un energia vitale della civiltà moderna." [The Ancient cannot serve as the rule, it must be the vital energy of modern civilization that does so.] [174] She was suspicious of technical novelty for its own sake, but in favor of architectural "audacity" and, in her own work, always harnessed the most contemporary technological means. Like Gropius, she asserted that teaching methodology is more important than teaching skills. The *purpose* of Architecture was most important, and the goal of teaching Architecture was to prompt the student to develop a professional conscience and to be "fully conscious of his own responsibility as a 'producer' of a real work, which *lasts* and is visible to everyone; work that will endure in the spiritual inheritance which every generation passes on to the next." Bo Bardi's own architectural conscience drew on her Roman education and the circle of modern architects and theorists responsible for cultivating her professional formation in Milan and São Paulo. That experience is inscribed on the surface of *Propaedeutic Contribution.*

172 Cathrine Veikos, "To Enter the Work: Ambient Art," *Journal of Architecture Education* 59, no. 4, Special Issue: Installation Art (Blackwell Publishing, 2006): 71–80.

173 Bo Bardi, quoted from an interview in the 1986 film *Lina Bo Bardi* by Aurélio Michiles and Isa Grinspum Ferraz.

174 *Propaedeutic Contribution,* p. 70/*Contribuição Propedêutica,* p. 16.

In the following, I have edited and restructured sentences to best convey the intended meaning of the text. I have corrected obvious typographical errors and bibliographical information. Given the importance of the visual associations intended by the author, I have corrected only obvious errors of positioning or orientation of the illustrations that appeared in the original text in this translated edition. I tried to preserve, as much as was possible, the original groupings of the illustrations and their relationship to both the text and the notes. For this reason I have maintained the format of the original text with the author's notes at the end. All my translations and editorial notes appear in brackets, { }. Source information for the illustrations has been updated where incomplete.

C.V.

PROPAEDEUTIC CONTRIBUTION TO THE TEACHING OF ARCHITECTURE THEORY

LINA BO BARDI

São Paulo, September, 1957

Translated and edited by Cathrine Veikos

Thesis presented to
the competition for the post of
chaired Professor of "Architecture Theory"
at the School of Architecture and Urbanism,
University of São Paulo. {1}

The illustrations that accompany this work form a basis for the discussion of
Architecture Theory and attempt to show the amplitude of possibilities for its
exemplification; chosen from diverse areas, from newspapers, to documentary photos,
to ancient drawings and contemporary technical drawings and depicting historical
references, customs, etc.; all are presented because interests in architecture and its
theory concern problems of history and criticism, interpreted, above all, in the service
of everyday life. Similarly, the references and the bibliography, realized using the
same criteria, again with the purpose of giving an idea of the amplitude of the
problem, are merely indicative.

All photographs without special indication were taken by the author.

1 The University of São Paulo, Faculty of Architecture and Urbanism (FAU-USP) was founded in 1948 by a group of professors from the Polytechnic School at the University of São Paulo. It was housed in the Vila Penteado, the Art Nouveau mansion on the rua maranhão, in São Paulo, which was donated by the philanthropic Alvares Penteado brothers, Sílvio and Armando. This was the first search for a Chair of Architectural Theory.

PREFACE

There is not a single piece of stone laid down by man at the center of any of our cities, that does not express an idea, that does not represent a letter in the alphabet of our civilization.[1]

2 A cover letter signed by Paulo Quadri Prestes, secretary, with the heading "University of São Paulo, Faculty of Architecture and Urbanism," announced the competition for the open position for the Professor of Architecture Theory. The letter introduces a four-page document dated May 25, 1957 that outlines topics to be addressed. See Appendix 1 for copy of original and translation.

I choose this romantic statement from Manuel Araujo Porto-Alegre, among the several definitions of Architecture that the reader will find in the pages of this essay, for two reasons: first, because Architecture is an art that must take into serious consideration the *land* on which it takes place—important because of the emotions it draws out of writers and artists;—and, second, because Architecture is the *product*, or better still, the *projection*, of civilized man in the world.

By adopting these principles as criteria, I propose to make an excursion through the vast theme that constitutes the field of Architecture Theory, offering my contribution. It starts from a point of view in accordance with the general principles outlined by the committee. [2]

In addition, I propose a methodology for teaching this complex discipline, especially in the very limited time that is available, just a single academic year.

Rather than choose one of the topics offered by the competition program and develop it in detail in a limited, technical sense, I thought it more appropriate to interpret the spirit of this program, to explain why a reworking of it, without change, of course, to its composition or to the structure of each one of its items, may make a contemporary contribution to the expression of a subject that has only recently been defined as Architecture Theory.[2] This avoids, from the outset, interference in the curriculum from other disciplines, and provides the student with an accurate idea of the unity of spirit—in other words, as Leon Battista Alberti has said, the *lineamenta*, the "cosa grande e divina"[3]—of Architecture. It is the sort of proposal that creates an impassioned student, a student with an incentive to think, a motivation towards research, and a conviction that modern architecture is, like all other human activities, the product of man's experience in time. There is no difference between "modern" and history; the "modern" is itself a product of history, and only through it is it possible to avoid repeating obsolete experiences. This history is not seen as a "cosa da forbici e colla"[4] [cut and paste] but as something alive and present, a history revived with fundamentals endowed with the capacity to transmit fruitful lessons. It is clearly not the history

1 Leonardo da Vinci, *Cataclisma*, black pencil drawing (Windsor Library, n. 12 382). *"Descrivi il paesi con vento e con acqua, e con tramontare e levare del sole"* (Leonardo, *Arundel Codex 263*, British Museum, v. 172). [da Vinci, Leonardo. *Leonardo da Vinci: Natur und Landschaft: Naturstudien auf der Koniglichen Bibliotek in Windsor Castle*. Stuttgart and New York: Belser Johnson Reprint Corp, 1983. p. 17, fig. 15.]

2–4 Allegory of Theory, Practice and Design (Ripa, *Iconologia*, Padua, 1625, pp. 166 and following). [D. J. Gordon, "Poet & Architect," *Journal of the Warburg & Courtauld Institutes*, London, 1949, vol. XII, pl. 30b., pl. 30c., pl. 30d.]

3 Lina Bo was a student at the Scuola Superiore di Architettura in Rome [the Architecture College of Rome University of Engineering] from 1933/34 to 1939/40. Renato Anelli describes the school as being based on the proposal of "total architecture" drawn up by Giovanni Giovannoni in 1916. The object was to produce architects with technical and artistic competence to formulate transformations for old Italian towns and cities in order to insure that modernization would not jeopardize the Italian cultural heritage. See Renato Anelli, *Rino Levi: arquitetura e cidade/pesquisa e textos*, São Paulo: Romano Guerra Editora, 2001.

4 A document bearing the letterhead of the University of São Paulo, Faculty of Architecture and Urbanism, dated September 20, 1957 and signed by Paulo Quadri Prestes, secretary, attests to Lina Bo Bardi's teaching contracts in 1955 and 1956. She taught a fifth-year course in Architecture called "Composição Decorativa," literally, "Decorative Design."

of textbooks, monotonous and second hand, merely capable of suggesting that the "past" is past, and no longer valid, suggesting that the world began today, and man, alone, has the task of reconstructing a "paradise lost." It is a history that is not "History" as a mere abstraction, but, like life itself, concrete and fecund.

It is true that the ideas transmitted to the young by their various professors form the foundation of education; but my experience, both in the College where I studied, [3] and in the one in which I taught, [4] has shown me the necessity for a department that is, to a certain extent, a place for meetings and for the cordial discussion of different points of view. It should have the goal of offering the future architect a unitary moral sense, a conscience or, in other words, the "spirit of construction." The stimulus to acquire a professional conscience, in other words, a philosophical point of view towards the relationship between the architect and society, an understanding of his activities in connection with other activities, the responsibilities, the limits, and the issue of not overstepping these limits, all this should be included in the teaching of Architecture Theory. It should be imparted with a sense of humanism; in other words, with those notions and reasons that animate the spirit, rather than with formal idealisms, old-fashioned positivisms and materialistic–scientific interpretations. This will give Architecture Theory significance for our times, for humanity, and, at the same time, provide for a stance that is critical and composed, devoid of utopian enthusiasms, but conscious of its own responsibilities. I summarize these principles by adopting some reflections from *The Architecture of Humanism*, by Geoffrey Scott,[5] reflections which I include in these first pages as a herald of a new type of humanism,[6] maybe "cold" or "scientific," but certainly conscious of its own "humanity".

5 Frontispiece from *L'idea dell'Architettura universale di Vincenzo Scamozzi architetto veneto, etc... .* Venice, MDCVX (1615).
On the frieze of the portal: "Nemo huc liberalium atrium expers ingrediatur."
At the base of the columns stand two statues, one represents *Theorica*, who holds a book, the other *Experientia*, who holds a compass.
The four statues we see at the top of the portal represent Praecog(nitio), Const(ructio) Expol(itio) and Restaur(atio). It is one of the finest allegories of Renaissance Architecture. (In "Poet and Architect: the intellectual setting of the quarrel between Ben Jonson and Inigo Jones," by D.J. Gordon in *Journal of the Warburg and Courtauld Institutes*, London, 1949, vol. XII, plate 30.)

6 Frontispiece from an eighteenth-century German treatise dedicated to the ornamentation of doors and windows. (*Grund mäßige Anweisung zu den Verzierungen der Fenster in kürzte Regeln verfasset, und Mit 100 kupferne erläutert durch Johann Rudolph Fäsch, etc... .*) J. C. Weigel, 1781. Frontispiece. Courtesy of Bavarian State Library, Munich, Germany.

Chapter 1

PROBLEMS OF ARCHITECTURE THEORY

Regarding a few treatises

Man, as the savage first conceived him, man, as the mind of science still affirms, is not the centre of the world he lives in, but merely one of her myriad products, more conscious than the rest and more perplexed. A stranger on the indifferent earth, he adapts himself slowly and painfully to inhuman nature, and at moments, not without peril, compels inhuman nature to his need. A spectacle surrounds him—sometimes splendid, often morose, uncouth and formidable. He may cower before it like the savage, study it impartially for what it is, like the man of science; it remains, in the end, as in the beginning, something alien and inhuman often destructive of his hopes. But a third way is open. He may construct, within the world as it is, a pattern of the world as he would have it.[7]

5 The sixth book of Serlio was published in 1967: *Sesto Libro. Delle habitationi di tutti li gradi degli homini* (Ms. Bayerische Staatsbibliothek, Munich, Cod. Icon. 189), ed. Marco Rosci, Milan 1967.

6 Both Artigas and Niemeyer used the V-column in their projects. See *Habitat* no. 1, 1950: 2–16 and *Habitat* no. 2: 6–11.

Throughout the present work, you will notice numerous citations regarding the theories of Architecture,[8] including texts from philosophers, treatise-writers and professors, in a kind of extension of the program's indications. By being in contact with the students, I have been able to verify their intense desire to learn, not only from a strictly technical point of view, but also from a historical point of view. Here, questions regarding the necessity of a knowledge of ancient treatises present themselves. It is possible to say, effectively, that such knowledge is only obligatory for specialists, that a contemporary architect could build by making use of Hamlin's treatise[9] without needing to know, for example, Serlio's *Libri*[10] (one of which still remains unpublished: Library of Munich). [5] Perhaps this is the same problem that exists in the teaching of archaic languages, a pedagogical problem now being discussed in certain countries. Regardless, it is obvious that reading *The Iliad* should serve as a source of knowledge of a timeless poem and not as an example of the rules of Greek grammar. Sullivan, when young, was annoyed with 'architecture theology,'[11] precisely because, at the Architecture Department of the Massachusetts Institute of Technology in Boston, they taught the "orders" as a grammar. It is a student's right, as it is a professor's duty, to know that the 'V'-shaped pillars, so popular nowadays [6] and, in our time, first used by Le Corbusier, were actually designed by Viollet-le-Duc in 1872.[12] It is possible that a young architect, with the help of some calculations, can support the entire structure of a building with such pillars, ignoring

7 Loading stone in Dimapur, the state of Assam (J.H. Hutton, "Assam Megaliths," *Antiquity, A Periodical Review of Archeology* (September, 1929), plate XIII. Gloucester, Eng. Antiquity Publications).

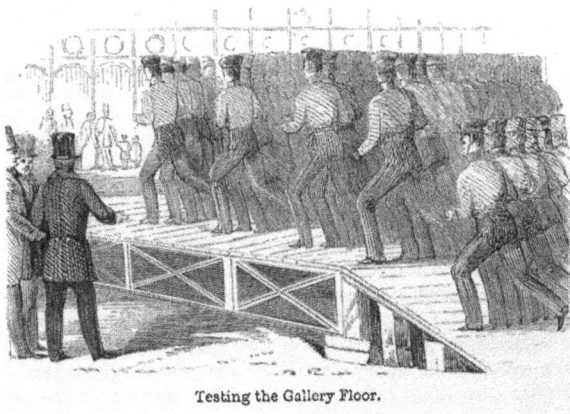

Testing the Gallery Floor.

8 Soldiers employed as weight to check the strength of a platform in the Crystal Palace. Peter Berlyn and Charles Fowler. *The Crystal Palace: Its Architectural History and Constructive Marvels*, London, 1851, facing p. 88: James Gilbert, Elibron Classics Reprint.

9 Plate of Caryatides in *A Treatise on Civil Architecture: in which the principles of that art are laid down, and illustrated by a great number of plates accurately designed, and elegantly engraved by the best hands*. London: Printed for the author, by J. Haberkorn; To be had at the author's house in Poland-Street, near Broad-Street in Soho . . . et al., 1759. After page 36. William Chambers, London MDCCLIX.

Man is always the constructor of Architecture. Today, the machine alleviates human exertion, but it cannot do everything.

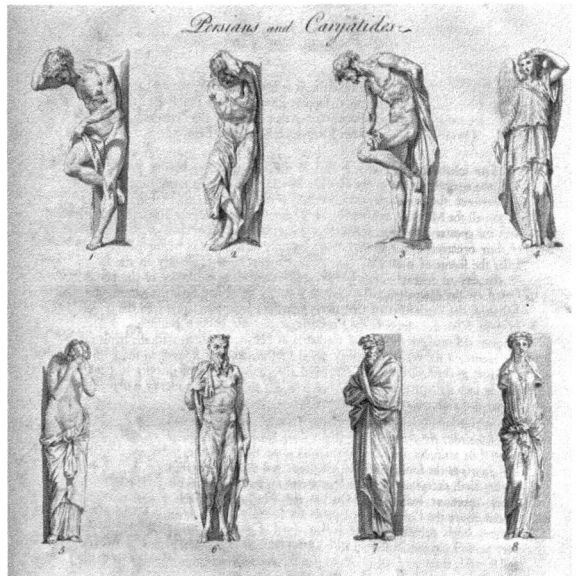

Persians and Caryatides

the precedents; however, were he to boast of such a feat, we would have the right to smile, evoking history.

It is a professor's obligation to keep abreast of the developments in his discipline, since students need not only to learn about concepts, but also to receive interpretation and clarification from the professor. It is for this reason that programs need to be constantly re-examined, especially since they are often based on a single treatise. For example, as with the case of the well-known Lurçat,[13] we should ask if such a treatise is considered, by the critic or even by the European university, as a work that contains ideas that are concurrent with present developments or if it is useful only from a historiographical point of view. Is it capable of stimulating current and active thought? This is especially important in a country such as Brazil, whose new architecture has unique characteristics. I offer here, for example, that one of the particularities of this treatise is that it does not cite authors or offer notes, and maintains a categorical tone that is not consistent with university studies.[14]

It is not an eclectic taste that leads me to observe the existence of innumerable treatises that are worthy of consideration or susceptible to criticism: in this field the literature is vast and it is the professor's job to critically analyze the content of a treatise that is suggested as the main text for a course.

I recognize the difficulty which lies in the development of a treatise for a course, and the loss of vitality which occurs when the words spoken in a classroom are transcribed into the pages of a book which is not directed to the same students but, rather, to an undifferentiated audience of young individuals that may be from other countries (as is our case). This international audience receives treatises from the most famous centers of art, treatises, for example, like Gutton,[15] in which an ignorance of geography can instantly be detected as well as a failure to attribute works to authors, and vice versa. Naturally, it is not my intention to deprecate these texts, as I acknowledge the complexity of such tasks. However, I insist on professorial autonomy, or at least on the possibility to criticize treatises that follow philosophies or methods that have been clearly superseded, a demand already expressed in one of Sergio Bettini's observations following a controversy concerning Architecture Theory.[16]

With regard to the implicit problems mentioned above, it is clear that these ideas, at times explicitly denied or categorically asserted by distinguished professors, can and should be discussed again, in honor of the Lodolian principle of not "confining" Architecture.[17]

Where treatises are concerned, it is our duty to respect the right idea and to reject that which, in our understanding, is wrong. We should discuss it with the purpose of finding its true meaning, substituting the method "treatise or theory to be officially followed" with the method "treatise to be discussed."

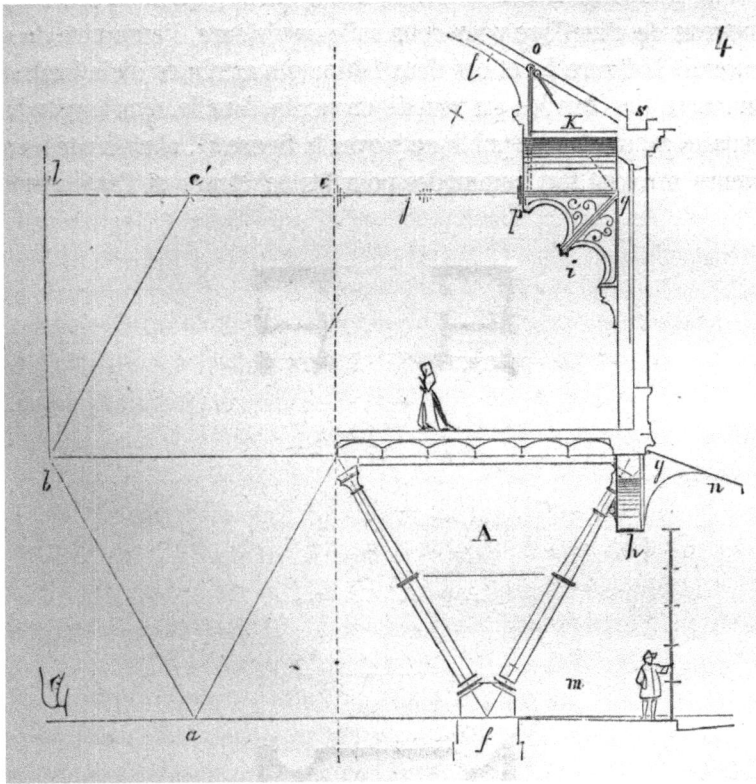

10 Viollet-le-Duc, Design of a structure (Viollet-le-Duc, *Entretiens sur l'Architecture*, Paris: A. Morel et cie, 1863, p. 65, fig. 4).

Example of collaboration between an architect and an engineer, which in the near future should emerge into a single discipline.

11 Roof of a building by Oscar Niemeyer, in Pedro do Rio, 1954. Structural Engineer, Amrein (Stamo Papadaki, *Oscar Niemeyer: Works in Progress*, New York: Reinhold, 1956, p. 81).

"Substituer à une colonne de granit, de marbre ou de pierre, une tige de fonte de fer, cela n'est point mauvais, mais il faut convenir que cela ne saurait passer pour une innovation, pour l'introduction d'un principe nouveau. Remplacer un linteau en pierre ou en bois par un poitrail en fer, c'est très-bien, cela n'est pas non plus le résultat d'un grand éffort de l'esprit. Mais substituer à des résistances verticales, des résistances obliques, c'est un principe que peut, s'il n'est complétements neuf, puisque les maitres du moyen âge l'avaient déjà admis, prendre une importance majeure et amener des combinaisons neuves" (Viollet-le-Duc, Eugène Emmanuel, vol. II, p. 64, op. cit.). Viollet-le-Duc himself admits that he gives no priority to this type of structure; I cite it as an example of "historical consciousness" (though this critical position is typical today).

By means of an example, it is possible to explain what I mean by discussion. I refer to one of the most serious treatises of recent times, Guadet.[18] This theoretician offers us, as a first image, a T-square, demonstrating his concern with teaching the ABCs of drawing; and, after dedicating four volumes to the norms and elements, he concludes the work with an ample chapter about the dignity of the architect. In my opinion, this chapter should come first, since the idea precedes the instrument. Guadet apologizes for any lacunae:

> mon excuse c'est que pour traiter complètement un sujet aussi vaste que la théorie de l'architecture, il faudrait une bibliothèque entière, et la vie de plusieurs hommes ... En matière d'art, en effet l'enseignement didactique ne peut guère dépasser les éléments ... J'entends souvent répéter ces inanités sonores: "école supérieure, enseignement supérieure, études supérieures"... Ce que faut l'étude supérieure c'est la supériorité de l'étudiante ou la méthode et non pas de l'objet étudié ... Ce qui fait l'étude inferieure au contraire ... c'est l'étude incomplète hâtive et légère, inferiorité cette fois encore de l'étudiant ou de la méthode et non pas de l'objet étudié.[19]

> [my excuse is that, in order to treat a subject as vast as Architecture Theory, one would need an entire library. And the lifetime of many men ... In matters of art, a pedagogy can barely go beyond the basics ... I often hear the inane repetitions: "higher education, elevated teaching, elevated studies" ... What makes elevated studies is the superiority of the student or the method, and not of the thing studied ... what makes inferior learning is the inverse ... it is incomplete study, hasty and superficial; again the inferiority lies with the student and the method and not with the thing studied.]

The methodology of the time consisted of an unbridled eclecticism, to which Guadet, as Garnier's assistant in the construction of the Opéra de Paris, had, of course, contributed. The famous master, who naturally could not rebel against the Parisian school, observes that at the beginning of Architecture Theory,

> nous devons être judicieux, persuasifs, mais non pas pérentoires. Dans ce que nous pouvons dire il y aura toujours a prendre et a laisser, un choix a faire selon le goût et le tempérament de chacun. Mais du moins le professeur aura rempli une grande partie de son rôle s'il a fait comprendre qu'en architecture tout est sujet de penser, de penser autrement que lui, soit, mais en se pénétrant du moins de cette conviction qu'il faut savoir pourquoi on fait ce qu'on fait, ainsi, et non autrement.[20]

The study of structures and their history is of obvious importance to the understanding of architectural organisms. Here are some examples given from diverse periods.

12 Brick found in excavations behind the "Duomo" in Milan, dated 1386 (Camillo Boito and Filippo Salveraglio, *Il Duomo di Milano e i disegni per la sua facciata*, Milano, 1889, phototype no. 1).

13 First figure of the Treatise of Andrea Palladio: A. brick corner, B. bands of bricks for firmness of the wall, C. "opus reticulate", D. Courses of brick extending through the depth of the wall, E. mortar (*I Quattro Libri dell'Architettura*, Andrea Palladio, Venetia, 1570; p. 11. Palladio, Andrea. *I Quattro Libri dell'Architettura*/Andrea Palladio; a cuora di Licisco Magagnato e Paola Marini; introduzione di Licisco Magagnato. Milan: Il profilo, 1980, p. 22. Translation: Palladio, Andrea, *The Four Books on Architecture*, tr. Travenor, Robert. Cambridge: MIT Press, 1997, p. 12).

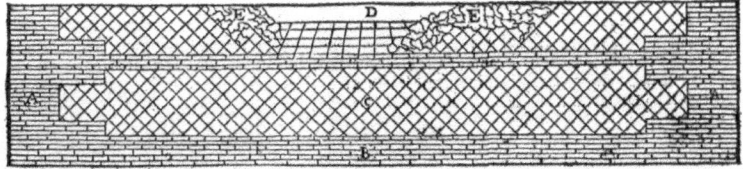

14 Example of good workmanship with brick. The façade of the Hyde House, Washington, DC, 1798 (Deering Davis, Stephen P. Dorsey and Ralph Cole Hall, *Georgetown Houses of the Federal Period: Washington D.C., 1780–1830*. New York: Architectural Book Publishing Co., Cornwall, NY, 1944, p. 8).

15 *(Right)* Erechtheum: viewed from the north through the door of the west wall (George Wicker Elderkin, *Problems in Periclean Buildings*, Princeton: Princeton University Press, 1912, p. 29, fig. 8).

7 "Ninguem nasceu com a pedra
filosofal no bolso," meaning "no one
can achieve perfection."

[we have to be judicious, persuasive, but not absolute. In what we can say, there will always be a give and take, a choice to make regarding the taste and temperament of each individual. The professor will have accomplished a big part of his role if he has succeeded in conveying that, in architecture, everything is subject to thought, to thinking outside oneself; this, or, at the very least, in inculcating in his students the conviction that one must know why one does what one does in one way, and not in another.]

No one was born with the philosopher's stone in their pocket, [7] and for precisely this reason the master admits a polemical "contradiction," another point of view, and directs students to a splendid and passionate recommendation, one that is already a principle of any "theory" that is useful against the rampant culturalism of his time (a "clientèle de prétendus amateurs et connaisseurs pour imposer la fameuse recherché des Styles") ["clientele of pretenders to the role of amateur and connoisseurs eager to impose the infamous search for Styles"]; he affirms that ultimately: "S'affranchir de la servitude du passé, de tous les passés, c'est libérer l'avenir."[21] ["To free oneself from the servitude of the past, of all pasts, is to liberate oneself to the future."]

Naturally, to free oneself from the servitude of the past does not mean to ignore the past. This is evidenced by his treatise, which is full of examples, interpretations and discussions about the history of Architecture.

It would be easy to continue to analyze treatises, and even interesting to follow their evolution from the appearance of Vitruvius and the imposition of the "Orders" to the first reactions following the Baroque demand of "freedom," and on to the polemics which favored the re-establishment of the magisterial Classicism of the Gallaccini[22] type; from the restoration of the official Napoleonic style to the race towards individualism that, in the nineteenth century, transformed the "Rules" into a cascade of solutions, whose entanglement left the masters—whether they were inclined towards the Gothic or the Renaissance—to focus once again on the past.

In more recent times, treatises have met with theoretical systematizations that are both temporary and incomplete. I make allusions to this problem with these reflections.

Concepts and meanings of architecture

What is meant by the term, Architecture? At first glance, it might seem safe to limit it to the art of construction and, in a narrower sense, to the construction of buildings; but architecture is almost implicitly every type of structure and representation, from the structure of rocks, the skeleton, the infinitesimal figure of the atom, to the appearance of the spheres that compose the planetary system. Nature has offered Man the means to

16 1889 Universal Exposition: Cave Reconstruction (Charles Garnier and A. Ammann, *L'Abitazione Umana*, Milano, 1893, p. 17). Originally published as Garnier, Charles and A. Ammann. *L'habitation humaine, par Charles Garnier et A. Ammann. Ouvrage illustré de 335 vignettes et contenant 24 cartes.* Paris: Hachette, 1892, p. 37.

17 Flint, Pressigny le Grand, Loire, France (John Evans, *The Ancient Stone Implements, Weapons, and Ornaments, of Great Britain*, London, 1897, p. 29).

18 Celtic amulet with inscription (*ibid.*, p. 61).

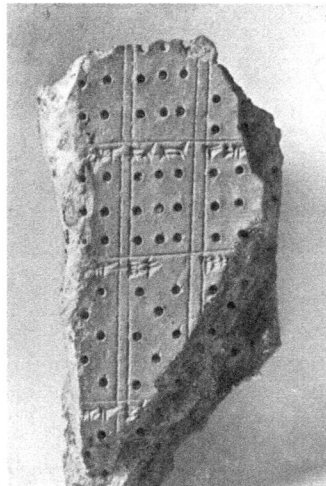

19 Geomantic signs on a fragment of a terracotta tablet, Africa and Asia (Sir Ernest Alfred Wallis Budge, *Amulets and Superstitions*, London, New York: Oxford University Press, H. Milford, 1930, p. 462).

modify and reorganize it, and Man has striven to do so; he has slowly created infinitesimal architectures that, once refined, form new architectures all over the world, from the chipped rock to the interplanetary satellite, from the cave to the skyscraper, from the amulet to the cathedral. It would be irreverent not to begin with Vitruvius, who gave to the Renaissance the rules of construction, just as Horace had given those of *ars poetica*, not to mention the influence exerted by the Aristotelian *Poetics*. According to Vitruvius,[23] Architecture is the *Aedificatio*, the construction of all public and private buildings, excluding all the works that belong, first and foremost, to the realm of engineering; it is the same understanding of architecture later indicated by Quintilian (*in omnibus quae sunt aedificio utilia, versatur*)[24] [as everything that is useful for the purpose of building]; but engineering is included in the last two books of Vitruvius' treatise, dedicated to *Machinatio* and to *Gnomonica*, and the book in the eighth part deals with topics related to hydraulics. As is known, Vitruvius even talks about clocks and many other techniques, sciences and arts in his treatise. He arrives at this because of his intuition for the vastness of the art, spatial and without definite limits.

The search for a definition occupied the minds of all the wise men. In order to bypass a purely historiographical problem—which would exceed the limits of our discipline—I present a definition that can be considered exhaustive, taken from one of those "anonymous figures" who never appear in dissertations, because today's haste limits research to encyclopedias:

L'Architettura è quell'arte e scienza insieme che fabbrica edifici d'ogni fatta, dalla casipola più modesta alla reggia ed al tempio della maggior sublimità, per avvantaggiare gli uomini rendendoli attivi, inventori e intraprendenti; costruisce vascelli incominciando dal più piccolo battello, sino alle grandi navi corazzate da guerra, le quali in sé compendiano in grado eminente l'ingegno e la maestria di tutte le scienze geometriche e fisiche nella loro meravigliosa applicazione; apre strade dal più angusto e picciolo sentiero di uso private, alle vie di ferro, nelle quali colla velocità del vento, si corre attraverso i fiumi, sui mari e nelle viscere della terra. L'Architettura eziandio è quella che agli uomini insegna a prosciugare paludi, onde somministrare all'agricoltura fertili terreni, che formano la ricchezza delle civili nazioni; a perforare ed appianare montagne; colmare valli; gettare ponti su fiumi e mari, onde facilitare le comunicazioni e gli scambi, con che prosperano le industrie e i commerci; a scavare canali attraverso incolte campagne, per dar corso all'acque stagnanti, a miglioramento della pubblica igiene; e a fortificare un luogo qualunque contro gli assalti delle armi nemiche, rendendo se non sempre vani, almeno lenti gli attacchi dell'ambizione sfrenata; e finalmente a produrre tante cose utili ad ogni fatta di persone, che opera non

Here is confirmation of the clear fusion between engineering and architecture in naval construction. It is significant that one of the major contemporary civil engineers has built a vessel making use of reinforced concrete, "ferro-cement" in particular.

20 Transatlantic ship, the *Empress of Australia* (Moholy-Nagy, László, *Von Material zu Architektur*, Munich: A. Langen, 1929, p. 47, fig. 31).

21 P.L. Nervi: concrete frames of a 400-ton ship after 30 days of construction (Ing. P.L. Nervi, *Nuove possibilità per le costruzioni navali in cemento armato*, Roma, 1945, fig. 16). Nervi, Pier Luigi. *Works of Pier Luigi Nervi*/preface by Pier Luigi Nervi; introduction by Ernesto N. Rogers; explanatory notes to illustrations by Jurgen Joedicke; translation by Ernst Priefert. New York: F. A. Praeger, 1957, p. 49, fig. 6.

picciolo sarebbe ad una ad una accennarle. Con grande ragione dunque si è dato all'Architettura questo nome, che secondo l'etimologia della sua voce significa, arte e scienza direttrice di tutte le altre; e quindi l'architetto è l'ordinatore supremo di tutti i lavori e di tutte le opera che concorrono alla formazione di qualsiasi edificio. La parte di Architettura con la quale si intende quella dedicate alle costruzioni di edifici per gli uomini riuniti in società, siano essi di uso private o pubblico, o per pubblica utilità è l'Architettura civile.[25]

[Architecture is the art and science that together produce buildings of every kind, from the most modest hovel to the most sublime palace temple, to benefit mankind by making active and enterprising inventors, to build ships starting from the tiniest boat up to the largest armored ships of war (which in itself sums up in an eminent degree the talent and expertise of all the geometrical and physical sciences in their admirable application) and to open a small private route off the narrower streets that are used to convey iron inland from the bowels of the earth through rivers and seas at the speed of the wind. Architecture teaches men to drain swamps in order to create fertile agricultural land, which constitutes the wealth of civilized nations; to drill iron mountains; to fill valleys; to throw bridges over rivers and seas, facilitate communication and trade with thriving industries and businesses; to improve public hygiene by digging channels to drain the stagnant waters of the barren countryside; and to fortify any place against the assaults of enemy weapons, slowing down, if not completely vanquishing, the attacks of unbridled ambition. Finally, to produce many useful things for every kind of person, none of whose work is insignificant. With good reason, then, this name has been given to architecture, which, according to its etymology, is the directing art and science of all else, and therefore the architect and chief officer of all work that contributes to the formation of any edifice. That portion of architecture by which is meant the construction of buildings for the use of society, whether for private or public use or for public utility is Civil Architecture.]

I choose this sensible definition because it anticipates that Architecture will increasingly take on the meaning of the Vitruvian *utilitas*. Of course, the elaboration came from long ago: from Mengs, [8] and from the Neo-Classical critics that followed Father Lodoli ("Devonsi unir e fabbrica e ragione e sia funzion la rappresentazione")[26] [Construction, reason, and function should be united in the representation] [9] and from Milizia ("qualunque fabbrica, per potersi dire compita, deve sempre avere i tre requisiti seguenti: 1° Bellezza, 2° Commodità, 3° Solidità")[27] [Any construction, to be called competent, must have the three following requirements: 1 Beauty, 2 Convenience, 3 Solidity]

Today, we cannot think of architecture as separate from urbanism; history shows that the past was conscious of this.

22 Aerial view of the Acropolis of Athens (photographer unknown).

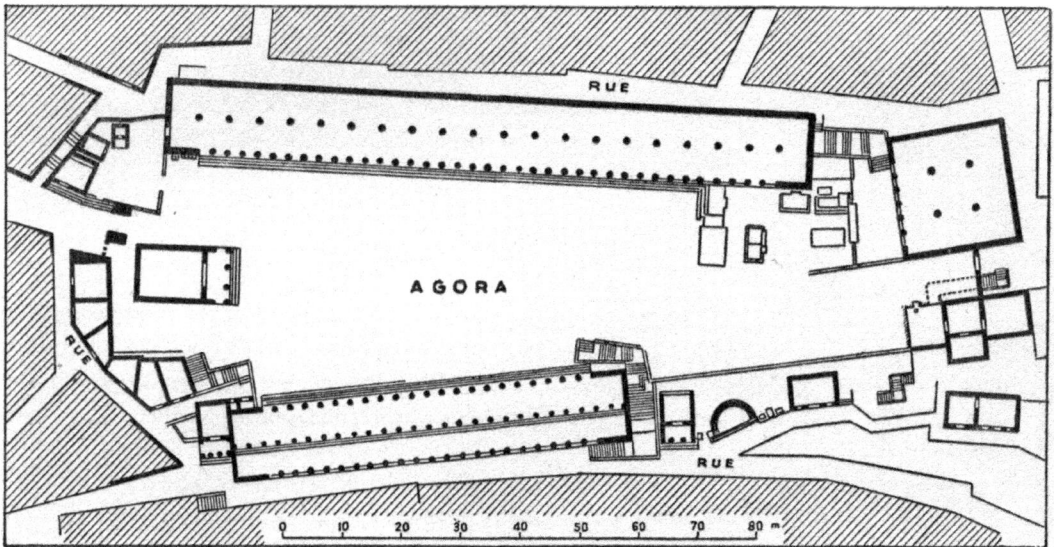

23 Assos: plan of the "Agora" (Roland Martin, *L'Urbanisme dans la Grèce Antique*, Paris: A.&J. Picard, 1956, p. 274, fig. 60).

24 Leonardo da Vinci, section of a building in a city with stacked roads (Manuscript B, Institut de France, Paris: Alberto Tallone editeur; detail of folio 36 recto. Reproduced from Alberto Sartoris, *Léonard Architecte*, Paris, 1952, p. 95).

10 Italian art historian and professor, editor of the magazine *seleArte*, Carlo Ludovico Ragghianti (1910–87).

I. Che tutto il suo bello prenda il carattere della necessità stessa: tutto vi deve comparir necessario. II. Che gli ornati hanno da derivare dalla natura stessa dell'edificio, e risultare dal suo bisogno. Niente ha perciò de vedersi in una fabbrica che non abbia il suo proprio ufficio, e che non sia parte integrante della fabbrica stessa. III. Quanto è in rappresentazione, dee essere in funzione.[28]

[I. Everything that is beautiful should follow the character of necessity. II. Ornament should be derived from the nature of the building and as a result of its needs. Nothing should be part of a construction if it does not have a proper function, and is not integrated in the construction. III. How it is in representation, it must be in operation.]

Amidst so much "functionalism," one must not forget the voices that appeal to nature, such as Algarotti, who compared architecture to metaphysics, recommending that in it there was:

Varietà ed unità; così che l'animo di chi vede nè sia ricondotto sempre alle medesime cose, onde si genera sazietá, nè distratto in diverse, onde confusione; ma risenta quel diletto che dallo scorgere negli oggetti che gli si presentano novità ed ordine, ha necessariamente da nascere; perfezione che ravvisano I filosofi nelle opera della Natura madre primiera e sovrana maestro d'ogni materia d'arte.[29]

[Variety and unity, something that animates it but always brings it back to itself, generating satisfaction, rather than the distraction promoted by diversity. The object of our creation should present order and novelty as well as the perfection of Mother Nature, the Master of Arts.]

Such are the principles of the Vitruvian treatises.[30]

In keeping with my intention to clarify the meaning of Architecture Theory, I should note that I consider the theory of "internal space," so fashionable today, to be far from clear and definite. I would tend rather towards a theory of "space total space," in which space takes on the disposition of man, is part of the human sense of life and posits man as the main protagonist in the space of the world.

Here, I take the opportunity to extend the idea of architecture to urbanism. Ragghianti [10] rightly says: "All'urbanistica che ha una forma sia da riservare il termine di architettura."[31] [For all urbanism that has style we should reserve the term architecture.] Architecture is clearly an expression of urbanism. For this very reason, it is necessary to consider it as part of the urban whole, and not as a separate entity. Examining the matter carefully, it is apparent that, in the majority of cases, Architecture

25 Praça do Comercio, Lisbon with the statue of Márquez de Pombal (nineteenth-century lithograph, author's collection).

26 Panoramic view of Bahia, in 1759. Drawing by José Antonio Carlos (Smith, Robert Chester. *Arquitetura Colonial Bahiana*. Salvador: Livraria Progressio Editôra, 1955, Plate I).

27 View of a plaza in Ajaccio, Corsica. Original drawing (author's collection).

Here a study is being proposed on the transfer of the theories and practices of architecture since "the Portuguese established in Brazil the world they had created in Europe. The best proof that Bahia offers is the city itself, which became the most faithful replica of Lisbon and Porto. During a period of almost 215 years, from 1549 to 1763, it enjoyed the privilege of being the first metropolis in the Lusitanian New World." (Robert C. Smith, *Arquitetura Colonial, 1 Parte, na colção Evolução histórica da cidade do Salvador*, Salvador, 1954, vol. IV, p. 11).

11 Bo Bardi is making reference to the fact that the house numbers are all obscured by the vegetation.

has been the appearance, or the façade, the evolution of the decorated tent of primitive people. Today, the problem is radically different. The architect has become the executor of someone else's decisions and recommendations, decisions that should be his in order that he can create form, space, appearance, functionality and efficiency, not only for the occupants of a building, but also for the entire neighborhood, for the entire city; henceforth, Architecture can no longer dispense with a science and art of public life, and accordingly, a science and an art of collective responsibility.

Palladio and Borromini paid more attention to the exterior plasticity of the form than the arrangement of the floor plan; the architecture of all the great "formalists" is a monumental "call for attention," so much so, that nowadays, despite the fact that it is a rigorous consideration of form to follow function, formal external harmony is never renounced. Often good architecture is lost and, even more often, "ruined" by the structures that surround it, mediocre products of builders who never imagined themselves to be contradicting an ignorant client, not seeing how ridiculous it is to put some abstractly twisted iron on a façade (so attractive to nostalgics) or to install terracotta sculptures representing Diogenes and Plato in niches. To be convinced of this it is enough to go for a little walk around our city. Residential neighborhoods, well planned from the point of view of urbanism, lose sight of the need for deliveries; [11] they are rich in that lush Brazilian vegetation that often hides ugly walls and, happily, redresses ridiculous façades. These are often, with regard to Architecture *in the strict sense* a representation of cosmopolitanism and a polymorphic language filled with curious incongruities: the Moorish style alternates with the one that is (for some strange reason) denominated "colonial" but which is, deep down, nothing more than a tired repetition of the Portuguese "little Baroque." The small palace whose style attempts to imitate Florence's "Palazzo Vecchio," with towers and intricate coats of arms of presumed ancestors (ridiculous imitation of the Italian), is next to a Nordic-style house with a very inclined roof. Then we come across the generic Gothic style of rock and lime, which is not even Victorian; second-hand Vignolian "orders"; not to mention the painful rendition of the "Capitol" style, which justified a revival of Jefferson's new Washington,[32] but that, in our luxurious "gardens," does not even have the good sense to "evoke" an idea of the New World. In these residential complexes, driven by a vain desire to impress a random passer-by, which nature can always successfully fix and adapt, the few beautiful residences that have been built with, rather, the criteria of "living for living," seem wholly out of place.

If a theory must depart from an unconscious critical attitude, we must all, at least, be aware of the enormous responsibility that lies in the casual choice of "styles," and the many ways to waste ornamentation on façades and decorate interior spaces. Are we perhaps carrying forward the ancient polemic between the aesthetic and the moral of Lodoli[33] and Milizia?[34]

Nature and architecture

Architecture is both inspired and governed by nature, from which it receives the materials and the instruments necessary to form it and give it harmony; nature pacifies, and for this very reason the study of nature[35] should be the primary source for the study of architecture—the product and creation of man. I do not mean the issue of art imitating nature, or the Wildean notion of nature imitating art. Even if it is not my aim to match imitations and paradoxes, so favored by the followers of the ideas of Nietzsche (and, in general, of the avant-garde movements of this century), studious reflection on the natural order of things will, without a doubt, favor permanent contact with this determinant reason of our being.[36] With reference to a problem related to this last recommendation, I should like to point out the current isolation of the house relative to any vegetation or green areas; it is easy to imagine the consequences of this problem. In reality, all who perceive architecture as something intimately connected with urbanism are perfectly aware of the problems that result from this issue; the contemporary human habitat must be planned with a view to creating a connection with nature, not only by designing green areas, but by reconstituting entire forest strips in areas where there is extensive deforestation (as has been foreseen in Russia). The proceedings of the Conference organized in Caracas in 1952 by the International Union for the Protection of Nature [12] and the VIII International Scientific Conference of the Pacific, in Manila[37] (with the presence of personalities such as Julian Huxley and Harold Coolidge) record discussions related to reforestation, laws for protection against forest fires and the dangers of diverting large water sources. The problems addressed included a reconciliation between the requirements of "hydro-electric man" and the preoccupation with the extinction of the *"Pinus insularis,"* which nature put in certain places not only for reasons of beauty but, more importantly, to consolidate the terrain and avoid erosion. This clearly shows that man is beginning to think seriously about the topic of the architectural environment.

The modern architect, absorbed by the search for further and faster solutions for our cities, our houses and our mechanical problems, due to the increase in the world population, should urgently attend to the call of Prof. Roger Heim of the Academy of Science in Paris, [13] who laments the destruction of twenty extremely rare, six-hundred-year-old willows of the species *"daphnoides,"* sacrificed due to the elevation of Lake Oregon, or the extinction of the *"Lycopodium annotium"* in the region of the Pyrenees. It is crucial that we listen to the warning, which is profoundly important and necessary for the physical and spiritual survival of man, and very different from the militant proclamations made by Simon Bolivar, notwithstanding the recommendations of Buffon and Humboldt.[38]

12 The conference took place September 3–9, 1952.

13 Roger Heim, *Destruction et Protection de la Nature*, 1952.

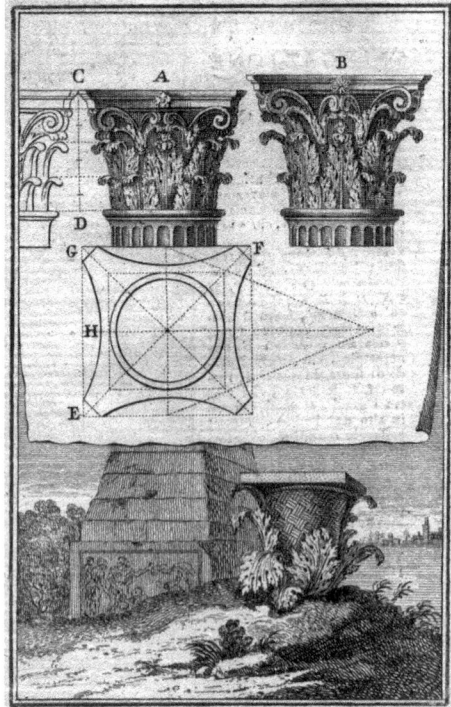

29 Proportions of the Corinthian column (*Vitruvius Pollio. L'Architettura Generale di Vitruvio ridotta in compendio dal sig. Perrault dell'Accademia delle scienze di Parigi, ed arricchita di tavole in rame. Opera tradotta del francese, ed incontrata in questa edizione col testo dell'autore, e col commento di Monsig. Barbaro, alla quale in oltre si è aggiunto la tavola e le regole del piedestallo*. Venice: G. Albrizzi, MDCCXLVII (1747), plate X).

28 Allegory of forest (Eugene Muller, *La Forêt*, [*son thistoire, sa légende, sa vie, son rôle, ses habitants.* P. Ducrocq]. Illustrations de Andrieux, Bellecroix, etc. Paris, 1878, p. 31).

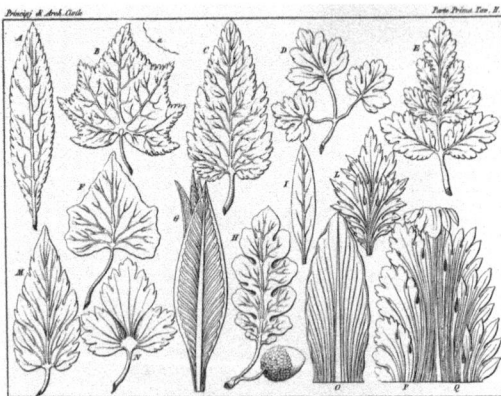

30 Folios proposing architectonic compositions (*Atlante di Trentasei tavole in rame per l'opera di Milizia Principi di Architettura Civile.*
Not dated, but end of XVIII, part I, plate II).

31 Architecture and material dependence. Ionic capitol that Jefferson tried to exact, without success, from a stone in Virginia; agora of the gardens of the University of Virginia (I.T. Frary, *Thomas Jefferson: Architect and Builder*, Richmond: Garrett and Massie, 1931, plate LI).

32 Interior of the Church of São Francisco, in Salvador (Pál Kelemen, *Baroque and Rococo in Latin America*, New York: Macmillan, 1951, plate 165b).

33 Old Church of Missionaries of Para. The roots of the Apuizeiro (Amazon tree) interlace with the construction (São Paulo, *Habitat*, no. 1, 1950, p. 83).

34 Nature invades Architecture (Federico Hermanin, *Giambattista Piranesi*, Rome: Pompeo Sansaini, 1922, plate 10).

From the intimate space of the house, the family nucleus, to the omnipresent space of nature, the problem of architecture—an activity of man in the contiguous space defined by earth and undefined by air—appears to us full of facts and anxious doubts; of assurances because of what has already been achieved; and, simultaneously, questions and fears. History is implicit in these thoughts; history, whose living presence is synthesized in our actions precisely because we are its result, even if we are convinced that "l'Antico non deve servir di norma, esso deve essere un energia vitale della civiltà moderna."[39] [The Ancient cannot serve as the rule, it must be the vital energy of modern civilization that does so.]

These preliminary reflections, springing from a quotation that could appear to be a mere literary elegance, do not indicate my preference for the Romantic. One of the characteristics of Romanticism, to a certain extent, is to subject oneself to fate; to accept "events" as unavoidable facts and allow them to turn into habits and fashions, rather than to overcome what is sent to us by destiny. For a Romantic, destiny is a master that cannot be dismissed but, rather, must be tolerated with patience. The insistence on the binomial term architecture–nature, knowledge of the fact that history relies on a reconsideration of Enlightenment questions that are now under the aegis of science and technology and increasingly removed from the scope of the arts, is a reaction having nothing to do with a Romantic attitude, particularly when one takes this complex term in the ordinary sense that it is assigned today.[40]

The measure of man

The restrictions of specialization, the renouncement and reduction of problems and their subdivision into a series of detailed fields makes us lose sight of the unity of an idea, and this is also not Romanticism. One of the fathers of Architecture observes, for example, the following:

> E veramente noi considerando questa bella macchina del Mondo di quanti meravigliosi ornamenti ella sia ripiena, & come I Cieli co'l continuo lor girare vadino in lei le stagioni secondo il natural bisogno cangiando, & con la soavissima armonia del temperato lor movimento se stessi conservino non possiamo dubitare, che dovendo esser simili i piccoli Tempii, che noi facciamo; à questo grandissimo della sua immense bontà con una parola perfettamente compiuto, noi siamo tenuti a fare in love tutti quelli ornamenti, che per noi siano possibili.[41]

> [Indeed, if we consider what a wondrous creation the world is, the marvelous embellishments with which it is filled, and how the heavens change the seasons of the world by their continuous revolution according to the demands of nature, and how they maintain themselves by the sweetest harmony of their measured movements, we cannot

"... modern poetry ... consists in not looking at anything carelessly, and recognizing meaning in all things and life in all its possible forms, in other words to animate nature by means of analogous poetic ideas" (Giacomo Leopardi, *Zibaldone*, Milano, 1937, vol. I, p. 26, cited by Lodovico di Breme).

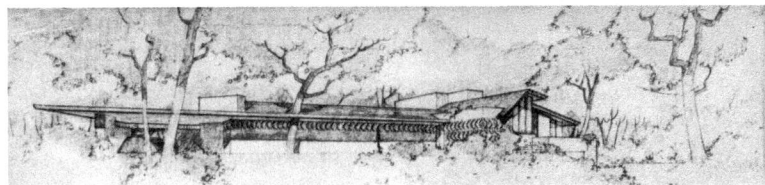

35 F.L. Wright, House in Middleton, Wisconsin, 1948 (Henry R. Hitchcock and Arthur Drexler [eds.], *Built in the U.S.A.: Post-War Architecture*, New York: Distributed by Simon & Schuster, 1952, p. 120, fig. 4). [© 2012 Frank Lloyd Wright Foundation, Scottsdale, AZ | Artist's Rights Society (ARS) NY.]

36 Respect for Nature in the house of John O. Carr in Taliesin, architect F.L. Wright (*Taliesin Drawings recent architecture of F.L. Wright: Selected from His Drawings*. New York: Wittenborn, Schultz, 1952, p. 12, fig. 4.] [© 2012 Frank Lloyd Wright Foundation, Scottsdale, AZ | Artist's Rights Society (ARS) NY.]

37 The same type of respect that Wright has for a tree and which is manifested in the figure earlier mentioned we find in the modest house of Mrs. Bullen, London, Ontario, Canada (*The Times*, London, May 15, 1957).

14 Andreas Palladio, *The Four Books on Architecture*, trans. Tavernor and Schofield, Cambridge, MA, 1997. This citation is from the "Foreword to the Readers" from *The Fourth Book on Architecture*, "In which the ancient temples in Rome and some others in and outside Italy are described and illustrated," p. 211. The sentence continues: "and build them in such a way and with such proportions that together all the parts convey to the eyes of onlookers a sweet harmony and each church fulfills properly the use for which it is intended," p. 213.

15 The "facocchio" is highlighted in an unsigned article titled "Frei Lodoli and the Chair" in *Habitat*, no. 1: 52. "Speaking of the furniture illustrated on the page immediately following, we consider it interesting to quote that passage of the so-called 'Socrates of Architecture,' Father Carlo Lodoli (Venice 1690–Padua 1761) who should be considered one of the most enlightened spirits of the prophecy of rational and reasoned architecture. Carlo Lodoli hinged his thought on a famous couplet: 'Both fabric and reason should combine, Its function then would be the outline,' and he said that it should be constructed 'with scientific solidity and sober elegance.'" The photograph of the chair that accompanies the essay is described: "probably a seat like the one which an Italian critic, a friend of ours, photographed in 1930, in Rome." See also, Joseph Rykwert, *The First Moderns*, for a discussion of the "facocchio": "The shoulders, Lodoli maintained, should dictate the form of the chair back, and the bottom, that of the seat. He therefore had made the prototype of a novel armchair, based closely on an ancient Roman one, which had not yet become common at the time . . . Lodoli's chair, however, not only had a concave back like the French models, but was curved in the part where you sit, as later became customary in England" (p. 317).

doubt that, the little temples which we build ought to resemble this vast one which He, with boundless generosity, perfected with but a word, we are bound to include in them all the embellishments that we can.] [14]

For a theory of Architecture, the idea that the measure of architecture means *the measure of man* is at least a starting-point, if not a rigid law, acting as reference to a vital principle such as it was in the past. If this principle is now outmoded, it is a consequence of the variability of the "units of measure"; and yet, there has always been a correspondence with the vital principle, an expression in accordance with each period: if the Parthenon is, to a certain extent, a small temple, Karnak is immense, St. Peter's Basilica is enormous rather than grandiose and Notre Dame possesses measures that we would call "mild" by contrast. Architecture that celebrates a political idea inspired by an obsolete past or the "deification" of man[42] is completely out of scale; although the Mies van der Rohe skyscraper currently being built on Park Avenue in New York City presents "grand" proportions, it expresses the reach of humanity and, furthermore, the fact that today man is no longer an isolated being but, rather, a sentient member of society.

Fra Giocondo, the Neo-Platonic Francesco di Giorgio [Martini], Leonardo, all inscribed the human figure in their circles, squares and triangles, an indication that an Architecture theory and harmony should express the average "human-building-measure," all inscribed within the limits of those indispensable geometric figures. One of the floor plans of Palladio, for example, is a "monument" that does not take the inhabitant and his exigencies into consideration, even though that "grand format" was the expression of the "human scale" of that time period, set out from "the exterior," from appearances, and not from the internal organization. In contrast, today I would substitute *Divina Proportio* with *Humana Proportio*. Luca Pacioli[43] says that it is necessary to have man as a starting-point for the measure of architecture. Humanism discovered and venerated man and exalted him according to the Platonic concept. This is a theory that still subsists today, a sort of axiom; nonetheless, it is possible that the dimensions have changed. Today, the necessities of man, his comfort, his material and spiritual pleasure, seem to be the primary consideration.

The Renaissance was followed by the Enlightenment, with the "facocchio" [15] of Carlo Lodoli,[44] the desperation of Romanticism, Positivism and its enthusiasm for the industrial civilization, and then contemporary Materialism and Scientism, which persuade man to claim hedonistic and utilitarian novelties in the establishment of a new society— a society that appears to be at the end of an era rather than the beginning of a historic period.

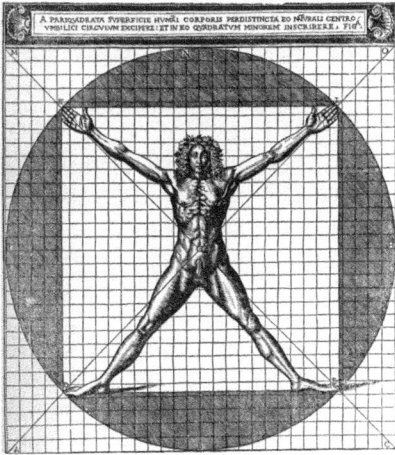

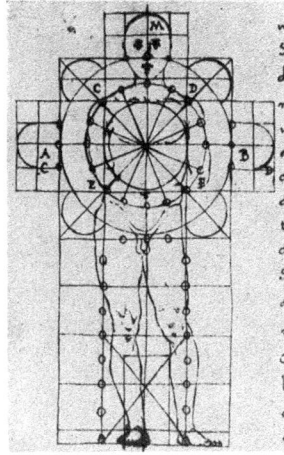

38 Figure in Cesare Cesariano, *Di Lucio Vitruvio Pollione de Architectura, etc.*, Como, 1521. [Wittkower, Rudolf. *Architectural Principles in the Age of Humanism*, 2nd ed. London: A. Tiranti, 1952, fig. 4.]

39 Francesco di Giorgio, drawing of human body in the plan of a church. Drawing of the codex Magliabechiano, fig. 1a., reproduced in Rudolf Wittkower, *Architectural Principles in the Age of Humanism*, London, 1952.

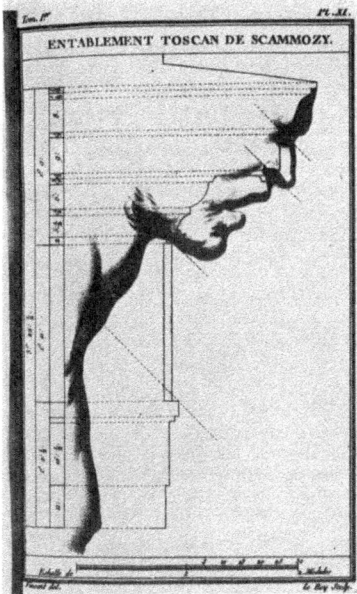

40 Architectural profile— Tuscan order (Jean-Francois Blondel, *L'Architecture francaise 1752–1756*, Paris, 1752, plate XI: "L'ordonnance la plus conforme à la nature ... peut seule constater les règles du bon gout dans l'architecture" (Emil Kaufmann, *Three Revolutionary Architects: Boullée, Ledoux and Lequeu. Transactions of the American Philosophical Society. New Series.* Vol. 42, pt. 3. October, 1952, fig. 2. Philadelphia, 1952, p. 438).

41 Head of Constantine, actually in the Palazzo dei Conservatori, Rome. Popular print (E. Lesbazeilles, *Les Colosses anciens et modernes*, Paris, 1878, p. 133).

42 Colossal head, Easter Island (*ibid.*, p. 255).

16 This letter is also quoted in Rudolf Wittkower, *Architectural Principles in the Age of Humanism,* New York: W. W. Norton & Company; First Edition edition, 1971, p. 60, note 3. (Originally published in London: Warburg Inst., 1949).

Theoretically, history is useful only as an old bridge that allows us to cross a river; in other words, man's exigencies have become *suddenly*, rather than *gradually* (an adverb that was well liked by the Science Academies of the eighteenth century) diverse. The architect is called on to create new, *other*, values that do not correspond so much with particular ideologies, but with certain necessities, implicitly aesthetic; in the same sense that we demand chemically pure and well-bottled milk from the farmer and industry, and a color TV simply because we are tired of the black-and-white one.

Man's necessities have changed. According to Le Corbusier's well-known concept, man eats, drinks, sleeps, works and lives in a manner that is different from that of yesterday; the phenomenon of speed and the rush for physical well-being has revived cities, while life in rural areas continues as before. The architect must adapt, must update his "theory," especially if his theory is to be communicated to the young.

Every professor of architecture may think of his School in the same manner that Aldo Manuzio thought of the Trissino Academy, in Cricoli, where the young Palladio had become captivated by the discovery of the Classic as a "new" form. He writes to Bernadino Partenio (on May 20, 1555): [16]

> con noi mi rallegro, e con quella magnifica città [Vicenza] dell'honorato pensiero intorno all'academia; della quale usciranno, come dal cavallo Troiano, in poco tempo eccellentissimi giovani, ch'empieranno non più Vicenza, loro patria, ma Italia tutta della Gloria del nome loro. . .[45]

> [I congratulate ourselves, as well as that magnificent city [Vicenza] for all the honorable thought produced inside of that academy, from which will very soon emerge, as from a Trojan horse, outstanding young men. And they will fill not only Vicenza but the whole of Italy with the glory of their name.]

In School, it is not sufficient to merely teach Architecture; it is necessary to transmit to students the enthusiasm of predecessors and masters. In this sense, I still remember—for the way he exercised his profession or posed a difficult problem—Professor Enrico Calandra, Professor of Architecture Theory at the University of Rome; his understated intelligence, essential and anti- rhetorical, his seemingly pedantic method, lacking in easy enthusiasms but rich with a profound sense of human inquiry,[46] will be with me always.

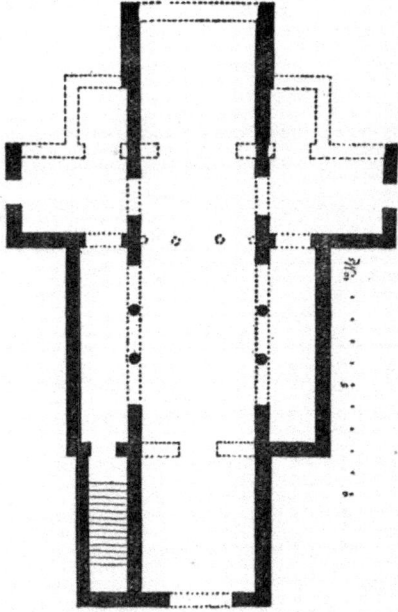

44 Representation of the Christian trinity (Santissima Trinidade. R. Pettazzoni, "The pagan origins of the three-headed representation of the Christian trinity," *The Journal of the Warburg and Courtauld Institutes*, London, vol. IX, 1946, pp. 135 and following).

The determination of number in architecture.

43 Plan of the three-aisled Basilica Laurosa, Portugal. Jurgis Baltrusaitis (*L'église Cloisonnée en Orient et en Occident*, Paris, MCMXLI, fig. 31).

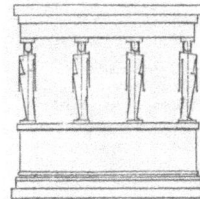

46 Study of Viollet-le-Duc concerning the position of caryatids in Greek architecture.

45 Original drawing in sepia of an autonomous architect's building of the end of 16th century, presenting on the last floor a series of caryatids that support the cornice (author's collection).

17 This is also quoted in Wittkower, *Architectural Principles*, p. 101, note 2.

Also relevant with respect to the sense of architecture as human measure, are Lomazzo's intentions that the measurements of the human body be used as criteria for the construction of ships: [17]

> il corpo umano il quale è un'opera perfetta e bellissima fatta dal grande Iddio a simigliannza della sua Immagine, con grandissima ragione è stato chiamato mondo minore. Perchè contiene in se con la più perfetta composizione, e con la più sicura armonia, tutti i numeri, le misure, i pesi, i moti, ed elementi. Onde da lui principalmente e non da altra fabbrica che uscisse della mano d'Iddio e dalle sue membra fu tolta la norma, ed il modello di formar i Tempi, i Teatrii, e tutti gli edifici con tutte le sue parti come colonne, capitelli, canali, e simili; navigli, macchine, e ogni sorte d'artifizio.[47]

> [the human body, a perfect and beautiful work made by God in his image, with great reason has been called a small world, because it contains within itself the most perfect composition and, in the most certain harmony, all the numbers, the measures, the weights, the motions, and the elements. Therefore it is from it [the body] and not from any other work that came out of the hand of God that we take the norms and measures to construct temples, theaters, and all the other buildings with all their parts, columns, capitals, channels, and so on; ships, cars, and all sorts of machines.]

In antiquity, it was easier to establish a "theory" because architecture was primarily based on the bilaterally symmetrical plan, which facilitated the external adornment of the façade as much as the internal distribution of the spaces: "Simmetry as wide or narrow as you may define its meaning, is one idea by which man through the ages has tried to comprehend and create order, beauty and perfection"[48] observes Weyl.

Nowadays, the taste for Vitruvian symmetry,[49] as well as the Renaissance's *proportio* and *commodulatio*, an observance of the "década" [*sic*] or the "tríada," eurythmics and the entire theory of a human measure as related to the physical man rather than to the moral man, seem to us like stages in the process of human thought. The manner of thinking and, so to speak, of "architecture-ing" an architecture is totally new, totally rediscovered, mainly because today's architecture is based on the metric system—a very important fact—while classical architecture was measured according to the "Greek foot," a form of measurement that was given different dimensions by individual countries. Viollet-le-Duc[50] insists upon this reasoning through new, unexpected "canons" that have nothing to do with the *commisuratio*, the absolute principle of Classical art that has not fully disappeared from architecture, since the "last hold-outs" continue to reach for Vignola's *Cinque Ordini*.[51] Here is one of the many problems to

47 Perspective of the second project of the monument to Vittorio Emanuele II, designed by G. Sacconi Acciaresi, *Giuseppe Sacconi e l'Opera sua grande.* [*Massima: Cronaca dei Lavori del Monumento Nazionale a Vittorio Emmanuuele II. Illustrata da 330 Incisioni.* Roma: Tipografia dell' Unione editrice, 1911, p. 89, fig. 91].

On monumentality beyond the human scale: when the monument to Vittorio Emanuele II in Rome was published (P. Acciaresi, *Giuseppe Sacconi e l'Opera sua grande*, Roma, 1911) the preface writer Guido Cantalamessa wondered intelligently: "Avrà censori quest'opera di cui io ho scritto tali parole? Quest'opera che aggiunge una si spiccata linea nuova al panorama della città? Certamente si. Sarebbe, non dico strano che non ne avesse, ma singolare. Anzi io prevedo denigrazioni aspre" (p. 5).

48 An equestrian statue of Vittorio Emanuele II being transported to its location on the monument, 1911 (*ibid.*, p. 148, fig. 171).

49 Banquet organized by architects, technicians and other workers in the belly of the horse of Vittorio Emanuele II, of the same monument (*ibid.*, p. 146, fig. 169).

18 *De Docta Ignorantia [On Learned Ignorance/on Scientific Ignorance]* refers to the fifteenth-century book of philosophy and theology by Nicolaus Cusanus on the notion that rational knowledge of God is impossible.

19 Yannis Xenakis is most probably the mathematician to whom she refers.

20 This is also quoted in Wittkower, *Architectural Principles*, p. 154.

which I allude in this work that could become the subject of a series of pedagogical discussions about a theme that is simultaneously historic, aesthetic, moral and technical. Historically, for example, Euclidean geometry proceeds to the "golden ratio." The golden ratio was praised by Pacioli, who considered it to be "divine" in accordance with the spirit of the Renaissance and his discovery of the "geometric" world and *de docta ignorantia*, [18] not in reference to Architecture, but in regard to the perfection of painters who had distinguished themselves in the technique of perspective.[52] Then come all the current interpretations and deductions of the *proportio*; Le Corbusier and his *Modulor*, which, when put into practice by a great mathematician (whom he does not mention), [19] provoked the following exclamation: "Faire appel simultanément à la géométrie et aux nombres, c'est le vrai but de notre vie . . ."[53] [Appealing simultaneously to both geometry and number, this is the true purpose of our lives]. With all that is invested in it, Geometry is a theme of considerable interest to the architect, notwithstanding what Guadet says— and here we see one more example of the "contradictory observations" presented in certain treatises: [20]

> On a cherché des combinaisons en quelque sorte cabalistiques, je ne sais quelques propriétés mystérieuses du nombre ou, encore, des rapports comme la musique en trouve minent les accords. Pures chimères . . .
>   Laissons là ces chimères ou ces superstitions . . . Il m'est impossible, vous le concevez bien, de vous donner des règles à cet égard.

> [We looked for somewhat esoteric combinations, I know but a few mysterious properties of numbers or, even, that music undermines the harmonies. Pure chimeras . . .
>   Let us leave these as myths or superstitions . . . I cannot, you understand very well, give you rules in this regard.]

Quite true; and he concludes: "Les proportions c'est l'infini."[54] [Ratios are infinite.]

Architecture and science

Lest I be accused of deviating from a systematic approach, I should like once again to indicate that my main purpose here is to denote the problems and ideas [of a contemporary Architecture Theory] while respecting, consciously or unconsciously, the peculiar spirit and character of our time, a time that is, even in its literary and artistic preferences, agitated and eclectic, innovative, anxious for syntheses and speed, and nearly distraught due to the sheer accumulation of facts, thoughts and actions with which it is now palpably overloaded.

Thus far, I have made only indirect reference to the term "science," although it is apparent that the fusion of art and science has increasingly characterized the development of Architecture. On the one hand, the fusion helps to achieve harmonious solutions to aesthetic ideals and, on the other, provides the certainty that comes with the progress of scientific research. The eventual fusion of art and science will certainly be realized, although, in the second half of the nineteenth century, it seemed impracticable to the great critic Fiedler:

> When the artist develops his visual conception to the point where "this way and no other" becomes a necessity for him, this process differs from that of the scientific investigator who regards a process of nature as a necessary. He who does not contemplate the world with the interest of the artist, if he at all feels the desire to take notice of the appearances of objects, attempts but to investigate the conditions of their origins. Only with difficulty, however, will he come to understand that there is a need of visually comprehending appearances as such, independently of a knowledge of their origins. To quote Goethe: "Thus a man, born and trained to the so-called exact sciences, will not easily conceive, at the height of his intelligence, that there could likewise exist a fantasy that is exact, without which art is essentially inconceivable."[55]

But the reconciliation between a concern for external appearances, sometimes regarded to be of superfluous, aesthetic interest, and an accommodation of the interior, may, at the very least, afford something inevitably of interest—a hedonist–utilitarian. The architect (Fiedler was writing about the artist and the scientist in a broad manner) will one day reconcile these two human activities, and be the mediator of approaches that exceed their disciplinary boundaries, because it is said that, despite growing warnings about the prevalence of scientific progress, there is nothing approaching a reaction in art, throughout its continued presence. During the Athens Conference, Le Corbusier drew the graphic[56] found on page 21, [21] which meant to represent the fact that scientific development was diverging from the state of consciousness, and therefore from the arts. Perhaps he was thinking about his polemic of the "maison machine-à-habiter," where the scientist battled against the artist, perhaps against himself, the author, whose "rooftop" on the Champs-Elysées [22] appeared to be the Romantic nostalgia of an artist who was concerned only with problems related to "taste." Le Corbusier observes that the architect must depend on collaborations with the scientist in order to be enlightened and rescued when he cannot find the necessary solution himself. Nervi has also adopted this point of view in his definition of "construction"—

21 Lina is referring here to Figure 54 in her text, which has a caption referring the reader to note 56, following.

22 The Charles de Beistegui apartment, 1930. "... in a letter to the Italian modernist P.M. Bardi in 1933, Le Corbusier had no qualms in setting the apartment de Beistegui alongside the Pavillon Suisse as paradigmatic examples of his urbanistic principles" and indicating that the apartment is a "coda and critique of the 1920s villas." Tim Benton, *The Villas of Le Corbusier 1920–1930*, New Haven: Yale University Press, 1987, pp. 209–210.

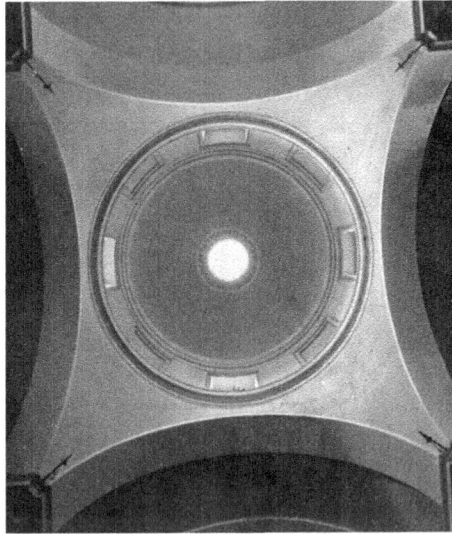

Historical antecedents of the correlation between science and architecture. It must be remembered that a correlation between science and architecture had already begun in antiquity, around the subject of ballistics.

50 The Platonic geometric precision of "everything is numerical", a Pythagorean architecture designed by Raphael, but executed by Baldassare Peruzzi: Sant'Eligio degli Orefici, Rome. Adolfo Venturi, "L'architettura del Cinque-cento", in *Storia dell'arte italiana*. Vol. II, pt. 1. Milano: U. Hoepli, 1938, p. 196, fig. 168.

51 Skyscraper on Park Avenue [New York]: Mies van der Rohe and Philip Johnson.

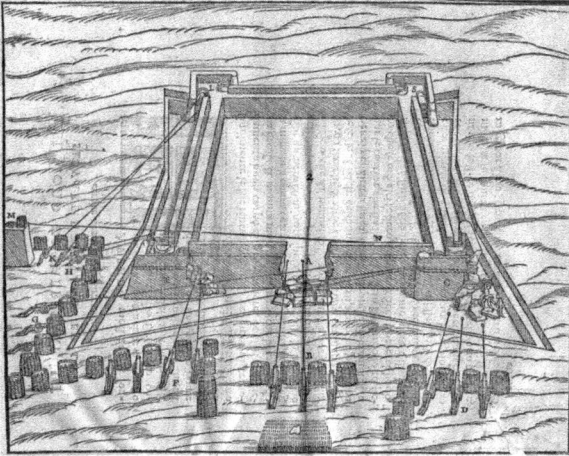

52 Fortress (Zanchi, Giovanni Battista de'. *Del modo di fortificar le città/trattato di M. Giovambattista de Zanchi da Pesaro*. Venezia: Per Plinio Pietrasanta, 1554, p. 29).

53 Representation of various operations that the architect performs to measure the terrain (L.B. Alberti, *op. cit.*, plate XXX).

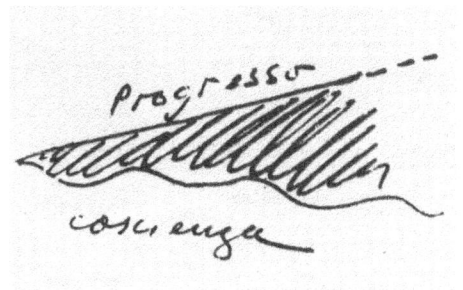

54 See note 56, and following [Le Corbusier sketch, redrawn from the original, in *Quadrante*, no. 5, 1933, p. 20 (issue on CIAM Athens)].

23 Radio Corporation of America
(1919–86). The company was taken
over by General Electric.

a definition I will return to in the coming pages—as his allusion to "scientific theory" seems to suggest that the builder should be aware of the field of science.[57]

One day, the architect will follow recommendations made by the dental hygienist; he will install a device that automatically adds fluoride to the water, will fulfill the demands for proper air conditioning, and study, in all aspects, the necessary paradox of the fall-out shelter. In this sense, the future of the architect lies in science. However, above all, the architect should be the designer of the house of man, and even his advocate, and he should rebel against this "prison" when he realizes that many of his colleagues, perhaps unconsciously, are reducing human life to a fantasy-less adventure, separating it from nature, divorcing it in a way that contradicts organic necessities and, in a moment of specious arrogance, defies our origins.

In this case, the architect is an artist, interpreting not merely vague worlds, but life itself; he is inspired by ideas worthy of being proposed and defended. His influence may be even more essential in the future than it has been in the past, and, naturally, more diverse. To a certain extent, only poetry, music, painting, sculpture and dance do not change—although they are the expressions of historical crises: nonetheless, Architecture changes, as it is now responsible for designing a house for man instead of building the Pyramids and the Louvre. Today, the architect's biggest problem is the small house and not the cathedral. Even geniuses were not able to project the cathedral well enough; it is no longer a problem because today's mystics seek a different form of silence, one that cannot be found in eternity or prayers, but in physics laboratories where scientists photograph matter in movement. We have not yet witnessed the birth of a new Saint Francis, who can find hints of a celestial and mysterious kind of poetry amidst the bombardment of atoms. Despite the rush to conduct atomic investigations, the architect, even as he is ready to receive, from RCA, [23] that atomic fire that will replace electricity, just as coal and gas have replaced firewood, continues to be the builder of a house and, if the term does not sound excessively romantic, a home.

In our houses, science has provided us with "leisures": the TV, the radio, the gramophone, the telephone. However, science should also promote self-reflection, since this ability to be excessively communicative has imprisoned us in a world that has ceased to reflect.

What power does the architect's theory have against another's pretentious ideas? While exercising our profession, we have all come across cases that have weighed on our consciences: a client, animated by absurd fashionable exigencies, leaves an architect's office not understanding why his project has been deemed unfeasible, while a line of "architects" appears, ready to satisfy this client's aesthetic wishes, even if what he asked for was a house in the shape of a ship, to remind him of the sea.

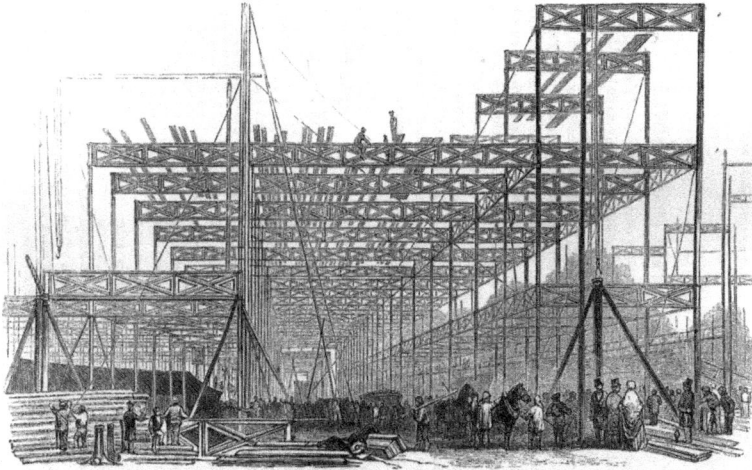

General View of the Works in Progress.

"England was the birthplace of the whole Industrial Revolution" (Siegfried Giedion, *Space, Time and Architecture, etc.* . ., Cambridge, 1956, p. 166).

55 The Crystal Palace during construction; Joseph Paxton, architect (Berlyn, *op. cit.*, facing p. 69).

56 Structure of house, "Meister häuser" no. 17 at the School of Bauhaus, in Dessau: Walter Gropius, architect: (*Bau und Wohnung: Die Bauten Der Weissenhofsiedlung in Stuttgart Errichtet 1927 Nach Vorschlägen Des Deutschen Werkbundes Im Auffrag Der Stadt Stuttgart Und Im Rahmen Der Werkbundausstellung "die Wohnung."* Stuttgart: F. Wedekind, 1927, p. 63, top).

57 Queensboro Bridge, New York, 1909; Gustav Lindenthal, engineer.

24 Heinrich Wölfflin, *Classic art, an introduction to the Italian Renaissance*, trans. Peter and Linda Murray, New York: Phaidon, 1968, 3rd edn, p. 231.

Architecture Theory begins precisely by renouncing those architectures that all architects have or should have renounced. The science that promotes "habitation" and community living should be an exact science, at least with reference to categories, climates, countries, etc. However, if this science is also an art, as it appears to be, how many "artistic paths" (to use a Romantic expression) are there? The polygon has many facets; however, aesthetics may be singular, such that, amidst a series of doubts and questions, we try to define it by deducing and synthesizing: but what is aesthetically pleasing for the vast array of clients who are both indifferent and undifferentiated? On the other hand, who will take it upon themselves to judge, in such a fluid and transient field, the expression that is synonymous with creativity, art and with the definition of a style?

It is apparently quite dangerous to talk about style; remember certain reflections made by Wölfflin:

> Quando si dice che é nato un nuovo stile si pensa sempre a una rivoluzione negli elementi architettonice. Ma se si consider ail fenomeno più da vicino si vede che non sono soltanto e grande architettura, il mobilio e le vesti, a subire una transformazione, ma l'uomo stesso nella forma del suo corpo è mutato e, proprio nella nuova maniera di sentire questo corpo . . . di animarlo e di muoverlo, si ha la manifestazione più profonda di uno stile. Certo bisogna dare a questo concetto maggior valore di quell che non I faccia oggi giorno. Nel nostro tempo si muta di stile come si proverebbe in una mascherata, un vestito dopo l'altro. Ma questa confusione degli stili data appena dal secolo decimonono e noi non abbiamo neppur più il diritto di parlare di stile ma soltanto di mode.[58]

> [When we speak of a new style arising, the first thing which occurs to us is that there has been a transformation in the architectural sense, but if we examine it more closely we find that the change is not confined to the environment of man—major or minor architectural features, furniture or costume—but that man himself has changed even in his outward, bodily form; and the real kernel of a style is in the new outlook upon the human body and in new ideas about deportment and movement. This conception of style is a much more weighty one than that which obtains nowadays, when styles change like fancy dresses being tried on for a masquerade. However, this uprooting of style dates only from our own century and we have really no longer any right to talk of styles, but only of fashions.] [24]

On styles and fashion (see reference to Wölfflin),
three examples:

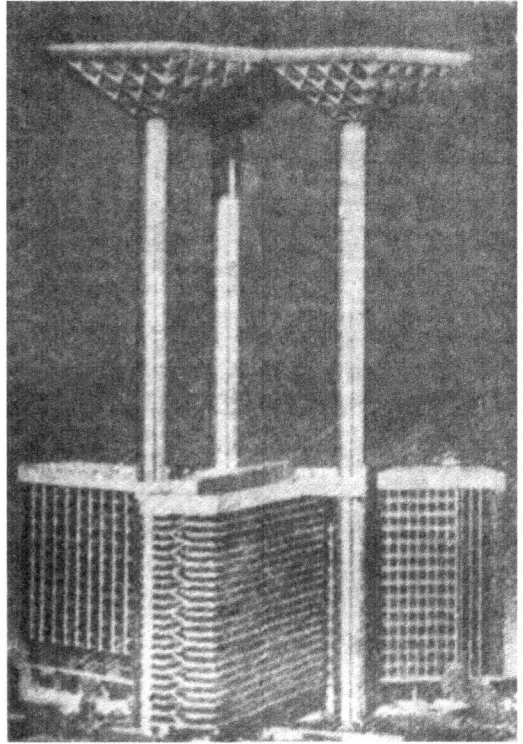

59 Adaptation of the Tuscan order through the
Baroque (*I cinque ordini di architettura di Andrea
Palladio, etc.*, Venice, MDCCLXXXIV (1784), plate 1).

58 Project for a skyscraper with helicopter pads;
James Dartford, architect (*The New York Times*, March
15, 1957).

60 Adaptation of a Jugendstile ornamental plan;
"Entrance to the new world" by Joseph M. Olbrich
(*Ideen von Olbrich*, Wien: Gerlach u. Schenk, 1899,
plate 1).

25 Bo Bardi is referring here to
Neutra, repeating a phrase from the
catalog of the Neutra exhibition at
MASP, October 1950.

A century ago, a surprised and emotional Ruskin gathered together
the fragments of the adornments of St. Mark's Basilica in Venice, asking
himself whether that "art" was not something sacred. It certainly *was*
sacred; *today* it is sacred once again, but what about tomorrow? Today, the
value of certain pieces of art, produced in the past, cannot be contested;
nevertheless, in the nineteenth century, painters such as Giotto and the
Primitives were considered to be inexperienced and inexact painters. In
the future, what will people think of our Cubism—which prides itself in
having "visually" anticipated the discovery of the mysteries of the atom—
of our Futurism, of our Concretism, which believes itself to have abolished
Figurative Art? Or will man, who is simply a man, continue to perceive
himself as a demigod? It is fitting that, in their process of elaboration, our
theories are simultaneously illuminated by conviction and overcast by the
shadows of doubt that are so characteristic of our times. If the scientist
may offer some safety, if the sum of his experiments may lead to some kind
of certainty and truth, then what is art's truth? By appearances, its truth
is quite relative: the *Venus of Willendorf* and the *Venus de Milo*; the Dolmen
and the Parthenon; the San Vitale mosaic and The School of Athens;
Caravaggio's *The Calling of St. Matthew* and David's *The Coronation of
David*; the Malatestiano Temple and the Eiffel Tower; Fallingwater and
Rio de Janeiro's Ministry of Education; Cézanne and Picasso, Klee and
Wols are expressions of a single historical truth. However, the preferences
were and continue to be infinitely varied, even more so than the variations
of each artistic production: man-made productions that have nothing to
do with nature. Fiedler starts his essay—which has been cited already—
by observing: "Because a work of art is a product of man it must be
explained and judged differently from a product of nature."[59] The scientist
investigates the immutable nature, and from this investigation he extracts
the truth; what the artist finds in nature is only inspiration. The architect,
while an artist, makes use of these motifs: he began by building columns
that were inspired by tree trunks, and today, the most forward-looking [of
them] place gardens at the heart of their houses. [25]

In conclusion, if the unity of nature lies in the inexorable invariability
of its laws, in the constancy and immutability of its phenomena, the unity
of history lies in a process that is marked by countless diverse moments;
it is therefore impossible to consider the validity of either one of these
unities to be absolute.

When properly understood, Architecture is and should be the clearest
awareness of this truth. For this reason, it should be considered the greatest
inspiration to a truly moral attitude.

61 Drawing by Ruskin (John Ruskin, *The Elements of Drawing & the Elements of Perspective*. London: Dent; New York: Dutton, 1907, p. 65).

62 The urban geometry of New York inspires one of Mondrian's compositions entitled, *New York City*, 1942 (Piet Mondrian, *Plastic Art and Pure Plastic Art 1937 and other essays, 1941–1943*, New York: Wittenborn and Company, 1945, after p. 20, "New York City 1942").

63 Internal spaces dug into the rock: Naqsh-e Rustam, West Asia, (Garnier, *op. cit.*, p. 345).

Materials and architecture

The idea that the materials, and not the various *milieux*, determine the architecture (an idea clearly seen in a lecture by Selvatico)[60] is currently being demonstrated in North America by the radical change in the appearance of façades: in the last century, we saw the introduction of superimposed metal staircases, due to new fire regulations; recently, we have seen the appearance of air-conditioning units in the windows; and today, façades have been modified by the introduction of walls made almost entirely of glass. The façade is no longer opaque, no longer an architectonic element constituted by the play of shadow and light, as it was up until the Neo-Classical period. Today, the façade tends towards transparency and acquires a picturesque value, due to the reflections on the glass walls—of the surrounding buildings, of the movement on the streets and even of bystanders. A demonstration of this profound change in the "artistic" state can be seen in New York City on Park Avenue, in the area surrounding 40th Street. Here, the architects responsible for new buildings have decided to make the façades transparent, following the example of Lever House (one of the first to follow Mies van der Rohe). The glass façade, soon to be replaced by plastic, is a consequence of the widespread use of air conditioning. Air conditioning has become an important factor not only because of its great influence on the development of architecture, but also because of the protection it provides against harsh climactic conditions.

New problems and new "tastes" intervene in the formulation of a new theory. We can already recognize an element that is usually sacrificed to "form": the color of architecture.

One of the difficulties in studying the theories of the past lies not only in the damage done to monuments, but also in the disappearance or modification of color—be it caused by man or by climactic conditions. Architecture is always a certain color which, regardless of the material, tends to change. It is difficult to imagine the Temple at Cape Sounion, [26] the Pyramid of Cheops, [27] Bernini's Colonnade, at the time when they were built, as the original colors of these architectures cannot be reproduced on our retinas; and attempts to color the reconstructions, prerogatives of the philology of German archeology, serve only to confuse our ideas. We should assume from the beginning that the destiny of an architectural structure is to change color. In twenty years, the bronze façade of the Mies van der Rohe skyscraper can become a stupendous turquoise, just as has happened to the color of the roofs of many basilicas, due to oxidation. At the time of the first aluminum roof (Church of Saint Joachim, Rome, 1897), the architect envisioned a silver cupola, but a few

Facades continue to change, no longer due to a stylistic evolution, but because the pure and simple facts of life demand it, and require aesthetic transformations to adapt to those same facts.

64 The UN Building, New York, whose façade, entirely of glass, reflects the facing building (Photo: Ernst Haas).

65 Façade of a building in New York with fire escape.

66 Façade of a building in New York with air conditioners visible.

67 Another building in New York, with air conditioners embedded.

years later, the oxidation of the aluminum had turned the cladding the
color of lead. Anodizing was only discovered later. Today, aluminum
seems to resist oxidation and retain its natural color.

These observations lead to the reflection that architecture, like other
things, is mutable and, because it is an art amongst the noblest productions
of man, generations learn to love it, despite the transformations brought
on by time. The façade of the Igreja da Ordem Terceira in Bahia, remains
valuable to us even though it no longer possesses the brilliance that it had
when it was first sculpted; we consider it valuable not only because of its
antiquity and our reverence for the past, but also because we find the color
of the stones, transformed by the sun and bad weather, to be beautiful. On
the other hand, the painting of many northern churches, with that
disfiguring lime whitewash, is a pity.

Industrial cities cannot sustain architecture of an intended color, due
to the modification of atmospheric factors by smoke. The innovation of
glass seems to signify a desire to confer a certain degree of durability to
the color. However, as we have seen, it is a color that mirrors the surroundings, the everyday, the weather.

We should be conscious of another evolution in the current
development of architecture: the transition from a hand-made phase to an
industrial phase. Architecture now depends on the aesthetics of a product
that has been mass produced, and on the pre-fabrication of the parts that
compose the architectural whole. Everyone knows that every industry
possesses a *fine art* element and every kind of art possesses an industrial
element.[61] Overcoming William Morris's paradox that architecture is
synonymous with applied art, we should nonetheless notice the inter-
dependence between industry and architecture and, consequently, another
unforeseen "theoretical" element that emerges from industrial practice:
the catalogs of materials, machinery and systems produced by industry
remain unmentioned in bibliographies and are considered to be—if not
"interesting reading," as once entertained such individuals as Anatole
France—occasional publications that are only of technical and financial
interest, whose data present values that are transitory and cannot be sys-
temized in scientific discourses. At first sight, it would seem that catalogs
are not important enough to appear in theoretical treatises; nonetheless,
it is important for us to highlight the opposite, because architecture has
been, for more than a century, the result of the reading and consultation
of catalogs of building materials. Furthermore, I must mention that
in the heyday of the discovery of new machinery and the novelty of
standardization, architectural structures were, in great part, built from

Industrialization, the new systems and new construction materials, continuously modify technique, because they modify the "representation" of Architecture.

68 Detail of the glass façade of a skyscraper in New York that reflects surrounding buildings.

69 São Paulo, Direita St., nos 162–196; Walter Brune, architect (*Solution to a construction problem*, São Paulo, 1910, plate 1).

"pattern books," which contained even the most minute details. The turn towards pre-fabrication and automation, especially now that commercial advertisements continue to drain individuals' capacity for judgment, will lead the consumer of architectural products and, consequently, the architect, to consider commercial catalogs as extremely useful tools. This statement is not supposed to be controversial, but historical. We must remember that in the sixteenth, seventeenth and even in the nineteenth centuries, Vignola's "Five Orders of Architecture"—in the most varied combinations and according to what is fashionable and the volatility of the exegetes (and it would be enough to recall the Five Orders "ombreggiati secondo il recente metodo della Accademia di Belle Arti del Regno (italiano)")[62]—were a sort of catalog, the great catalog of architecture, just as the several "Grammatik der Ornamente" were during the period of individual uncertainty.

70 Interlocking wall, France, Coignet System. European Productivity Agency, O.E.E.C. European Productivity, no. 25. Paris: European Productivity Agency, O.E.E.C., 1957, p. 39, middle left.

71 Placement of pieces of flooring in a prefabricated building. European Productivity Agency, O.E.E.C., *ibid.*, p. 15.

72 Pieces of prefabricated concrete, reconstruction of buildings on the island of Santorini in the Aegean Sea. European Productivity Agency, O.E.E.C., *ibid.*, p. 29, bottom.

73 Prefabricated stairs, Coignet System. European Productivity Agency, O.E.E.C., *ibid.*, p. 39, top right.

Another category of catalogs must also be mentioned: the great booksellers specialized in architecture and related fields that, in the period of Art Nouveau, were very important in shaping the style as well as the mentality of the architect. We still have not dealt with this issue, because Architecture Theory continues to be seen as a philosophical speculation—which it is as well—and not considered to be based on the positive facts which inspire it. I was able to get the most famous of these catalogs, Hessling's *Dekorative Malerei und Flaechenverzierung.*[63] Hessling was an international bookseller from Berlin who, in the late nineteenth and early twentieth centuries, exercised great influence, due to his branch office in New York City and the assistance of salesmen who traveled all over the world. His search for illustrated and well-regarded books to suggest to architects and decorators was not based on a commercial strategy, but instead on an aesthetic concept; therefore, this catalog is more useful than a history book about a period and its aesthetic ideas, as it offers a panorama

74 Floor of the Baptistry of Florence.

75 Floor for weekend trailer
(*The ground on which we
stand*, Amsterdam, Linolen
Krommenie, 1957, pp. 27).

"Serial production, which must now be taken into account as a basis of modern
architecture, exists in nature itself, and intuitively, in 'popular work'."

76–79 Salvador, Fair of the "Agua dos Meninos" (Photos:
J. Medeiros, O. Tavares, A. Brill).

28 Lina is likely referring to the destruction of many buildings of architectural distinction during the post-war rebuilding effort.

of the "construction" of new concepts, with hundreds of newly discovered authors working together to create, if only briefly, a sense of style. Therefore, we should not underestimate the number of works that were inspired by the catalogs of great booksellers. On the other hand, it is impossible to face the history of architecture of the recent past, and therefore the theory of Architecture that originates from it, without considering the series of manuals that was destroyed, as is well known, due to the frailty of our current sense of history. [28] The catalog that I mention contains hundreds of titles; the authors range from personalities who continue to be highly esteemed, such as Morris, Hoffmann and Crane, to professors who have been forgotten, even though they were powerful influences in the shaping of a style. This proves that the elaboration of theory may originate from practice and be its consequence.

Where should we place the investigators of new forms and the elaborators of the atmosphere that will determine the style of a time period? The catalogs—including, as I have already mentioned, the "catalogs of architectonic ideas"—are the products of amanuensis, often uncontrolled, that suggest forms and materials that have already been made and are often decorations for the construction of architectural structures. Some may argue that the determiner of stylish architecture does not take advantage of it; however, I must affirm that there has been an increasingly widespread preference for manufactured materials and for collaboration between the architect and industry.

The architect and society

The question of judgment in art, as we know, is as old as man; in the past, there was a constant need to identify the judge and the public. According to Aristotle, the public is the judge of artistic productions.[64] The question is, when is the public considered to be the judge: in the first moment of contemplation or after adapting to the work of art? If there exists a literature of the Aristotelian "applause" upon the discovery and inauguration of the masterpiece, there is also another [literature] that records the public's dissatisfaction, or incomprehension of the work. In ancient times, judgments proceeded slowly because artistic styles lasted for centuries. Thus, the public was accustomed to slow revolutions—even though they witnessed rapid political ones—in which the new stylistic period was incorporated into the one which had preceded it. The lack of immediate stylistic fractures prevented the awakening of any feelings of repulsion, or solely negative judgments.

Judgment is carried out when errors are apparent. The public is the first to notice the errors, but it is aesthetes that denounce them: after all,

FRONT ELEVATION OF BUILDING—Scale, ⅛ inch — 1 foot.

80–81 *Catalog of Architectural Parts in Metal: Designs and Prices of sheet-metal Cornices, Window Caps, Dormer Windows, Mouldings, Gutters, Ridgings, Raised Letters, etc... etc , pp. 365 and 481 (Catalog manufactured for the trade by Kittredge Cornice and Ornament Co., Salem, Ohio (c.1880)).*

the development of the history of art surrounds a restricted number of individuals, mainly artists and aesthetes, and the public only appears to be allowed to judge according to Cicero's well-known distinction.[65] In favorable periods, artists created a "moral atmosphere" that was accepted by the public, with only occasional exceptions.

A theory of architecture should, therefore, rely on general and basic ideas: the first would regard its scope, already very wide, with criteria to bring it in harmony with the times, the climate, and the national spirit. It is easy to demonstrate that the "Tudor" style has nothing to do with our century, and even less with the tropics and Brazil. Unfortunately, there is no law or regulation that allows us to forbid someone from building his house, eventually painting (not *sine cera*) the façade to imitate wood.

Are we living the last part of Eclecticism, that some Italian critics
also call "culturalismo?" [29] This was a trend that emerged at the margins
of Neo-Classicism as a natural consequence of the newly regained democratic will, and, for nearly a century and a half, distorted theoretical
considerations and architecture styles. Even today, there are aspects of our
cities that seem to pay tribute to the renowned manual, *Il Proprietario
Architetto* by Vitry, which was directed

> a tutti i proprietari che vogliono da sé medesimi sovrintendere ai loro
> edifici e dirigere i lavori dei loro artisti; non altra cognizione
> richiudendosi se non quella dei primi elementi di aritmetica e
> geometria, vale a dire la mistura della superfice e dei solidi.

> [to all the owners who want to oversee their buildings and the labor
> of the artists they supervise; no other knowledge than the primary
> elements of arithmetic and geometry are needed, in other words, the
> combination of surfaces and solids.]

Like other improvisers of his time, he offered this to human stupidity:
"modelli di qualunque genere architettonico, poiché anche l'egizio e il
gotico hanno le proprie loro bellezze inoltre perché con tutto l'omaggio
renduto al genio creatore di Atene e Roma . . ." [architectural models of
any kind, since even the Egyptian and the Gothic have their own beauty
as tributes to the creative genius of Athens and Rome. . .], as well as other
architectural styles with certain qualities; so—and note that, in a sense,
the situation continues—the proposed classic style in all of its adaptations,
even Gothic ("Malgrado quella specie di riprovazione di cui il gotico fu
in certa guisa colpito dai *puristi* dell'architettura moderna" [Despite the
disapproval of the Gothic style, which was in some way affected by *purists*
of modern architecture], because "il cantor della Grecia, lord Byron abitava
uno dei castelli più gotici della Gran-Bretagna" [the bard of Greece,
Lord Byron, lives in one of the most Gothic castles of Great Britain]),
the Turkish style ("la sua ripartizione però interna non armonizzerebbe né
co nostri bisogni né tampoco con le nostre abitudini, non comportando
menomamente le nostre costumanze fabbricati disposti a guisa di quelli
che usani nell'oriente," [its internal distribution, however, did not
harmonize with our needs, still less with our habits, and did not result in
changing our manner of building to the manner of those in the east]), and,
as if that was not enough, here is his excuse for an Egyptian style
("L'obbligazione impostaci di offrire modelli di ogni genere di architettura

82 "Moyamensing Prison" of Philadelphia (*Philadelphia Architecture in the Nineteenth Century by Theo B. White, editor, William P. Harbeson and others*, Philadelphia, published for the Philadelphia Art Alliance by the University of Pennsylvania Press, 1953, plate 29).

83 Project for the Academy of Fine Arts of Philadelphia, Pennsylvania, 1811. Project by John Dorsey and drawing by W. Strickland (*ibid.*, plate 7).

84 Academy of Fine Arts, New York, which imitates the Palladian style.

85 Palladio, Villa Cornaro, Piombino Dese (G.K. Loukomski, Lukomskiĭ, G.K. (Georgiĭ Kreskent'evich) *Andrea Palladio, sa vie, son oeuvre*, Paris: A. Vincent & Cie, 1927, bottom. MCMXXVII, plate LXXVI.

The nineteenth century created the Bank style, the Stock Exchange style, the School style, the Courthouse style, the prison style; while for the former the Greco-Roman was considered desirable, for the latter the Egyptian style was chosen. The fortress style was mostly used for barracks.

30 Cf. Pietro Maria Bardi, "Architettura, arte di stato," *L'Ambrosiano*, January 31, 1931.

fu quella che ci ha obbligati a produrre anche il presente")[66] [The obligation imposed on us to provide models for each type of architecture was what forced us to produce all this]) etc.

I have included these quotations in order to allude to a very important problem: it concerns the relationship between architecture and urbanism, or the scientific art of creating harmonious cities, surpassing the spirit of the urbanism of the past, which was based on "fortresses" rather than on the human logic of an ideal city—from houses on stilts that defended individuals from beasts to Haussmann's magnificent plans (despite their questionable motives).[67] It is still, in other words, the relationship between aesthetics and order/authority that governs. Thus, we necessarily touch on that fallacious concept of "architecture as art of the state." This concept has already had horrible consequences in several European countries, where politicians exerted its power to assert obsolete ideologies. [30] Therefore, would it not be dangerous for an administration to regulate aesthetics, thus confusing it with "political aesthetics"? It is important to have in mind that, in a democratic country, the means to affirm ideas—even the ideas we consider the best—are always available, and these means are education and example, rather than intellectual constraint and control. That is why theory cannot exist without criticism, especially the everyday criticism that has its rudiments in good sense and good taste.

The compulsion of all builders to adopt inclined roofs in Nazi Germany and in Fascist Italy, the requirements that builders use cut stone instead of concrete and that 2 percent of the cost of the construction be destined for picturesque decorations will continue to exemplify the intervention of political power[68] on the free development of civic life, because Architecture is the field that best represents a country, an era, a civilization. Due to the democratic standards of our time, these political interventions may seem quite strange. In highlighting the necessity of artistic expression, especially in our discipline, we must not forget to reflect on the historical characteristics of a past—the period preceding the appearance of the liberal and democratic ideals that mark our historical period—in which the activities of artists and architects were regulated by authorities in accordance with the peculiarities of the political societies in which they worked. I will have an opportunity to explain this problem later, but first, by way of example, I offer the most important treatise of the 1600s, as decreed by Louis XIV with his creation of the Royal Academy of Architecture:

> Jugeant fort à propos que c'est soit l'unique moyen de dépouiller l'Architecture de ses ornements vicieux, de retrancher les abus que l'ignorance de la présomption des Ouvriers y avoient introduit & de

86 "Ewige Wache" (Eternal Vigilance). Monument to the Nazis in Munich. German Library of Information, ed. *A Nation Builds: Contemporary German Architecture*. New York: German Library of Information, New York, 1940, p. 9.

87 The same monumentality in the façade of a factory in Germany, *ibid.*, p. 115.

l'enrichir de ces beautés naturelles & de ces grâces qui l'ont rendue si recommandable parmy les Anciens.[69]

[Judging aptly that it would be the only means to strip Architecture of its vicious ornaments, and to eliminate the abuse that the ignorance and presumption of workers had introduced and to enrich it with those natural beauties and graces which rendered it so commendable among the Ancients.]

Today, however, the School, with its role as a venue for free investigation, discussion and intellectual exchange, is the only place from which a clear orientation to Architecture can be given. These are important resources for the work of current and future architects. Only the school works in opposition to all types of dogmatic and restrictive attitudes. The controversial innovation that happened in this century was realized by some isolated spirits and unofficial, short-lived schools [Bauhaus] and it was kept alive only in some American schools: Gropius, Mies van der Rohe, Le Corbusier, Wright, were some of the masters of this polemic.

We can consider the Athens Charter of 1933[70] as a point of departure as well as a synthesis of all the demands encompassed by that passionate controversy in which, for the first time, Architecture and Urbanism became one and the same problem.

The architect and the client

Amongst the determining elements of a theory [of Architecture] is the role of the client, which, once again, brings us into the realm of practice. It is obvious that the architectural style of any construction, be it a modest house or a great factory, is greatly influenced by economic factors: the architectural structure is the result of innumerable factors that appear in the course of the architect's work, such as the request for the project, the choice of architect, the architect's agreement with the owner, the consultations with governmental authorities and the changes that they impose, the possibility of achieving the desired details. Taking these factors into consideration, it is very possible that at some point in time, there will appear a house in the form of a pagoda or a factory in the form of a cathedral: constructive freedom does not impose limits on individual freedom. After all, a theory of Architecture could be aesthetically established by constituent economic groups. The position of the architect, who is, *in fieri*, a theorist or a professional, who should possess a theory, is extremely complex. It has ever been thus, as historical examples show; nonetheless, I will limit these examples to one that refers to the Middle Ages, the

31 Known as "The Rotharis Code" of 636–652.

32 Leader Scott, *The Cathedral Builders: The Story of a Great Masonic Guild*, New York, Charles Scribner's Sons, 1899, p. 62.

period in which, following the fall of the Roman Empire (responsible for the intermingling of the oriental and occidental styles), the role of the professional architect was re-established. This happened because the Lombard kings acknowledged and invested in a group of builders from Lake Como, who eventually dispersed all over Europe, and came to be esteemed not only as master masons and builders, but as artists as well.

The Germanic kings' statutes and norms were passed on to the Comacini masters by means of an extremely important document, the *Memoratorio de Mercedes Comacinorum*,[71] promulgated by King Liutprand. (This succeeded King Rotharis' Edict of 22 November, 643, [31] which included rules, tariffs, and provisions for occupational hazards, etc.). The *Memoratorio de Mercedes Comacinorum* was a sort of "construction manual"; I leave aside its purely practical aspects in order to deal with its theoretical aspects, and thus to confirm the view that the architect should be subject to the client. It should be noted that [the articles of the Edict suggest that] the architect is not only responsible for the important and representative edifices but for the humble and ancillary works as well. For example, of the seven articles [in the Edict] meant to guide the [Comacini] masters one refers to *De Furnum* [the oven] and the other to *De Puteum* [the well], with practical norms regarding their solidity, functionality, etc.; this explains the phrase at the beginning of article CLX: *Similiter romanense si fecerit, sic reportet sicut gallica opera* ("Roman work shall be accounted of equal value to Gallic work" [32]).

This shows that the architect was expected to design and build in two different styles, or in other words, with two different theories. We should recall this fact today, when many architects are perfectly willing to build a house in the colonial style and simultaneously build another in a "modernistic" style, depending on the preferences of each of their clients.

The architect trained under Lombard law was supposed to dictate— *ad opera dictanda*, as it appears on paragraph CXLV, meaning to show, to draw or to explain the works that are going to be made—in two different theories. In that period, a theory meant a stylistic norm, or more specifically, the type of arch used: acute, round and horseshoe. At a time when culture was secreted in the monasteries and there was a shortage of materials and little participation on the part of local masters (a phenomenon similar to that experienced by Portuguese builders in Brazil in the sixteenth and seventeenth centuries), intermingling of styles, transposition of norms, and indecision on the part of clients, the unique art of the "Comacini" masters became commonplace, opening the door to evolutions, confrontations and technical and structural improvements; ornaments acquired

90 Chartres, cathedral constructed by Bispo Fulbert in the eleventh century, reconstructed based on a miniature by Andrea de Mici (Otto von Simson, *The Gothic Cathedral: origins of Gothic architecture and the medieval concept of order. With an appendix on the proportions of the south tower of Chartres Cathedral, by Ernst Levy.* New York: Pantheon Books, 1956, plate 30). On the anonymity of the medieval architects and the lack of documentation concerning the construction: "Si l'on cherche dans le Cartulaire des renseignements relatifs à la construction de l'église de Notre-Dame, on est surprise de n'en trouver d'aucune espèce" (Guérard, *Cartulaire de l'église de Notre Dame de Paris*, vol. I, pref. 52, p. clxvii).

91 Stonemasons and carpenters of Westminster Abbey, drawing c. 1270 (Manuscript "Life of the Confessor" in Cambridge (*Memoires of W.R. Lethaby, Westminster Abbey and the King's Craftsmen*, New York, MCMVI (1906), p. 114, fig. 65).

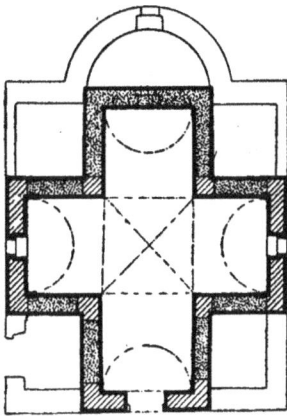

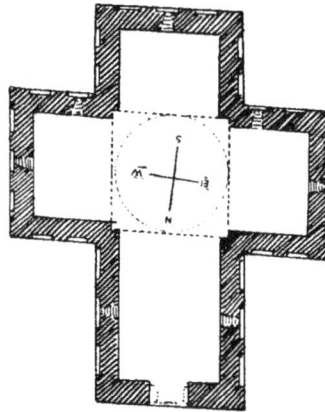

92–93 Plans of the "Sacelli" simple cruciform: a) Ravenna, Mausoleum of Galla Placidia; b) Halvadere, (Asia Minor) small church in ruins (Sergio Bettini, *L'architettura di San Marco, origini e significato*, Padua, 1946, plate III).

33 Bo Bardi relies on the interpretation in the book she cites by Giuseppe Merzario, *I Maestri Comacini—Storia artistica di Mille duecento anni (600–1800)*, Milano, 1893.

34 In *The Cathedral Builders: The Story of a Great Masonic Guild*, Leader Scott makes a case that the Comacini masters were the Medieval link between Classical and Renaissance art. Furthermore, she concludes that "the famous artists who formed the rise of the Renaissance were not each a separate genius inspired from within, but a brethren of one guild whose education was identical and whose teachers passed onto them what they received from their predecessors—the accumulated art-teaching of ages" (p. 423).

original shapes, based on Nordic-meridional grafts; the *Opus Romanense* and the *Opus Gallicum* became part of history, whilst the predominance of the craftsman led Architecture to become a product of its time.

The Romano-Lombard style was a convergence of many diverse influences and styles. [33] Therefore, how much of a role could it play in defining the Romanesque? [34]

I did not intend to engage the subject philologically, but I think it is fair to present these [historical] problems in order to demonstrate how difficult it is to define a theory of Architecture, even retrospectively.

Romanticism and architecture

Contemporary architecture is the result of a process of renovation and research; a near convergence of particular motives leads us to a state of transition. One of the problems that more clearly expresses our uneasy state is no doubt represented by Romantic ideas and experiences. The most interesting part of this problem is that, to a great extent and concerning innumerable aspects, we are still experiencing the consequences —maybe the last ones—of all things that characterize Romanticism, understood above all (in the manner in which it is possible to synthesize its many and at times contradictory manifestations) as an indeterminate state of anxiety, a dissatisfaction and, for this reason, a polemic against all fixed and definite regulations; it was in this manner that the contemporary historicist conscience was born.[72] From this reference comes architectural and artistic Romanticism. How better to celebrate Architecture than with these verses:

> Earth proudly wears the Parthenon,
> As the best gem upon her zone,
> And Morning opes with haste her lids
> To gaze upon the Pyramids;
> O'er England's abbeys bends the sky,
> As on its friends with kindred eye[73]

This poem explains Emerson's "*adventitious beauty*," or casual beauty. Observing, from the temple of Venus, the roofless houses of Pompeii, Emerson relates architecture with nature, and nature with Creation; that which is built by man with the mysterious capacity for its destruction (perhaps as a reminiscence of the polemics that surrounded the Lisbon earthquake, with its two most forceful protagonists: Leibniz, and his "pre-established harmony," and Voltaire, who ridiculed this principle); the view of the rediscovered Pompeii is a casual beauty, originating from an

The reproduction of designs from afar was common throughout the Renaissance, and we can say that through the circulation of specialized magazines, the practice continues today. To illustrate this fact, which must be taken into consideration in the history of the Theory of Architecture, I reproduce the following figures.

94 Example of an unfinished architecture of Palladio interpreted today as a "symbol" of a "sculptural element." Palladio, Palazzo Porto Breganze, Vicenza, (Loukomski, *op. cit.*, plate XXXIII).

95 Casa Ralph Allen, derived from the style of Palladio, Bath, England, 1727 (Walter Ison, *The Georgian Buildings from 1700 to 1830*, London: Faber and Faber, 1948, fig. 31).

96 Original design of Bernardo Belloto, reproducing a mid-eighteenth-century palace in Prague, with a caption that shows how the painters were in charge of architectural reproductions so that they might be used as models (author's collection).

35 Emerson, lecture on Art and Nature (1879) listing the five orders, asks, "where was the Chinese, and the Hindoo, and the Persian, and the Saracenic? Five is a very narrow counting for the styles of men."

36 The first line of this paragraph is omitted. It reads, "To show man's dwelling as an epitome of his human needs, Emerson employs an anatomical figure."

unforeseen cataclysm; but it is the same beauty that the Romantics discover in the ruins of Greece, Rome and Egypt. The Romantic, for example, had not yet considered Mexico and all other civilizations [whose art] did not lead to a literary tradition, as it was the case with Etruscan art. [35]

Besides this, Emerson also deserves to be remembered by virtue of his perception of the future of American architecture. In relation to this, he observes:

> In architecture, height and mass have a wonderful effect because they suggest immediately a relation to the sphere on which the structure stands, and so to the gravitating system. The tower which with such painful solidity soars like an arrow to heaven apprizes us in an unusual manner of that law of gravitation, but its truth to which it can rear aloft into the atmosphere those dangerous masses of granite, and keep them there for ages as if it were a feather or a scrap of down. Then, great mass, especially in height, has some appreciable proportion to the size of the globe and so appears to us as a splinter of the orb itself.[74]

This idea of "architecture as a splinter of the World," that led some American architects to make their skyscrapers resemble forests of an ideal nature, even golden, suggests to the aesthetics of Boston the idea that architecture must make friends with the elements of sun, wind and rain, as well as the physical laws of gravity:

> Lest it be in turn destroyed by the very force of nature.

In this manner, Emerson sees the function of the architect in relation to the universe and, since he alludes to the Egyptians, his reference becomes clear—the architect as priest. However, when he turns his attention to the *flats* of Philadelphia or New York, there finding an absence of the ideals of hygiene and decorum, he pursues an architecture that is no longer purely romantic (meaning "pure aesthetic pleasure"). It is a case of re-asserting the anatomical definition so that it is increasingly inspired by the architecture–nature concept: [36]

> Every work repeats in small the nature of the workman, a house is a sort of statue or mask of the builder, the underpinning being the feet; the cellar, the abdomen; the kitchen, the stomach; the windows, the eyes; the chimney, the nose; the sitting room, the heart; the library,

The idea of Architecture in a spatial sense could be given not by a single style of architecture, but by an ensemble, that is, by urbanism. And that is the reason why we dedicate a section to some romantic interpretations.

97 Architecture as a "shard" ("The Present Revival of Christian Architecture," from *Pugin's Apology in the Gothic Revival, an essay in the History of Taste*, by Kenneth Clark, London, Constable, 1928.

98 Panorama of the West Side of New York—view from the city reservoir.

37 Emerson calls him "Ruskin's scholar." Quoted in Hopkins, *Spires of Form*.

38 Hopkins says, "It is not until our own time, however, that his application of the organic principle to architecture becomes crystallized in the practical functional theory of Frank Lloyd Wright."

39 "selfish and cruel aspect" is from Emerson, "Art", *Works 1*, 1868.

40 This is Emerson's summary of Greenough's theory, from *English Traits*.

the brain; and the lower members with their uses are not wanting in the vents and vaults of the house.[75]

Wright's architecture will be influenced by this idea, already organic, since it was born as a biological symbol, interweaving conceptions made by Garbett,[76] Ruskin's student, [37] and by Greenough,[77] a Romantic who theorized about functionalism, both of whom were capable of comprehending the part that industrialization and the machine would play in the new architecture. [38]

I insist on the analysis of this transitional period, characterized by the abandonment of an imitative architecture, especially in America—due to the importation of a culture that, with Napoleonic ostentation, leads to Neo-Classicism—because of a new perception of human life and of aspirations for an organic and functional well-being that would result in the industrial movement, having as its consequences the current domestic appliances and even household *loisirs*; I insist on this because I see in this fracture the emergence of a theory of Architecture that, it is true, is still unable to define itself, but is already searching for the fundamental bases— moral and technical—of the problem.

For the Romantics, the expectation of the new "Machine Romanticism," the industrial production and the subsequent contraposition between industrial work and handicraft, has a selfish and even cruel aspect, [39] Garbett states: "Is not a non-architectural building ugly simply because it looks selfish?"[78] [40]

Here, selfishness opposes generosity; it is selfish to demand functionality, *commodity* instead of dignity and appearance. Generosity is, in essence, an expression of "nobility." It is these social problems, the reconfiguration of cities, the migration, that transform urbanism, leading it in the direction of a science of "existence."

In my understanding, the most correct way to face architecture is precisely to not reduce it to a circumscribed and specific sphere, but rather to consider it as part of a larger realm, or as a simple component of urbanism or even of a vast geography. The modernists pose a certain resistance to this conception, perhaps influenced by the old habit of subdividing and separating the parts of the world into things and thoughts. On the contrary, the Romantics understood architecture in a cosmic sense, although in practice they fragmented their own ideas when they adhered exclusively to memories of the past which they understood only as abstractions. Thus the ivy was allowed to grow over the ruins, reinstating the picturesque mystical Gothic, giving way to that period after which industrialism and the machine would outline the rational path of new ideas. This path will perhaps end by up offering us a style.

99 Skyscrapers and chimneys in downtown New York.

100 Sharp architecture, from the enduring hardness of the Egyptian obelisk (for example, the mausoleum-obelisk honoring the heroes of '32 in São Paulo). Project for a monumental column in a park; Italian architect of the seventeenth century (author's collection).

Nevertheless, the concept and, I would add, the literary error of the Romantics, also has its value, making it impossible to ignore the importance of the ideas that are aroused by the "Kosmos," and by the near-angst that I prefer, in the philosophical plane, though fruit of the eclectic, to the decisive tone typical of Victor Cousin.[79]

101 Scene from the opera *Andromeda and Perseus* (seventeenth-century manuscript, Library of Baron de Landau, Milan, 1948, n. 207).

102 Grandjean de Montigny: Project for the Temple of the Muses (Museu Nacional de Belas Artes; in the journal *Estudos Brasileiros, Rio de Janeiro*, no. 11, 1940, after p. 486). "In the second quarter of the nineteenth century, the French architect Auguste Henri Victor Grandjean de Montigny, educated in the prestigious academic tradition then in vogue, was able at last, after many years of painful trials and thinly veiled hostility, to begin the regular teaching of architecture in the building that he had designed for the headquarters of the newly founded Academy of Fine Arts. It was thus officially integrated into the architecture of our country in the modern spirit of the time . . ." (*Artigos e Estudos de Lucio Costa*, Center for Architectural Studies, Porto Alegre, 1954, p. 53).

Seventeenth-century architecture, besides being "constructed" is also "drawn"; one could say that in the seventeenth century, architecture became confused with scenography.

Chapter 2

PROBLEMS OF METHOD

The example of the masters

Thus far, I have carried out a kind of excursion across time and through "theories" of architecture, focusing on one of the aspects and methods of its interpretation: the critical; however, the experience I have had in teaching has led me to understand a certain impatience on the part of students.

This impatience is well known: they no longer feel connected to the past; their "roots have been cut," the natural habit of studying calmly and methodically no longer exists, nor the awareness of an acquired and natural cultural inheritance. It is the impatience of those who do not want to know about things *that do not produce results immediately*, about things that do not provide us with solutions to everyday problems. At this point, we must recall the words of a young, recently graduated architect from Rio de Janeiro: "I feel as if I am hanging by a thread, with no knowledge of where to find solid footing." In previous centuries, no student of architecture who had his solid technical manuals and books with "theories" of architecture felt "as if hanging by a thread"; concrete rules sustained them—a young architect's convictions were the basis for his works.

Consequently, his dilemmas were comprised from the art of fixed rules and, in an analogous sense, the consideration of human solidarity, in the sense of "charity" and "philanthropy." Today's architect, on the contrary, feels a confusing tension between the "pure" or abstract problems of architecture and the burden of the discipline's responsibility to address social problems. The more sensitive individuals can be inhibited by this. In this century, architecture can no longer be characterized as an "exhausted" art form—to use the Romantic classification scheme of Antonio Tari[80]—it has lost its character as a product of fantasy and fixed linguistic rules, and turned into an art that reasons and expresses itself through the emotions and through practices that lend to its development a new, unforeseen character, unpredictable by virtue of the evolution of science, of technique and of customs, which are evolving vertiginously.

Between the Baroque and the nineteenth century, there were a whole series of theories. [These theories] must be examined because they suggest reasons for the evolution of a theory that may prove to be of interest. I wish only to mention two cases by way of example. The study of Boito deserves special mention, *Sullo stile futuro dell'Architettura italiana, op. cit.*

103 Allegory from the frontispiece of Blondel, *Cours d'architecture enseigné dans l'Académie royale d'architecture . . . par M. François Blondel. 2 Ed., augm. & cor.* Paris: Chez l'auteur, 1698. Frontispiece. (cit. vol. I, see note 28), representing his own design for the Arch of S. Denis. The title of Chapter VI (*op. cit.*, p. 618) is: "La Porte S. Denis à une seule ouverture est le plus grande ouvrage du monde de cette nature." Also found in Blondel: "Plus considérable par ses proportions que par les ornements." The academy founded by Louis XIV was based on this principle.

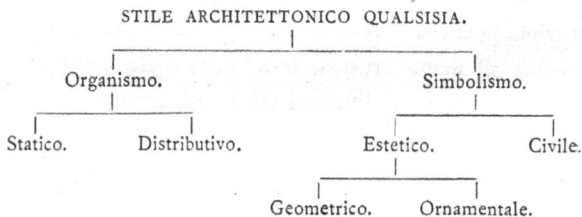

104 Synoptic Table to interpret any architectural style, according to Camille Boito (Camillo Boito, *Architettura del Medio Evo in Italia, Con Una Introduzione Sullo Stile Futuro Dell'architettura italiana: Ricerche.* Milano: U. Hoepli, 1880, p. XI).

41 Bo Bardi references a passage from the *Nicomachean Ethics*, in which Aristotle uses the term Lesbian rule both literally and figuratively: "For when the thing is indefinite the rule also is indefinite, like the leaden rule used in making the Lesbian moulding; the rule adapts itself to the shape of the stone and is not rigid, and so too the decree is adapted to the facts." The *Oxford English Dictionary* describes a "Lesbian rule" as "a mason's rule made of lead, which could be bent to fit the curves of a moulding." In the seventeenth century the phrase was commonly used in English in a figurative sense, referring to "a principle of judgment that is pliant and accommodating." The word "Lesbian" refers to a pliable mason's rule, an instrument for measuring curves that was made of a kind of lead found on the island of Lesbos. The material's pliability meant that it was flexible enough to be shaped to fit a curved edge.

The extreme precariousness and speed with which contemporary life flows impedes the formation of a stable method of teaching—a method which would already be obsolete in its initial stages. What, in buildings, is known as "flexibility"[81] [41] should be incorporated into the teaching method to avoid ossification—and this, of course, also in relation to the history of Architecture—thereby offering students a means which can become an instrument in their collection, or the solution to problems, when deployed, whose power would confirm, in a sense, the words of the celebrated treatise of François Blondel.[82]

Extremely critical positions and dogmatic doctrines, as well as every constructive "frivolity" that is positivistic in character should be eliminated. The task of the professor should be to awaken a critical consciousness, to teach the student the sense of history as continuity, not as a cultural elegance but as a vital source of real contributions. The young architect will find security not in notions that are *right* and *proven* but, rather, in the uncertainty, the timidity, with which he faces the moral responsibilities he will perceive intuitively in the profession, finding in those principles the strength and critical lucidity necessary to the professional today; will take care not to abandon himself to orgies of exhibitionism, but to find the reward for his efforts in his own sense of responsibility towards humanity.

We must, at this point in our investigation, broach the history of art itself (yet another demonstration of how vast the field of Architecture Theory could become and how many different disciplines it could encompass). It will therefore be necessary to engage extremely subtle issues, which concern not only the history of styles, but History itself. This problem will eventually be solved by the consolidation of all relevant disciplines into a single course, under a single professor. It would not be a course about "theory" or "character" or even "history of art"; it would be a course about History. How is it possible to effectively separate Theory from Character from the History of Art? How can a professor of Theory transmit to his students "concrete" and critically valid concepts if such concepts may be modified or even eliminated by the abstract interpretations given by the professors of analytical Architecture or History of Art? Wouldn't those abstract interpretations belie the interests of those professors?

The famous Gothic style, commonly referenced as an expression of the period, is a very well-known anachronism. The vicissitudes of its "manufacture," instituted by the people during the administration of Gian Galeazzo Visconti, and its construction lasted five centuries and continue today. It is a typical example of the impossibility of a style's moving beyond the historical period that characterizes it; the Baroque and Neo-Classical insertions prove the truth of this statement.

105 Milan cathedral in an engraving from 1735 (after Camillo Boito, *Il duomo di Milano e i Disegni per la sua Facciata*, Milano, 1889, phototype 43).

106 "Gothic Revival" in New York, 5th Avenue. A new construction rises on one side of the church. Should not a religious building be totally isolated?

The competition program refers to the "isms" as well as to the history of steel, concrete, glass, plastic, etc. Unless we treat them as isolated factors, these themes necessarily invoke the History of Art. As a practical example drawn from recent history, it is worth mentioning "Art Nouveau," considered to be increasingly important, since it refers to a historical *fait accompli*. In referring to this period, whose boundaries remain undefined by the critics, the professor of Theory will have to draw on concrete and determined facts, and not on vague abstractions; in the course of a lecture, he will have to work hard in order to transmit a constructive synthesis of this period based on its tangible aspects. It is only in this manner that Gaudi's inclined columns, "curves made of bricks resembling fish scales" and pillars of lava will acquire their real significance and contribute to the topic.

Nonetheless, how are we supposed to engage in such a complex subject without making it seem utopian? Today, we could criticize the program of most Schools of Architecture because almost all disciplines repeat the same themes, although in different ways: from "design" to "plastic arts" and "history of art," and even to "urbanism." That which is considered to be "theory" and provides the architect with a critical consciousness and a historical maturity—besides a technique—should make up a single subject matter and a single course. However, as we have observed, this is a problem as complex and delicate as the merger of civil engineering and architecture.

Simultaneously to the conveyance of theoretical notions and knowledge and in the pedagogic spirit to which I have alluded, I believe that it would be highly desirable to record and, to a certain extent, relive the history of the pioneers who opened new paths to the field of Architecture, facilitating and determining its new consciousness. In this way, even the least recognized articles, the ones that oppose the innovators, could be didactically useful. The task of affirming dissenting ideas that have been proclaimed is always arduous. True innovation is only slowly accepted and a long time passes before other individuals become proselytes —especially people in countries where tradition dictates a constant conformity to the established aesthetic orders. If we review the recent past, one that still seems recent in Europe, we will be able to verify that important architects such as Mies van der Rohe, Gropius, Mendelssohn

The search for "another type" of column began with the peculiar and fanatical approach of the Art Nouveau movement; from Gaudí, who was inspired by "modern" ideas and the foremost interpreter of the demands of the Spanish people, to Horta and the "constrictores" of the flower's stem, which was made to serve the dynamic function of horizontal bearing, made possible by the new advances in concrete [forms. These two architects] represent something on which one could base the "new"; while the "culturalistas" made use of [concrete] in the most banal manner, as exemplified here. [Fig. 109].

107 Crypt of the Chapel of Colonia Guell, Barcelona; Antoni Guadi, architect.

108 Staircase of the Goetheanum; Rudolf Steiner, architect (*Wege zu einen Neuen Baustil, fünf Vorträge von R.S. 1914*, Dornach, Switzerland, 1926, plate after p. 26).

109 Monumental column supporting lamps.

110 Façade of a house in Novara, Italy, in the Floral Style, dated 1907. See "lesena" (pilaster) formed by the stem of a flower that serves as a console.

42 A total of eleven volumes,
published between 1901 and 1940,
Adolfo Venturi's *Storia dell'Arte
Italiana*, vol. 8, *L'Architettura del
Quattrocento* (2 parts) and vol. 11,
L'Architettura del Cinquecento (3
parts) appeared in 1924 and 1938,
respectively.

and many others had to emigrate to America, for one reason or another, at the same time that Brazil kindly offered Le Corbusier the opportunity to design one of his best buildings—a fact that had positive repercussions elsewhere, especially in Europe. In order to demonstrate the difficulties that the new architecture found in the Old World, we must take note of the fact that Le Corbusier himself had often been the victim of misunderstandings and hostilities. This is made obvious by the following piece of news, an extract of an article about a "soirée" that appeared in *Salle Pleyel*:

> Le Corbusier monte à l'estrade. Il y a de la peine à se faire entendre. On siffle, on crie, on braille, on vocifère—c'est une obstruction systématique de la part d'une partie du public. Mais Le Corbusier est habitué à la lutte. "J'ai lutté contre vos maîtres depuis quinze ans" s'exclame-t-il . . . Interrompu à chaque phrase par des applaudisse-ments et par des cris hostiles[83]

> [Le Corbusier takes the stage. It is difficult for him to make himself heard. There is whistling, shouting, yelling—a systematic obstruction from one part of the audience. But Le Corbusier is used to the fight. "I fought against your teachers for fifteen years" he exclaims . . . Interrupted at each word by applause and by hostile shouts.]

The theory of internal space

To organize a program defined as "Architecture Theory" which is not the fruit of philosophical speculations but, rather, something destined to be comprehended by students, is certainly a difficult matter; it is clear that it would be a deception to base such a program on mere criticism, or even constructive criticism. These doubts arise by virtue of the famous polemic that developed in Italy between Gustavo Giovannoni and Adolfo Venturi[84] at the precise moment when the critique of architectural history was in search of an articulation of the foundations of its method-ology. [42] Since we are living in a moment of open discussion, it is opportune to debate a prospective tendency regarding the current critical definition of Architecture. For this reason, I express opinions not so much as a critic, but as an architect participating in the formulation of a theory. In this endeavor, I do not exclude the collaboration of students, which in this case might correspond to the "minors" mentioned by Serlio,[85] since I am convinced that a professor must continuously construct his experience.[86]

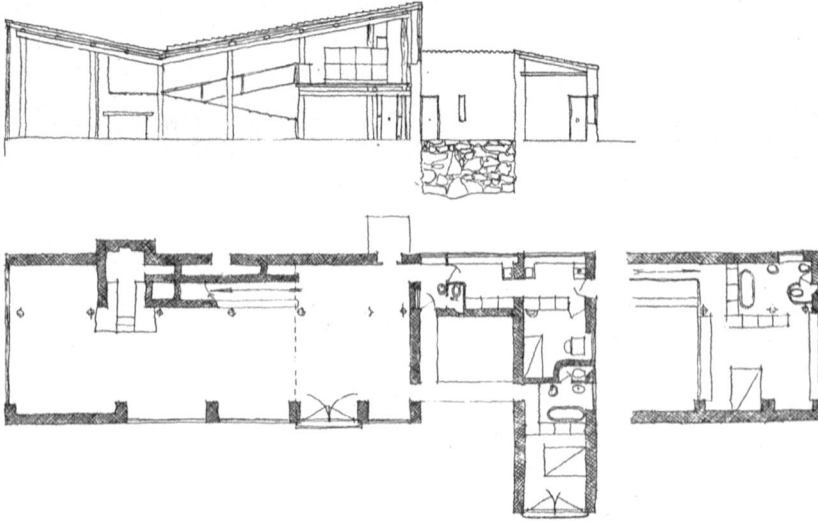

111 Casa Errazuriz, Chile, 1930; Le Corbusier, architect (Francis Reginald Stephens Yorke, *The Modern House*, London: The Architectural Press, 1934, p. 37, in which it is indicated that the architecture is "in South America" [*sic*]. But it is interesting to note that Le Corbusier located it definitively in Chile (Le Corbusier, *Oeuvre complète— 1929–34*, Zurich, 1935, pp. 48 and following) [© 2013 Artists Rights Society (ARS), New York/ADAGP, Paris/F.L.C.]. This project with its roof in "impluvium" (the most commonly used is "espluvium") created a real "school." It is certain that one cannot claim the "precedence" of a particular architectural solution, and that "creating a school" is for masters; but Le Corbusier responded politely, when A. Raymond was inspired by the project, with his construction of a house in the suburbs of Tokyo.

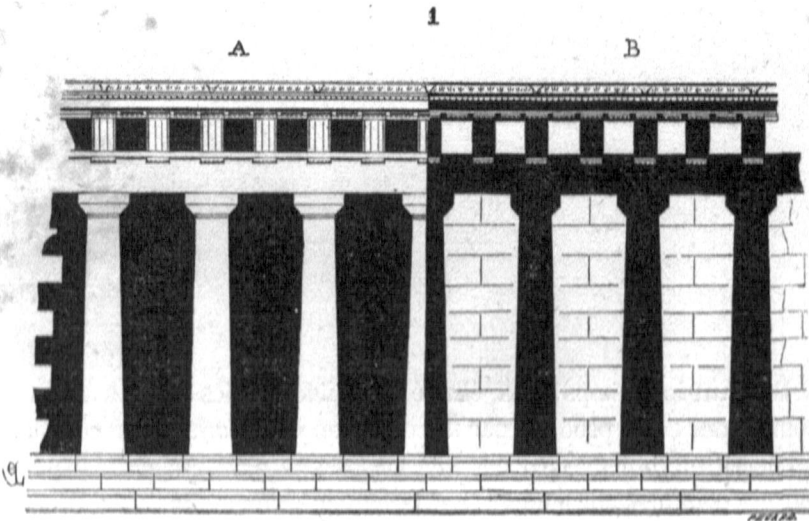

112 With regard to the consideration of color in Greek Architecture, Viollet-le-Duc suggests the following: "En Architecture, l'ordre prendra de l'ampleur; l'architrave, les triglyphes et la corniche, de l'importance, par la seconde, indiquée en B, les colonnes paraitront plus maigres, plus hautes, l'entablement perdra de son valeur. La coloration avait donc une grande influence sur l'effet produit par l'architecture, et nous pouvons aujourd'hui juger les édifices de l'antiquité grecque qu'en tenant compte de cette coloration. Tel ordre, qui nous semble lourd, pouvait paraitre svelte: tel autre, qui affecte des proportions grêles, présentait un aspect solide et ferme" (Viollet-le-Duc, *Entretiens, op. cit.*, vol. I, p. 250).

43 The chief proponent of the "Theory of Internal Space" is Luigi Moretti (1907–73), Italian architect based in Rome and editor of *Spazio* magazine. "Strutture e sequenze di spazi," *Spazio* 7 (December 1952– April 1953): 9–20, 107–108 sets out the main principles of the theory. Lina cites and summarizes the article in the caption to Figure 113, "Espaço Interno." Bruno Zevi, a life-time critic of the unrepentant Fascist Moretti, discusses the theory in his 1948 book, *Saper Vedere l'Architettura*, Torino. Giulio Carlo Argan, the Italian architectural theorist also discusses the theory in his review of Zevi's book, "A Proposito di spazio interno," *Metron*, no. 28, October 1948.

44 Moretti also cites these authors directly, and is known to have admired and often referenced the work of the Serbian architectural theorist Miloutine Borissavliévitch (1889–1969).

The most accepted definition of Architecture, and, I would add, the one that is most fashionable today as the basis of a "theory," is the "theory of internal space," [43] which comes from the more generic theory of "organization of space."

The "theory of internal space" may generate some confusion in those minds that are less experienced, with less critical sense and only little awareness of historical precedents. The first distinction to be made is that "internal space" is a term that can refer to spaces, to types and to various functions, from the "noble space" of the architectural monument—for instance, the Gothic cathedral—to the worker's house (*existenz minimum*). From the outset, two thoughts are apparent with regard to this theory: first of all, that the term "internal space" is self-evident when applied to architecture, not least because, and here is the second thought, space is a function of man, who constructs "architecture" in order to inhabit it. Once he does, he becomes the *protagonist* of his creation, moving *inside* and *outside* it. When he leaves, for instance, passing over a bridge, his "architectural adventure" continues, no longer inside, but outside.

Of course, this theory is not new, not even in the sense suggested by some recent interpreters. According to Hartmann and Ostendorf, the goal of Architecture is to "create spaces," external and internal. According to Schmarsow, architecture is a "space-creator," manifesting itself in three dimensions: (1) "the tactile space," (2) "the visual space," and (3) "the space of come-and-go." (The author uses the expression *Gehraum*.) These authors are mentioned by Borissavliévitch, considered an attentive historian, albeit a follower of the theories of Architecture.[87] [44]

There are other determinant factors besides the internal space, but none that would prevent the space from becoming a work of architecture. Ultimately Architecture is defined by both its internal spaces and the external spaces of urbanism. The definition can be found not only in the idea of "internal space," but also in the circumstance of "inhabitation," meaning that man is the constant "physical" protagonist of what I call the "architectural adventure." As long as this adventure is "useful" to man, it is considered to be Architecture; at the precise moment when it is no longer "useful" it ceases to be Architecture. The same holds for the chair in which we sit, the spoon we use to eat and the glass we use to drink, the sheet of paper on which we write or the package which we open and then destroy: man's real and intimate involvement with "architected" things is the essence of Architecture. The idea of internal and external space is subject to cavils that can lead to irrelevant discussions, similar to those about the distinctions between Form and Content.

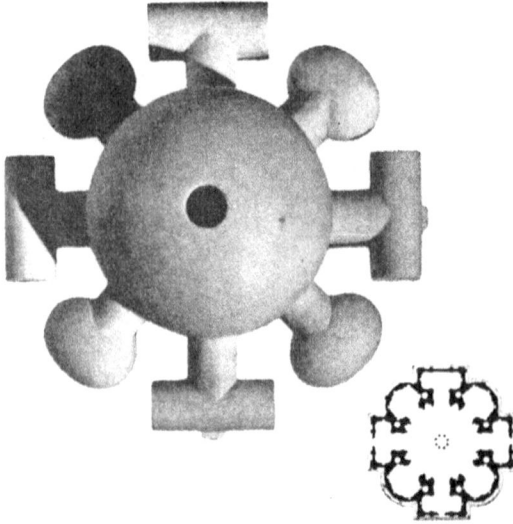

113 Michelangelo. Reconstruction of the project for the church of S. Giovanni de Fiorentini, Rome. Representation of the internal volumes from an engraving by Valerian Regnard (Luigi Moretti "Strutture e Sequenze di Spazi," in the journal, *Spazio*, Rome: Gruppo Editoriale *Spazio*, Rome (Dec 1952–April 1953): 20, figs 1&2.) This representation of the "internal space" (which becomes, paradoxically, "external space," in the chosen type of representation—the model— once it is impenetrable) of one of the five projects studied by Michelangelo for that church, can exemplify, let us say, the habit of contemporary hyper-criticism that, once outside the specialist sphere and in the vivid and active world of the academy, can lead to severe consequences, such as, for example, the creation of inhibition and the student's fixation in preconceived schemes and pseudo-scientific definitions (such as in the cited article): "pressure" and "energetic load," of the space.

114 "Internal space" or "external space"? (Giedion, Sigfried. *Space, Time and Architecture: the Growth of a New Tradition*. 3rd English Edition. Cambridge: Harvard University Press, 1954, p. 29, plate 17.)

45 Cicero, *De Oratore*. After *inventio*, the first of the five terms of Latin rhetoric, *dispositio*, the second term, means the organization or arrangement of the arguments put forth.

Architecture is a continuous adventure, human and real. When this adventure loses its physical character, it acquires a wide array of other values: its eternal Vitruvian essence, the *firmitas utilitas venustas*[88] of *De Architectura*, is replaced by values of judgment, feeling, literature, history, interpretation of all kinds, from customs to sociology, to "beauty" and pleasure, which have nothing to do with Architecture and the reasons why it emerged as the *dispositio* [45] of humans.

For example, the Coliseum is still considered architecture today because one can have an interpretation of it, even if it has a different character than it did at its origin; one must take into consideration the possibility of a romantic and literary interpretation that overlaps the purely architectural one. Can Filarete's unfinished project for a skyscraper, or the hanging gardens of Babylon, be regarded, therefore, as architectures?

Tangible existence, a real and utilitarian character, is the true character of Architecture, the only one that can embrace, in a single concept, the governor's palace, the working-class house, the school, as well as the design of a bed or a plate; the only one that justifies the humble, nearly eclectic, attitude of the architect today.

Citing anew an unjustly "anonymous" author whose fundamental concept of architecture still holds true, as presented in a lecture by the architect Pietro Valente, the chair of civil architecture at the University of Naples, on November 28, 1835:

Non vi è forse scienza, neppure sentierello di lettere, di arti belle, la cui essenza sia finora meno conosciuta o più vagamente e arbitrariamente definite, di quanto sia per la sublime e benemerita scientifica bell'arte l'Architettura. Ciò è fuor di dubbio la principale causa, non solo delle passate decadenze, ma si bene dello spaventevole presente svilimento, che par tristo foriero di una mai vista ignoranza del maggiore abbandono e del più significante dispregio per essa.

[There is perhaps no science of the arts, nor the fine arts, whose essence is less known or more vaguely and arbitrarily defined than the sublime and worthy scientific bell'arte of Architecture. This fact is no doubt the principal cause, not only of past decadence, but also of our present dreadful state, which seems a sad harbinger of further ignorance, neglect and most significant contempt.]

115 Terá Antonio Averulino, known as Filarete. In designing this fantastic architecture, was he anticipating the skyscraper? In the history of men of genius can be found the germs of all "anticipations." (Drawing from the manuscript "Fondo Magliabechiano," Biblioteca Nacional, Florenca, in *Domus* no. 193, p. 17) *Filarete, Treatise on architecture: being the treatise by Antoni di Piero Averlino, known as Filarete.* Translated with an introd. and notes by John R. Spencer. New Haven: Yale University Press, 1965. Yale Publications in the history of art; 16, v2.

116 Skyscraper in New York with Gothic-style ornamentation.

This statement was very audacious, especially because it was delivered in an Athenaeum where, one century before, the *Orazioni Inaugurali* of Gian Battista Vico had pronounced the criteria of a constrained and never-violent polemic. However, it is a good man that, as an architect, from his professor's chair, encourages students who aspire to "addirsi a si bella, utile e difficilissima professione" [adhere to the beautiful, useful and difficult profession] and, even in those early days, talks to them about "steel construction":

> esser l'architetto colui che obbligatamente debba saper progettare ed eseguire qualsiasi edificio civile; e dopo averne col tutto ogni minima parte antiveduta, guidarne la costruzione dalle fondamenta per fino alle piú piccole decorazioni, suppellettili e mobilie; onde l'insieme ne risulti corrispondente, unisono, coerente per ogni verso, uno in fine.[89]

> [to be an architect obligatorily implies that one has to know how to design any civic building, and by the anticipation of every detail, to be able to guide the construction from the foundation to the smallest decoration, to equipment and furniture, where the final result corresponds to a coherent end.]

Nowadays, there is an entire literature on the spatial interpretation of Architecture, the interpretation that delimits a certain category of architectures, including those characterized by "the internal space." Focillon, for instance, has a most felicitous "spatial" intuition of Architecture:

> Mais c'est peut-être dans la masse interne que réside l'originalité profonde de l'architecture comme tel. En donnant une forme définie à cette espace creux, elle crée véritablement son univers propre. Sans doute les volumes extérieurs et leurs profils font intervenir un élément nouveau et tout humain sur l'horizon des formes naturelles, auxquels leur conformité ou leur accord les mieux calculés ajoutent toujours quelque chose d'inattendu. Mais, si l'on veut bien y réfléchir, la merveille la plus singulière, c'est en quelque sorte d'avoir conçu et créé un envers de l'espace ... Le privilège unique de l'architecture entre tous les arts, qu'elle établisse des demeures, des églises ou des vaisseaux, ce n'est pas d'abriter un vide commode et de l'entourer de garanties, mais de construire un monde intérieur que se mesure l'espace et la lumière selon les lois d'une géométrie, d'une mécanique et d'une optique que sont nécessairement impliquées dans l'ordre naturel, mais dont la nature ne fait rien.[90]

Refuting the theory of "internal space," Gillo Dorfles said: "In realtà l'architettura è un'arte tipicamente spaziale che si costruisce e si manifesta nello spazio ma che è appunto in grado di valersi sia dello spazio interno che di quello esterno; e, anche, aggiungerei, d'uno spazio puramente immaginario purchè sia pensato e modellato architettonicamente." [Actually architecture is an art of space that is constructed and typically occurs in space but which, in fact, is able to make use of both the internal and the external space, and well, I might add, of a purely imaginary space, as long as it is thought and modeled architecturally] (*Discorso Tecnico delle Arti*, Pisa, 1952, p. 104).

"The greater the material apparatus, the more the material disappears, as in the Alps and Niagara, in St. Peter's and Naples" (Emerson, *Journal, op. cit.*, 1836).

117 Some North American critics take the dolomitic mountains of the Grand Canyon as precedents for the skyscraper ("Les Americans," in *Le Crapuillot*, October, 1930, p. 37).

118 Filarete, another example of a skyscraper (*Domus*, no. 193, p. 18).

[But it is, perhaps, in the internal mass that the profound originality of architecture, as such, resides. In giving form to the raw space, architecture creates its own universe. No doubt the exterior volumes and their profiles will offer a new, and altogether human, element to the horizon of natural forms, which, depending on their conformity or best-calculated agreement, always add something unexpected. But, if we really consider it seriously, the most singular and marvelous thing is that we have conceived and created an inverse of space . . . The unique privilege of architecture, among all the arts, whether creating residences, churches or ships, is not to shelter a convenient void and encircle it with safeguards, but to construct an internal world which measures space and light according to geometric, mechanical and optical laws that are necessarily implicated in a natural order, but do so while nature does nothing.]

It is not by mere chance that Focillon identifies construction in general as the "mobile construction" of ships. Architecture is a mobile construction; so is a ship and a locomotive, even if some people call them machines, they are special machines designed to accommodate man in "internal space." The railroads that began with simple cars destined to transport certain elements eventually had to be adapted in order to include hospitality cars, as a house *sui-generis*, with places to sleep, cook, rooms for dining and bathrooms. Maritime navigation preceded the railroads, and when the latter began perfecting the "hospitality" of its cars, the great transatlantic ships that resembled small cities already existed. In an attempt to solve a wide array of problems, which varied in dimension and permanence, different studies were assigned to different architects, who consequently were able to contribute to the study of the functionality of a house, especially that of the "minimal house." Here, I should also mention the example of airplanes for international airlines, in which new problems, especially those related to functional space, have already been brilliantly solved.

Also in reference to architecture as a modeled and accessible space, Scott observes:

But besides spaces which have merely length and breadth—surfaces, that is to say, at which we look—architecture gives us spaces of three dimensions in which we stand. And here is the very centre of architectural art. The functions of the arts, at many points, overlap; architecture has much that it holds in common with sculpture, and more that it shares with music. But it has also its peculiar province and a pleasure which is typically its own. It has the monopoly of space. Architecture alone of the arts can give space its full value. It can surround us with a void of three dimensions; and whatever

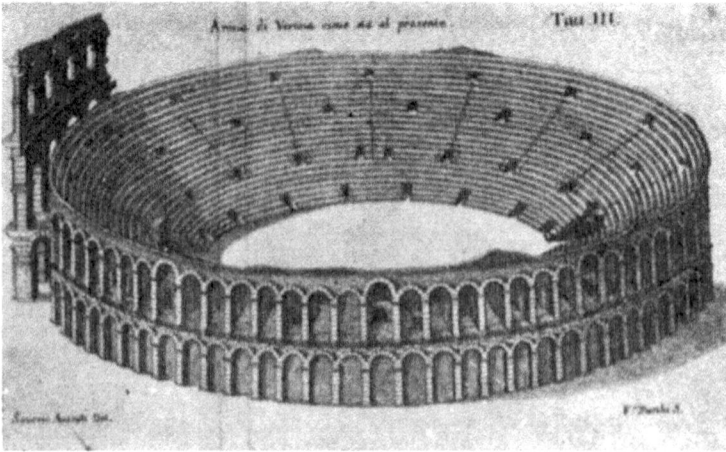

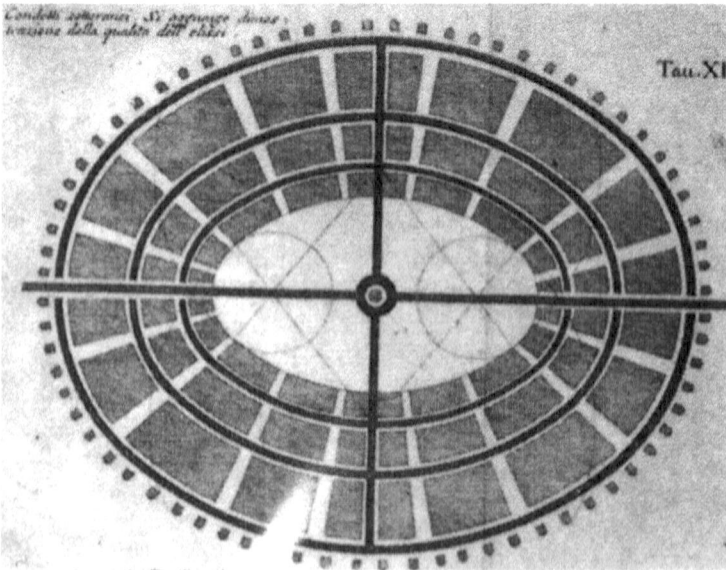

119–120 The arena of Verona and the ellipses that make up the plan of the amphitheater, eighteenth century. Today it is an outdoor theater for lyric opera. (*Degli Anfiteatri e singolarmente del Veronese, etc.* Verona, MDCCXXVIII (1728), plate III).

delight may be derived from that is the gift of architecture alone. Painting can depict space; poetry, like Shelley's, can recall its image; music can give us its analogy; but architecture deals with space directly; it uses space as a material and sets us in the midst. Criticism has singularly failed to recognize this supremacy in architecture of spatial values. The tradition of criticism is practical. The habits of our minds are fixed on matter. We talk of what occupies our tools and arrests our eyes. Matter is fashioned; space comes. Space is "nothing"— a mere negation of the solid. And thus we come to overlook it. But though we may overlook it, space affects us and can control our spirit; and a large part of the pleasure we obtain from architecture—pleasure which seems unaccountable, or for which we do not trouble to account—springs in reality from space. Even from a utilitarian point of view, space is logically our end. To enclose a space is the object of building; when we build we do but detach a convenient quantity of space, seclude it and protect it, and all architecture springs from that necessity. But aesthetically space is even more supreme. The architect models in space as a sculptor in clay. He designs his space as a work of art; that is, he attempts through its means to create a certain mood in those who enter it.[91]

Bruno Zevi defines architecture solely by its "spatial condition," thus creating a dangerous series of "categories" that lead to the distinction between architecture "with internal spaces" and another "without internal spaces." Evidently, Greek temples and bridges are not the only structures without internal spaces. And we could ask: if it is true that besides the Architecture that represents "great themes" there is another that is unfortunately referred to as "minor architecture"—a confusion between "greatness" and "great format"—in which category should we place con- structions of limited space that are not able to, for socio-economic reasons, resort to solutions of a plastic-spatial nature? It is clear that architecture cannot be distinguished in this manner; its values come from the human factor or, in other words, from its utility. This is also highlighted by Zevi, notwithstanding his contradiction regarding "internal–external."

Se incentriamo l'attenzione sugli spazi interni dell'architettura e dell'urbanistica, apparirà manifesta l'indissolubilità del problema sociale e del problema estetico. È bella un'autostrada senza auto- mobile? È bella una sala de ballo senza coppie che danzino?[92]

[If we focus attention on the internal spaces of architecture and urbanism, the obvious indissolubility of the social and the aesthetic becomes manifest. Is a highway beautiful without a car? Is a ballroom beautiful without couples who dance?]

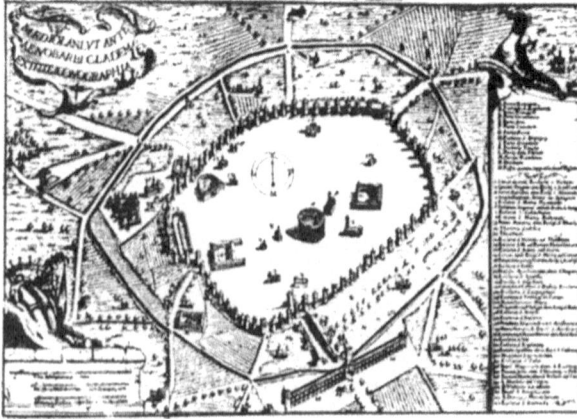

Exemplifications of spaces from the cell to the city.

121 Example of the distinction between monumental architecture and architecture destined for housing. The city of Milan before the destruction of Federico I, taking into consideration only the monuments (*De praeclaris mediolani aedificiis. quaeaenobarbi claden antecesserunt, etc., d. Pedro Gratiolio*, Mediolani, MDCCXXXV (1785); corresponding to p. 19).

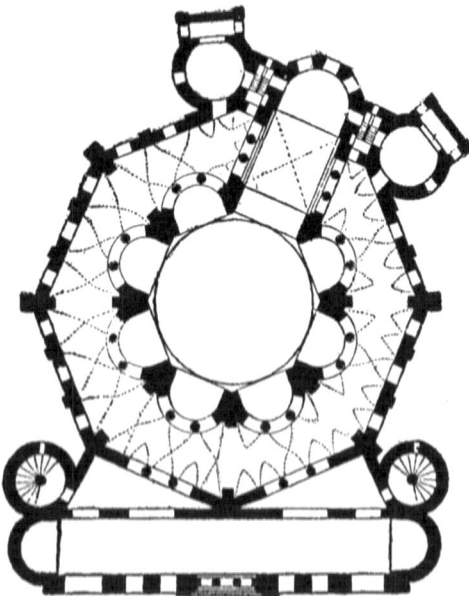

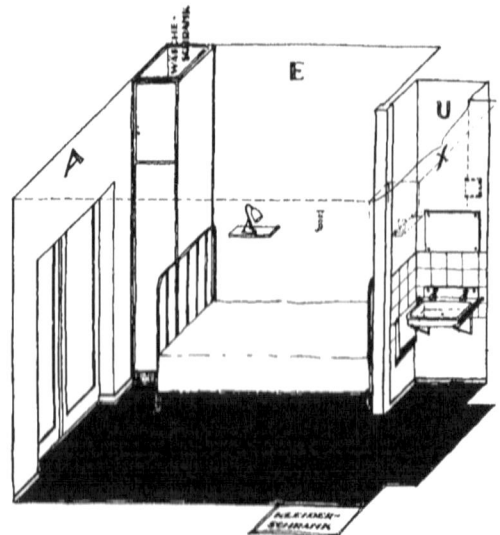

122 Plan of S. Vitale in Ravenna (Arthur Kingsley Porter, *Medieval Architecture, its Origins and Development with list of Monuments and Bibliographies*. New Haven: Yale University Press, 1912, p. 105, fig. 73).

123 Room; Bruno Taut, architect (Bruno Taut, *Ein Wohnhaus: Mit 104 Photos und 72 Zeichnungen, einer Farbenauf nahme und einer Farbenzusammestellung*, Stuttgart: Francksche Verlagshandlung W. Keller, 1927, p. 82, top left).

What difference is there between "passing over a bridge" and "a ballroom dance"? Man is still the protagonist, and the space, be it internal or external, is secondary: the architectural "fact" remains intimately connected with man. I insist on the issue of the spatial interpretation of architecture not only because it is fashionable but also because it is from these interpretations that programs are written and teaching activities developed. These can be dangerous, in the sense that they are biased and can misguide the creative tendencies of those who may be affected by literary presuppositions and, when not controlled by an intellect as critical as that, for example, of Zevi (who is an architect and practitioner) may lead to such deviations as "Organic Architecture," a stream of which was developed in Italy by Zevi himself, who, as a follower of Wright, founded an association in Rome in 1945, and in 1952 saw himself obliged to dismiss its results. This association produced stereotypical results, expressions of a deteriorating literature; the "organic" manifesto sterilized the creative act, bringing into existence dangerous architectures like the notorious "Mediterranean" architecture. The results of this "organic" campaign continue to be reflected in Italian architecture: how far from Wright, who flees from manifestoes and has confessed to stopping by the roadside during his walks through the fields, in order to learn from the structure of a tiny daisy.

This digression aims to clarify that I prefer to avoid manifestoes. As architects, we are interpreters of a vital "common sense" (notwithstanding the particular dread I have of this expression and the fear of its taint of cheap levity).

Almost spontaneously I am reminded of a master to whom I could attribute the architecture of today. I am referring to Pier Luigi Nervi, an architect with whom I have worked (not to mention collaborated). One day, in a heated discussion about the form of a concrete pillar, he said: "Enough! The architect is nothing but a stonemason who knows Latin." Such an observation appeared quite offensive, especially since it was followed by a series of criticisms concerning the "artistic" habit of architects who design without first accommodating preliminary project quotas. However, after some reflection, I found in that assertion no grain of truth that would impress me very much. Wright is looking at the structure of the daisy; it is self-conscious humility that goes *pari passu* [hand-in-hand] with ability, as opposed to baseless literary-critical assumptions, which in any case are so foreign to the educational field.

Our beloved master, Nervi, perhaps without the suspicion of drawing on Milizia,[93] gives us a concrete definition of Architecture which can give us much guidance:

Nasce dal soddisfacimento di esigenze materiali dei singoli e della collettività, e si eleva ad esprimerne i più profondi e spontanei

It is necessary to comprehend Architecture from the point of view of one's own country, bearing in mind architecture from other countries, in order to recompose the spatial panorama of this art, which is so varied and multiform. It is necessary to see in others' architecture the stimulus to develop Architecture in general.

124 Tripoli, Mosque of Carmelo; the roof of small vaults, particular to the East, occurs across the southern Mediterranean and in the tradition of folk architecture, from the house on the island of Capri, to the "trulli" of Apulia. This type of roof, along with whitewash, characterizes Mediterranean architecture. (G.T. Rivoira, *Moslem Architecture, etc. . . [its origins and development, translated from the Italian by G. McN. Rushforth]*, London, 1918, p. 172, fig. 148).

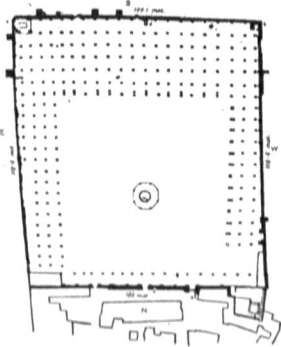

125 Plan of the Mosque of Amr, Fustat, Cairo (*ibid.*, fig. 12).

126 University College, Ibadan, Nigeria: façade of the library; Fry, Maxwell and Jane Drew, architects (*Tropical Architecture in the Humid Zones*, New York: Reinhold Publishing Corp., 1956, p. 279).

46 Pier Luigi Nervi, *Structures*, translated by Giuseppina and Mario Salvadori, New York: F.W. Dodge Corporation, 1956, p. 1.

47 Sigmund Freud, "The Dynamic of Transference," 1912.

48 Neutra makes this connection as well, in his "Architecture of Social concern: in regions of Mild Climate," São Paulo: Gerth Todtmann, 1948, pp. 212–218.

sentimenti riunisce in un'unica sintesi: lavoro manuale, organizzazione industriale, teorie scientifiche, sensibilità estetica, grandiosi interessi economici, e, per il fatto stesso di creare l'ambiente della nostra vita, esercita una muta ma efficacissima, azione educative su tutti. D'altra parte tutti con dilezioni o contrarietà verso particolari aspetti o tendenze di essa, o, infine con diretto intervento, concorrono a determinare I caratteri e le direttive dei suoi sviluppi. Per i tempo, per i fattori scientifici, estetici, tecnici e sociali che in essa si fondono, è più che giustificato considerare l'attività del costruire come la sintesi più espressiva delle capacità di un popolo, e l'elemento più significative per giudicare il grado della sua civiltà e lo spirito di essa.[94]

[It springs from the material needs of the individual and society, but in satisfying people's needs it broadens to express their most spontaneous and deep feelings. Construction gathers in a unique synthesis the elements of manual labor, industrial organization, scientific theory, esthetic sensibility, and great economic interests. Construction creates our physical environment, and thus exercises a silent but deep educational influence on each one of us. On the other hand, we all help to determine its characteristics and the direction of its development by passing judgments, by expressing preferences or dislikes, or by intervening directly in the construction process. Because of its varied aspects, of its persistence in time, and of the scientific, technological, esthetic and social factors which influence it, construction may well be considered the most typical expression of the creativity of a people and the most significant element in the development of its civilization.] [46]

With these words, Nervi did not want to give a definition of Architecture but of the "activity of constructing." Yet whoever it is that teaches "theory" cannot fail to be an architect, the "transference" (as a psychiatrist would say) [47] established between the professor and the student would immediately define this activity as the "construction of architectures."

Confronted by such an extensive topic, and the natural tendency to discover a new problem in a provisional solution, we return to the question: how to define a normative theory, especially if we understand that every theory is in transition, and in a state of becoming? The first statement would be that architecture should accommodate not only the social customs resulting from the most generous moral stream, but also the morality that opposes and competes with social ideas brought about by changing times. In this sense, I am reminded of the Encyclopedists.[95] For many centuries, this art was the expression of myths and political ideas, instead of the source of objective satisfaction and comfort that it is today. [48] In order

127–128 P.L. Nervi, Reservoir for naphta (*Storage tank for crude oil, and buildings—airplane hangars for the Air Force— using the minimum of iron*. Engineers, Nervi and Bartoli, Rome, 1944; distributed internally). P.L. Nervi, *The Works of Pier Luigi Nervi*, New York: Frederick Praeger, 1957, p. 26, plate no. 348, 774–6, 2,1937.

129 North American factory (from Làszló Moholy-Nagy, *on Material zu Architektur*, Munich: A. Langen, 1929, p. 227, fig. 198).

The engineer designing a silo or a reservoir is doing engineering work (in the sense of the term) if the emotional factors of art are not involved in its realization. If these are involved, the work now belongs to the immediate scope of architecture, regardless of whether it is a bridge, hangar, warehouse or dam. It is in this sense that one can wish for the fusion of engineering with Architecture. Indeed, an architect who designs a bad house is less of an architect than an engineer who designs a beautiful silo. Architecture is not classifiable, nor susceptible to crystallization in diagrams or artistic–academic preconceptions.

for it to become beneficial to everyone, it is fundamental that its point of departure be an expression and interpretation of the aspirations and material needs of the people and not a form of masking those things— especially from the classes that historically need more attention. In a sense, extravagance and wastefulness, the renouncement of contemporary ideas, and the passive acceptance of outdated formulas are to be considered, obviously, as negative and as the source of error. Accordingly, and in an opposite sense, the positive factors will include a rigorous consideration of the architectural elements useful within the general framework of urbanism, which slowly encompasses and integrates Architecture as its fundamental principle. Clearly, in the future, urbanism cannot simply be a meeting-point for the more or less disorderly rearrangement of the ideas of individual architects or builders who are usually not aware of the problems related to planning an ensemble: and here crops up, then, as a major exigency, that the architect also be a planner, and hence conscious of the innumerable problems which, if well analyzed, include substantially all "knowable" problems—problems which are far more complex than those recognized by Vitruvius.[96]

Because man is destined "to dwell," and as all his movements happen in an environment, unless he is outdoors following the paths, and therefore guided by "space," it is inevitable that the architect should be scrupulously aware of the contributions and innovations of each activity that, in connection with all others, promotes human advancement. It is therefore an extremely important activity that requires social, moral and aesthetic coordination and all the responsibility proper to it; I could say that the latter is the most sensitive, because of the human exigency that demands harmony of movement within the world's productivity.

After having examined some aspects of the theory of the "internal space," with reference to divergent definitions and to certain theorists, especially architects and engineers who deduce a theory of practice, I now conclude these theoretical reflections, which should be considered as taking a position, not as much as Architecture Theory but, shall we say, as "basic didactic principles" with the purpose of showing the danger of any teaching that is oblivious to life's problems, the *daily problems*. (I am not afraid of this expression because the solitary man who tries to solve his quotidian problems of existence will, at the same time, achieve a work of philosophy and criticism.) I feel that the architect, although a specialist and aware of the different methods of inquiry, *must* maintain constant contact with life, in the most common sense, without allowing this contact to be detrimental to his position.

These will not confine you, quite the contrary. Wright, drawing on the wisdom of ancient Japan said: "An artist's limitations are his best friends."[97] I want to conclude these suggestions about a method of teaching with this picturesque description, created by Wright himself. It is a

130 Urban center of Ipiranga, São Paulo; Bezzi, architect (photographer unknown).

131 Blocks of buildings in New York, between Second and Sixth Avenue and 108th and 109th streets, planned for demolition for the construction of a new neighborhood (*The New York Times*, March18, 1957, p. 29). [Headline reads, "Most of Neighborhood Businessmen Uprooted by East Harlem Project: Complain of Treatment by City." Article discusses the plan to build the Ben Franklin Houses in the five-block area outlined: "The merchants in these pictures were on Second Avenue between 108th and 109th streets. A sixth block will contain Junior High School 117 and a playground."]

49 *Eternit* is a brand of fiber board, a roofing and paneling material made of fibers and (asbestos) cement.

vision that could be used for our contemporary world—an image of an America destroyed by an imaginary catastrophe and rediscovered centuries later, for researchers and archeologists, like a new Pompeii, where they attempt to understand the sense of our civilization from the piles of wreckage:

> And this experiment in civilization we call democracy will find its way to a scrap heap into which no subsequent race may paw with much success for proofs of quality.
>
> Suppose some catastrophe suddenly wiped out what we have done to these United States at this moment. And suppose, ten centuries thereafter, antiquarians came to seek the significance of what we were in the veins of us—in the ruins that remained, what would they find?. . . They would dig up traces of sacred Greek monuments for banking houses. The papal dome in cast iron fragments would litter the ancient site of every seat of authority, together with [fragments in stone and terra-cotta of twelfth] century cathedrals where offices and shops were indicated by mangled machinery-relics of dwellings in fifty-seven varieties and fragments of stone in heaps, none genuine in character, all absurdly mixed. They would find the toilet appurtenances of former ages preserved as classic parlor ornaments in ours. They would find a wilderness of wiring, wheels and complex devices . . . But I think the most characteristic relic of all would be our plumbing. Everywhere a vast collection of enameled or porcelain water closets, baths and washbowls, white tiles and brass piping.[98]

The pessimistic panorama traced by Wright could seem outdated, since the book was written in 1930; however, we still see in our cities the construction of Gothic cathedrals in concrete, and the most "refined villas" are built in the pseudo-Palladian style with columns of Eternit [49] formed like greenhouse piping, in which no memory of the original "entasis" remains; and in the most "refined" ballrooms, if it's not being used as a bathtub, the marble oratory of a colonial church is put into service as a mobile bar. Nonetheless, this is not the only contemporary danger of "going beyond our own limits"; others, which are perhaps more harmful, exist: it concerns the "Romanticism," marked by an excess of technicality, which could lead us to a new "culturalismo," albeit one more refined and "intelligent" than the one that characterized the mid-1800s. In light of these characteristics, this "technical cult," a literary super-structure with "pure" positions and linked to materials and epochs could be even more dangerous than the previous one. An example can be found in the design of the Museum in the Castello Sforzesco in Milan, where the

132 Project of an anonymous architect of the seventeenth century, for the blending of architecture and nature (author's collection).

133 The harnessing of nature: the famous example at Tivoli (Charles Garnier and A. Ammann, *L'Abitazione*. Paris: Hachette, 1892, p. 565).

134 The Kaufmann House at Bear Run, Pennsylvania; F.L. Wright, architect (Photo: Museum of Modern Art, New York).

[© 2012 Frank Lloyd Wright Foundation, Scottsdale, AZ | Artist's Rights Society (ARS) NY.]

50 The architectural firm BBPR, Gianluigi Banfi (1910–45), Lodovico Barbiano di Belgiojoso (1909–), Enrico Peressutti (1908–76), and Ernesto Nathan Rogers (1909–68), was responsible for this project.

51 "Pau a pique" is a primitive type of house construction common in Brazil's northeast, sometimes translated as "wattle and daub."

52 The terms "dogmatism" and "impressionism" appear in quotes because they are listed in the "Edital" [Notice] under "B. Elements of Aesthetics," number 4. See Appendix 1.

53 The "Edital" [Notice] lists three points under "E. Caraterologia dos Edificios" 1. Carater [caractère] 2. Habitation 3. Classification of Buildings.

extravagance of the architects [50] is so violently imposed that the museum disappears behind replicas of hand-crafted seating, exhibition paraphernalia, and in the preparation of "environments": such as Leonardo's "Sala delle Assi," when it comes to the absurdity of hiding parts of the famous wallpaper behind vertical structures that are used for the exhibition of drawings.

Heritages are heavy and "non-heritages" are dangerous and difficult to overcome because of the lack of examples. In spite of everything, it is the examples that create "the atmosphere" of a culture. I am not advocating the "pau a pique" [51] house, nor a return to the culture which preceded architectural creativity; what I claim is necessary, now, is a fair middle ground, not "dogmatism" nor "impressionism" but a measure of criticism which takes into account history as heritage and continuity. This will provide the architect—who is the mediator responsible for man's "way of life" today—with the freedom of possibility. [52] And since I believe that School carries a cultural responsibility, I am convinced of the necessity for a non-dogmatic position on the part of the professor. A position that, while committed, and, at times, almost "rigid" with respect to certain problems, is characterized by the flexibility to which I alluded. A Professor should have a malleable comprehension of the human point of view, an extremely rigorous and critically constructive scientific point of view, and an unyielding intransigence with regard to a professional attitude which, without taking into account the discussions that the term may raise, is deemed "moral."

Theory of architecture and "caractères" of buildings

Following these reflections, I will proceed, "by points" [of the competition program] to try to express my ideas about programs and methods for teaching the "Theory of Architecture," while keeping in mind my experience as a student and a teacher. [53]

What would be a better plan for teaching the "Theory of Architecture," one that, while addressing, at least implicitly, all the topics indicated by the [competition] program's point-based classification system, would also contribute to the elaboration of a method constituted from the minimum number of essential elements germane to this very complex discipline? Although no longer appropriate, the subdivision of the subject "Theory of Architecture," integrated with the so-called "caractères of Buildings" continues to be used in order to provide the student with a unitary notion of architectural design. This criterion stems from the educational system of the second half of the nineteenth century, a time in which the new profession of the architect was slowly and painfully finding its definition.

Different aspects of the
archeological problem

135 "Greek
revival" on Wall
Street, New York.

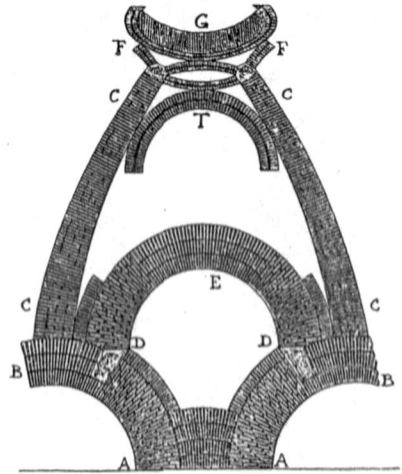

136 A section (one-
eighth) of the cupola
of the Pantheon,
Rome; relief by
Piranesi (Luca
Beltrami, *Il Pantheon
rivendicato ad Adriano*
[117–138 AD] Milano,
1929, p. 14).

137 Columns
found during
the excavation
of the Forum
of Trajan, in
1937.

54 Established in 1303, Sapienza
University in Rome has as its
motto, *"il futuro è passato qui"*
[The future was here]. Giovannoni
was Director of Architecture
from 1927 to 1935, and died in
1947. Lina attended from 1933
to 1939.

55 Lina uses the English term
"beach house" in italics.

I return once again to the treatises. First, I could cite Prof. Gustavo Giovannoni,[99] who was an engineer and architect, Professor of the School of Architecture of the University of Rome [54]—and also its Director. He was, without a doubt, a master endowed with a philological method of study and research that was rigorous and incontestable from a historical point of view; however, he was attached to an architectural intuition that was dependent upon traditional presuppositions and schemes. This led him to classify, and, I would even say, fragment, the whole of architectural knowledge into traditional, categorical, subdivisions: Architecture as theory and as "caractère" appeared, therefore, notwithstanding the current polemics, as something divisible. At a certain point, it was even proposed that the field be subdivided into Architecture and utilitarian Civil Engineering, attributing to the first courtly representational purposes and to the second, practical and everyday purposes. It is possible that this partition occurred to Prof. Giovannoni because of his work as a historian and expert restorer of ancient Roman monuments, work which inaugurated the more logical field of scientific restoration, surpassing the method advocated by Viollet-le-Duc, which attempted to "reconstruct the past."

Nonetheless, the theoretical position of this master was disadvantageous because it led the newly graduated student to maintain ideas that were rigidly classified by categories and that made him lose sight of the only immutable norm of the architectonic activity: the norm which calls for the consideration of the idea and the spirit such that they can be useful for all categories, from the "celebratory palace" to the prison, from the hospital to the news-stand, from the chair to packaging.

If we go from Giovannoni's "teaching" to those of other professors, such as Talbot Hamlin, the most renowned American author, we would confirm that the old method continues, even though necessary additions of "scale," "rhythm" and "color" have been made. In the introduction of *Forms and Functions*,[100] an updated exemplification of the architecture of our century, it is affirmed that this work follows and surpasses that of Guadet; and although I do not believe that Architecture should be divided in the manner suggested by Giovannoni—Courtly, or Monumental,[101] and Practical—this may also result in the student's feeling of confusion, especially when he finds that the Basilica of Constantine and the Chartres Cathedral are being compared to the Capitol of Lincoln, Nebraska and to a modest *beach house*.[102] [55]

From my point of view, there are no contradictions: I simply hope to highlight the complexity that surrounds the teaching of "Architecture Theory."

Will there be nothing between Guadet and Hamlin? Will there be no intermediate step between the fin-de siècle, a time in which the problem of hygiene was still under discussion,[103] and our presumptuously hygienic

138 Ground floor of the State Capitol, Lincoln, Nebraska; B.G. Goodhue, architect (Talbot Hamlin, *Forms and Functions of Twentieth-Century Architecture, Vol. 1*, New York: Columbia University Press, 1952, fig. 10).

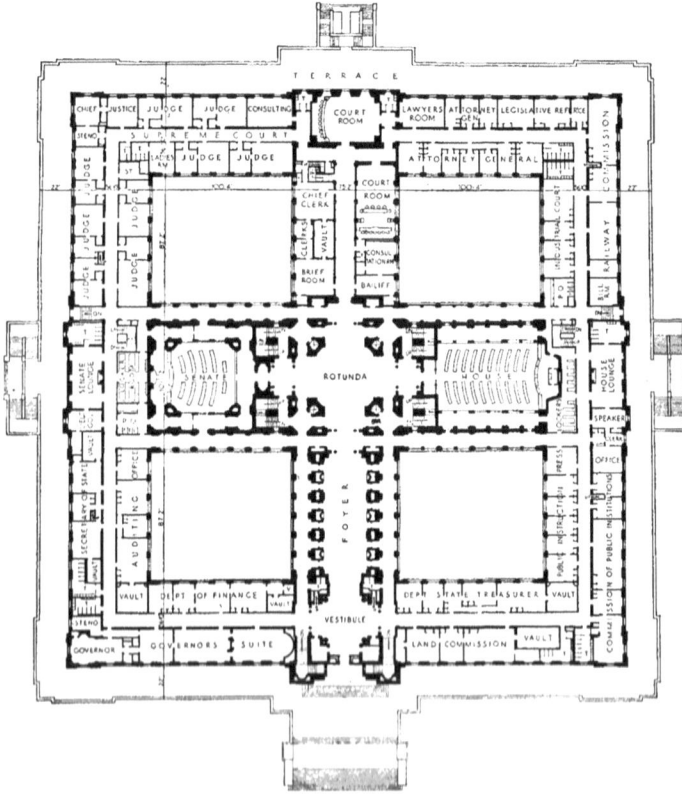

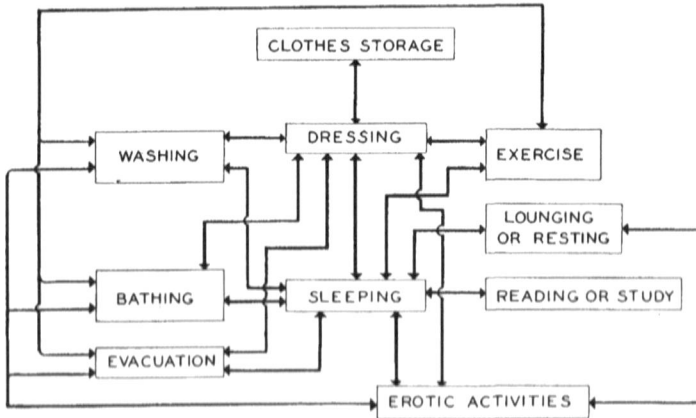

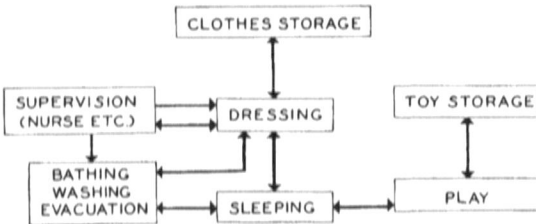

139 Diagram of the functions of a dwelling (*ibid.*, fig. 62).

56 This appears in the University of Rome, Faculty of Architecture, *Order of Studies*, 1956–57, p. 15. The instructor is Prof. Mario de Renzi (1897–1967), a *Novecento* Italian architect who worked with Adalberto Libera (1903–63), and in urban planning with Saverio Muratori (1910–73).

period, in which we have provided the "internal spaces" with a rigorous scheme for a bedroom?[104]

There is no irony in this, only a certain sadness in seeing the academy move so slowly. To this day, a sort of professional distinction between theory and practice still exists, and the architecture of Wright, Le Corbusier and Mies van der Rohe has not been interpreted in its real sense, even by the most modern manuals of theory, criticism and history.

All of the ideas that I have developed confirm the difficulty that lies in the theoretical systematization of architecture—of doubts that this art is becoming a science and extending its meaning beyond the inner and outer space to reach the space that characterizes all human production, finding confirmation in the history of ideas and the verification of the slowness with which the concept of "savoir vivre" evolves and remains to this day an illusion—all this leads us to a certain bewilderment and makes palpable the difficulty of codifying the ideas and principles of others, especially when making use of theoretical treatises. It is a consolation when ideas coincide, whilst errors are upsetting. Amidst so many achievements and clarifications, the division between Architecture and "decoration" leads to the corruption of the former. The equivocation that made Guadet wince,[105] the reason behind the current crisis in the teaching of Architecture, is mainly the insistence, in most the Universities, on adding the *complementary* course in "Decoration" to the course on "Architectural Design." In the current school year, the University of Rome has programmed this last course in the following manner:

> integrativo della "composizione architettonica" ha il compito di sviluppare, nell'allievo, le qualità espressive individuali, di raffinarne il gusto, di stimolarne le doti inventive. A tale scopo esso studia i rapporti fra struttura e decorazione e la loro sintesi nell'Architettura, ricerca i valori espressivi dei ritmi plastici e cromatici nella composizione architettonica, negli effetti di armonia e di contrasto dei materiali e dei colori e nel carattere stilistico dei particolari tecnici e ornamentali, nelle rifiniture artigianali e artistiche.[106] [56]

> [supplementary to "Architectural Design," [the course in Decoration] has the goal of developing in the student his personal expressive ability, of refining his taste, of stimulating his creative abilities. To this end, it studies the relationship between structure and decoration and their synthesis in Architecture, examines the expressive values of plastic and chromatic rhythms in architectural composition, in the effects of harmony and contrast of material and colors and in the stylistic quality of technical and ornamental details in handcrafted and artistic finishes.]

140 "Solution" for a bookshelf-bar-clock. (Francis Reginald Stevens Yorke. *The Modern House*, London: The Architectural Press, 1934, p. 23).

141 Skyscraper under construction on 3rd Avenue, New York.

142 New bridge link to Brooklyn, New York.

Of course, "lifestyle" is not regulated solely by the "Procrustean bed" [an arbitrary, but strictly enforced standard] of habitation; but must be considered, from an architectural point of view, in its continuity with its urban surroundings; we see very well in the example of New York, that an increased density of housing requires a corresponding increase in the width of roadways.

57 *The Lives of Celebrated Architects, ancient and modern: with historical and critical observations on their works and on the principles of the art,* by Francesco Milizia (1725–98); translated from the Italian by Mrs. Edward Cresy [Eliza Taylor] with notes and additional Lives, 2 vols, London: J. Taylor, 1826. The book is dedicated to Sir John Soane (1753–1837).

A theory is formed, or at least receives a strong contribution from academic programs. Thus, it is worthwhile to examine the syllabus of this course in order to establish some considerations. It is clear that "architectural design" should be designed and taught as a function of its expression, which means, in a manner which manifests the "taste" and "creativity" of the designer. However, this expressivity should never be conceived as an ornamental device, added *a posteriori*, but rather as an elaboration clearly anticipated by creative thought. This is a notion that has prevailed since the time of Priest Lodoli and Milizia, who said:

> In architettura l'ornato deve risultare dal necessario; niente ha da vedersi mai in una fabbrica, che non abbia il suo proprio uffizio, e che non sia integrante della fabbrica stessa: onde *quanto é in rappresentazione deve sempre essere in funzione* (emphasis added by the author).[107]

> [If architecture be the daughter of necessity, even its beauties should appear to result from such, in no part of the decoration should any artifice be discoverable, hence, everything extraneous is a proof of bad taste; nothing must be introduced which has not its proper office, and is not an integral part of the fabric itself; so that *whatever is represented must appear of service.*] [57]

In the expression "relationship between structure and decoration and its synthesis in Architecture" lies the obvious error inherited from the "culturalismo" of the last century, made explicit by the recommendation for "technical and ornamental details in handcrafted and artistic expressions." Take, for instance, one of those concrete pillars, clad—precisely in its "artistic" or "artisanal" period—with chiseled rock or mosaics, thereby nullifying the structural and functional idea, and the clarity of materials.

To teach someone to understand and design Architecture as something to be decorated *later* seems to divide Architecture, based on a theoretical error that, in more recent times, did prevail: the meaning of the decoration understood as the very meaning of architecture itself. The Doric temple was clearly defined in the minds of Greek builders, because its structure and its appearance were coincident; contemporary architecture should be taught entirely to the avoidance of the pernicious practice of decorative possibilities, regarded as dresses that can be adapted to fit any insignificant mannequin. In a period like this one, when "exteriorismo" plays an important part in the volubility of decoration—and is characterized by the pleasure of display and of standing out, by boredom with things already seen, by the constant renewal of fashion launched by the decorative industry, taking advantage of the phenomenon of its adaptability to variations of taste—in such a period, it seems absolutely necessary to look

Decoration, in itself, when misapplied to architecture, is without proper meaning. Today, we need another term. What we improperly call "decoration" in architecture is a human necessity, and in the great examples of history, decoration and architecture form a single whole. The [design] research of Wright follows this same trajectory.

143 Ornamentation of the ribs in the Chapel of the Cathedral of Noyon, France (Clarence Ward, *Mediaeval Church Vaulting*, Princeton: Princeton University Press, 1915, fig. 41).

144 Construction made entirely of concrete, imitating stone; it is an abuse of the material employed.

145 Curious degeneration of a functional necessity: the "keystone" of an arch applied in vain for pseudo-ornamental reasons.

146 (Moore, Charles Herbert, *Character of Renaissance Architecture*, New York, London: The Macmillan Company, 1905, p. 205, fig. 123).

with some distrust at an integration of decoration that corrupts an architectural unity. Architectural unity, in its clarity and wholeness, is already complete and detailed, and can be called, if necessary, "the finishing touch." Absolute unity founded in the wisdom and the heart of a sole master, that translates into the teaching of the many disciplines that compose Architecture.

Changing the subject, but still talking about treatises, I shall now return to Lurçat's treatise.

It seems to me that Lurçat, with all his merits as an architect, has not really come to terms with the issue of "didactic communication" that must be primary within the scope of education, showing, in other words, a minimum degree of intelligibility. In light of my own experiences, I am well aware that the reading of philosophical-literary texts can be quite difficult. Further worrisome with respect to students, is finding something that corresponds to their intuition about what "form" is beyond what they can find in the *Littré*.

We can observe that students, almost continuously, in a kind of reaction to unintelligible teaching with no basis in practice, resort to manuals that are easier and more modest, such as Melis' *Caratteri degli Edifici*,[108] Neufert[109] and like volumes of the genre *Manuale dell' Architetto*,[110] which constitute aids for the neo-architect who plans to "design" and not discuss the philosophy of designing.

If I have a preference for artistic-scientific literature, the manuals that present data in an accessible manner, it is because of their efficiency for professors who find themselves in the impossible situation of effectively developing the program for the "caracteres distributivos do edifícios" [typology of buildings] within a single year (or even in two, like certain foreign Schools), such a brief period of time to touch upon all the particular problems of the different kinds of construction and their respective functions and purposes. To the students, the syllabus of the "Character of buildings" seems to be composed of a series of different "topics," each dealt with in a different manner, according to the type of building being studied; therefore, it is difficult to perceive that the theme is *always the same*, because everything is about Architecture. Even if the data changes, the methodology and the procedure of designing remains the same. In effect, I do not believe that there exists, on one side, the "monumental" and, on the other, the "non-monumental," or, Architecture and civil construction.

At this point, we could ask: what can a professor of "Theory and Character" effectively do in the brief period of a year? I believe that in the following I will be able to summarize, and later develop, some of the basic problems faced by the architect. Though I will not address it here,

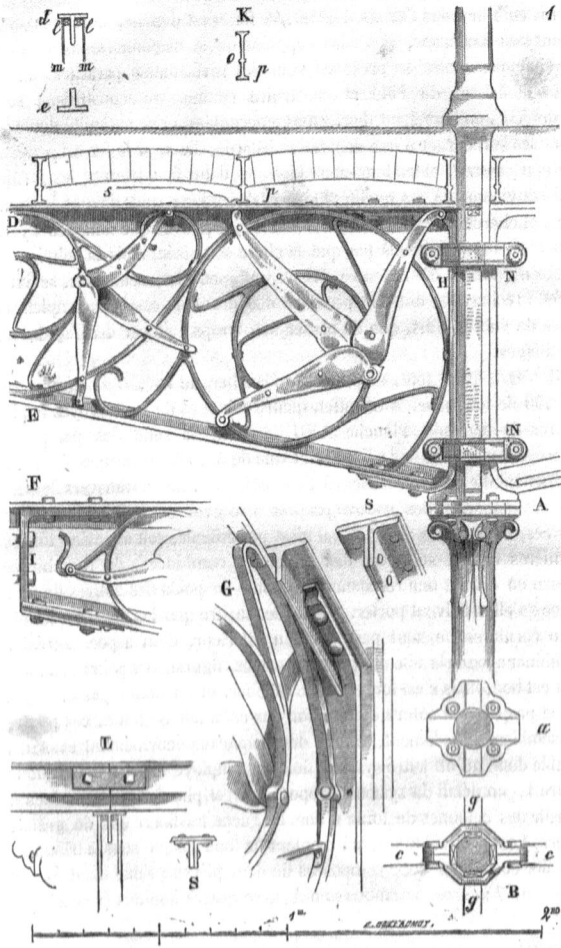

"On est toujours l'enfant de quelqu'un" says Brid'oison in the *Marriage of Figaro*. It could be said that Viollet-le-Duc is the son of the Gothic masters, but rest assured that this "descent" did not give rise to dependencies and constraints, because the nineteenth-century master recreated the spirit of the Gothic, and only occasionally fell prey to the "revival" that was the vice of that century.

147 Study for an iron structure by Viollet-le-Duc. The stiffening of the joints between the pillars is achieved with the naturalistic-mechanical forms of leaves and twigs [linking the] iron bolts and nuts, perfectly documenting the awakening of a "constructive conscience" that included decoration (Viollet-le-Duc, *op. cit.*, vol. 2. p. 126).

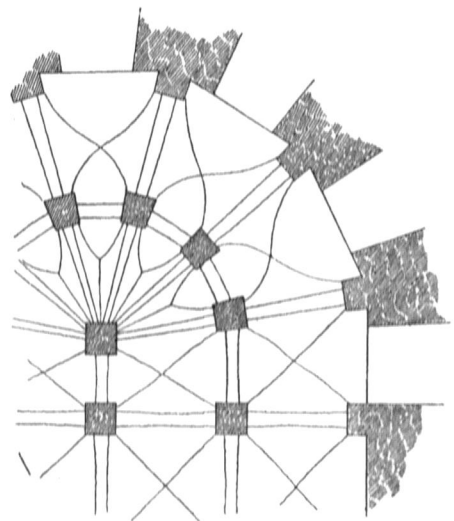

148 Relief of a curved vault in the crypt of Worcester cathedral, England, Norman-Romanesque (Charles Herbert Moore, *The Mediæval Church Architecture of England*, New York: The Macmillan Company, 1912, p. 8, fig. 5).

58 Pier Luigi Nervi, *Structures*, translated by Giuseppina and Mario Salvadori, New York: F.W. Dodge Corporation, 1956, p. 11.

removing an anachronism regarding the connection of Schools of Architecture with engineering is the more generic problem, discussed many times in Brazil and abroad, of any plan to reform Schools.[111]

Recently, when discussing the academic training of the designer, Nervi wrote:

> che la coesistenza di Facoltà di ingegneria edile e di Facoltà di architettura—notevolmente differenti non tanto nei programmi quanto nella mentalità e nei modi con cui i programmi stessi sono sviluppati, pur essendo le une e le altre dirette alla formazione di progettisti e di tecnici edilizi—non fa che aumentare la incertezza, mentre pone in piena luce la mancanza di un unitario indirizzo.[112]

> [The existence of separate departments of civil engineering and architecture increases our uncertainties and clearly shows our lack of unified purpose. In fact, these departments do not differ so much in the subject matter they teach as in their viewpoints and the training methods they use, while both types of Schools try to make designers and builders.] [58]

Methodological update

With regard to the specific theme, that the central problem of teaching theory is the *methodology* and, more specifically, the modes of "design," or the means by which to acquire those notions necessary to design. Without exception, all design submits to the following definition by Viollet-le-Duc, a characteristic expression, similar in its conception:

> La théorie et la pratique; la théorie comprend: l'art proprement dit, les règles inspirés par le gout, issues des traditions, et la science qui peut se démontrer par des formules invariable absolues. La pratique est l'application de la théorie aux besoins; c'est la pratique qui fait plier l'art et la science à la nature des matériaux, au climat, au mœurs d'une époque, aux nécessités du moment.[113]

> [Theory and practice; theory includes: the art itself, the rules inspired by taste, from tradition, and science which can prove itself with absolute, invariable formulas. Practice is the application of theory to needs; it is practice which bends art and science to the nature of materials, to the climate, to the customs of an era, to the needs of the moment.]

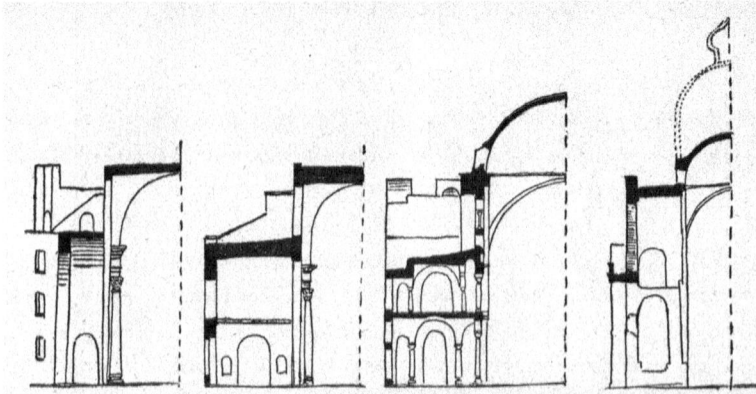

When the architect is an engineer, and vice versa.

149 The "thrust" in some buildings of the late Roman epoch: the Baths of Diocletian; the Basilica of Massenzio; Hagia Sophia of Constantinople; San Marco in Venice (Sergio Bettini, *L'architettura [di San Marco]; origini e significato*, Padua: Tre Venezia, 1946, plate LX).

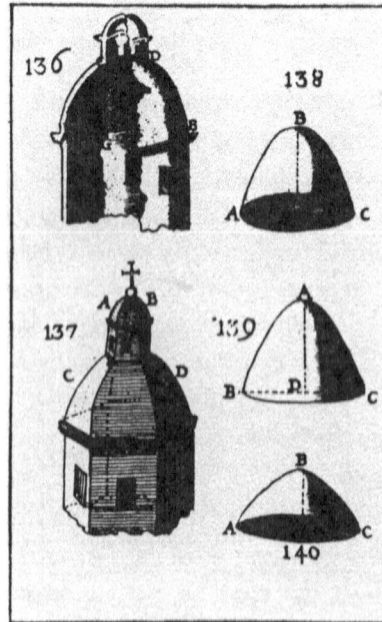

150 Examples of domes (*Trattato della misura delle fabbriche di G.A. Alberti, Bolognese, etc.* Perugia, 1790, plate XIV, p. 80).

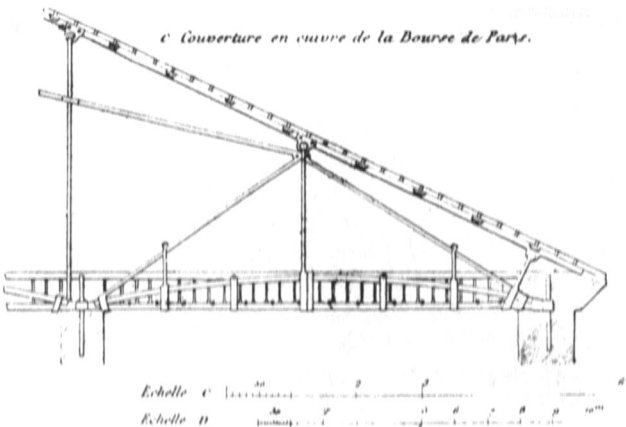

151 Drawing of the copper roof of the Palace of the Paris Bourse (M. Belmas, *Mémoire sur les couvertures des casernes et édifices*, Paris, 1837, pl. 13).

Here is what another master notes in relation to teaching:

> The teaching of a method of approach is more important than the teaching of skills. It should be a continuing process which must group concentrically like the annual rings of a tree. In all its stages the scope should be all-embracing instead of sectional, increasing slowly in intensity and detail in all fields of discipline simultaneously. The integration of the whole range of knowledge and experience is of the greatest importance right from the start; only then will the totality of aspect make sense in the student's mind. He will easily absorb all further details and place them where they belong if he progresses from the whole to the details, and not vice versa.[114]

It seems, then, that the themes to be considered are as follows:

1   A *methodological framework* is the only solid and invariable basis on which the student can work and be directed efficiently, since the necessities of modern life, of individuals and societies, to which architecture is closely linked, are developing rapidly and continuously, and are, as a consequence, unpredictable, even for the immediate future.

2   Architecture, like all other human activities, cannot go beyond the limits of nature; therefore, it is always wise to be inspired by it, using it as criterion for the validation of a work.

3   It is important to give the student the disciplinary means to subordinate the drive towards a primarily aesthetic statement—with its dangerous tendencies towards extravagance, exaggeration or an over-emphasis on rhetoric—by exacting from him a vision of the ultimate purpose of the work.

4   The basis of "design freedom," with regard to the formal aspects of [the building's] "appearance" is independence in the face of possible influences from existing work or, worse, from poorly assimilated and badly understood momentary trends.

5   The ethical sense of the architect's profession is based on a firm resistance to the sometimes illogical pressures, interests and ambitions of the client, whose competence is generally inferior to that of the architect.

6   It is necessary to overcome the historic "rupture" of the transitional conflict between the "ancients" and the "moderns," and search for clarity and comprehension in the continuity of history, thereby enlightening the mind of the student by means of instilling in him the habit of relating the profession to culture, in other words, to real life.

152 "Salle voutée, fer et maçonnerie," designed by Viollet-le-Duc, documented the sense of "constructive morality" associated with the Neo-Gothic, in which stylized forms were repeated only on the surface (Viollet-le-Duc, *op. cit.*, p. 60, fig. 18).

153 Plan of a seventeenth-century fortress (Pietro Sardi, *Corno Dogale della Architettura Militare/di Pietro Sardi Romano*, Venice: Appresso i Giunti, MDCXXXIX (1639), Part 3, plate XV).

Now, to review, briefly but in more detail, what I mean by a "methodological framework." *Method* is the capacity for orientation, study and apprehension of the intelligible creative scope that is necessary for science (in our case, Architecture) and for life, with the ultimate goal of achieving intellectual self-discipline and moral autonomy. These two aims should be the prerogatives of the academy, especially in their initial phase, and should never be abandoned to the idleness of practical life. Work is the only true source of any transformation of nature, or of man himself, ever to have been documented in history; all teaching that is based on abstract theories that dispense with man and ignore his existence and his work constitute a method that will undoubtedly lead to vague and unsatisfactory results. This is what happens, I repeat, in an accelerated course about "theory" which takes place in the course of a single year and is often based on superficial notions about aesthetics, which are "full of trends" because the professor rarely draws on "impartial" criticism but instead seeks to impose, although unconsciously, his own "idealistic," "positive," or "psycho-physiologist" point of view.

Note that only one section of the course is dedicated to the professional formation of the architect. This section is the "Caractère dos Edificios." [59]

What is meant by "Caractère" of buildings is well known in academic circles. The intrinsic characteristics of a Hospital are determined by the activities that must take place there, which are completely different from those that characterize a Museum or a Theater. However, it is not apparent that the position or the attitude of the designer, when confronting a problem either in its study phase or in its elaboration, is different for the various cases. By this, I mean to refute the notion that a consistent method results in a uniformity of "Caractère," and, to a certain extent, to an "Architecture Theory" of the same uniformity adopted from the Renaissance to the Neo-Classical period (not to mention the nineteenth-century "culturalismo," based on the generalizations of "Caractère of Style"). Especially with regard to the recent past, this presumed methodological unity is a pseudo-method which has led to the patchwork of absurdities, falsely aesthetic and functional, to which I have already alluded.

In other words, it is precisely because the architect is aware of the essential uniformity of his position in relation to construction that he must have a clear vision of the diversity of characteristics and functions implicit in various structures.

Although the classification of buildings into distinct categories may be useful to the differentiation of architecture, it can lead, as it once did,

Styles that have arisen spontaneously, and which are duplicated from memory [of foreign or distant sources].

154 Perugia, Church of Saint Bernardino, second half of the fifteenth century. "The Renaissance produced no theory of architecture. It produced treatises on architecture . . . But the style they built in was too alive to admit of analysis, too popular to require defense. They give us rules, but not principles. They had no need of theory, for they addressed themselves to taste . . ." (Scott, *op. cit.*, p. 40).

155 Charles Herbert Moore, *Character of Renaissance Architecture*, New York, London: The Macmillan Company, 1905, p. 231, fig. 134.

to another danger: the crystallization of architecture into types, which is highly detrimental to the autonomy of the student and does not encourage research. Due to the shortage of time allowed by the profession, mental laziness, or sheer habit, what results is a lifetime of work based on the insufficient schemes founded in the unduly short period of time spent at School. I believe that it is, in effect, a mistake, an inversion of the point of departure, to begin with "typologies," created by man, rather than focus on the protagonist of the architecture. As man is the protagonist, and Architecture the product of a well-lived life, if we focus our attention on what man has *accomplished*, we run the risk of quickly surpassing what has been made in light of new needs. However, if we focus our attention on the "protagonist" and his real and ever-changing life, we will not face this danger, as we will be moving forward together. As architects, we worry about choosing a method that will parallel the lives and the works of human beings. For a creative person, the fixation on distributive schemes, especially while in School, does not allow him to reap the benefits of his vital "impulses" and becomes completely useless and arbitrary. It is also important to note that students of Architecture are often exposed to themes that are not suited to their human experience; themes that are unintelligible and ridiculous,[115] especially when regarding "monumental and celebratory" themes. Consequently, the disoriented student starts designing at random, often basing his designs on resources such as magazines and never coming up with his own solutions: his goal is simply to complete the work, without concern for the manner in which this is achieved.

This is why it is so important to guide and initiate the students in the profession, as we are well aware of the consequences that the teaching of a wrong method or a professor's lapse may have on their formation. The simple "know how to study" formula could seem inappropriate when discussing a university education—which should constitute the most advanced form of education or, in other words, the specialization—since I assume that the students at this level possess a certain intellectual autonomy. Nonetheless, taking into account that our specialization requires an extensive body of knowledge and certain rigidity, I believe that, while at university and soon after graduating, these young architects cannot be fully independent. For this reason, it is advantageous to establish Schools that, through independent and practical courses, aim to improve the skills of young architects. Establishing a methodology that can teach students *how* to master the use of the instruments necessary for the planning of any kind of building—be it a school, station, stadium, skyscraper or chicken coop—is an essential aspect of effective teaching.

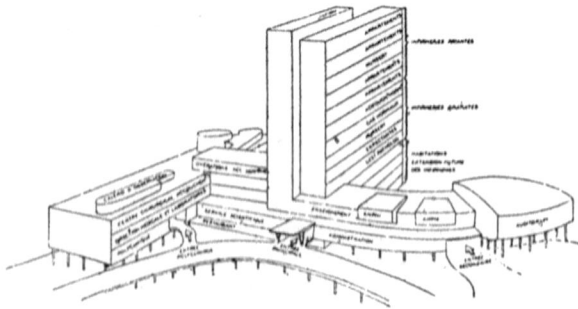

156 and 157 Hospital São Paulo; organizational model and schema; Rino Levi, architect. Example of the architectural complexity of the problem, the model of the idea of a plastic solution, and the organizational scheme of operation; however, only the "reality" is constructed and can be constituted as living architecture (Paul Vogler and Gustav Hassenpflug, *Handbuch für den Neuen Krankenhausbau*, Munich, 1951, figs 71 and 72).

60 The use of the term "organismo" to describe spatial organization, spatial design or arrangement of the floor plan, is consistent with Zevi's use of the term in *Saper Vedere l'Architettura*, Torino, 1948.

The methodology to which I refer could be practically based on the following:

a   A precise knowledge of the "spaces occupied" by the human body which, over time, can be considered invariable; an exact human measurement is assigned to each architectonic part.

b   Direct investigation, as well as consultation with worthy specialists and engineers, directly involved with the successful functioning of the proposed design. Subsequently, the specific "literature" on the subject is consulted.

In order to clarify some of the concepts mentioned above, I note that by (a) knowledge of the "spaces occupied" by the human body, I intend the perfect mastery of "human measure." How many students can actually say that they know the precise height of the armrests of a seat, or the height reached by the outstretched arms of a standing man, or the dimension of a passageway? This "space occupied by man," which I could also call the "economy of the space," provides the necessary limit and the basis for good design. Today, this limit is called the "human scale," a term that has already become a literary abstraction. To the students who asked repeatedly about heights and widths, I had to respond hurriedly (as it was not, indeed, our discipline) that they should carry a measuring tape in their pockets and measure everything: doors, corridors, chairs, tables, cabinets, beds, walls. While, in effect, the fact that the representative method and the metric scales will never provide us with an exact sense of real space might seem obvious, such an idea is not easily understood by students.

Together with the measure of man in space, it is necessary to develop a basic understanding of the dimension and limits of architectonic entities such as stairs, ramps and all other parts included in the architectural organism. [60] This is necessary because these parts are intrinsically connected to the "space occupied" by the human body and, therefore, not subject to variation. The mastery of human measure, or the economy of the space, transforms the student into a less timid designer, as he will be more certain of the dimensions of the different parts of the building, and more aware of the necessity to accommodate these requirements from the conceptual design phase.

By (b) "direct investigation," I mean comprehension of needs. It must be made clear that, when talking about needs, I am not only referring to practical "needs," which would shock the "artistic architects," but also "spiritual" ones.[116] Accordingly, when we study the design of a residential skyscraper, our considerations must go beyond the surface area, lighting and ventilation, means of communication, etc.; above all to the spiritual needs addressed by terraces, play areas for children, gardens, panoramic

158 Painting exhibition gallery. Royal Academy of Paris, 1789. "The Royal Family viewing the exhibition of the Royal Academy," etching by P.A. Martini after J.H. Ramberg, 1789).

159 Mobile Museum, installed in a truck and transported from city to city; realization of the Museum of Fine Arts, Richmond, Virginia.

160 Midway Gardens, Chicago; Frank Lloyd Wright, architect (in Lewis Mumford, "The Social background of Frank Lloyd Wright," *Wendingen*, publication of the association of Architecture et Amicitia, Amsterdam, no. 5, 1925). Frank Lloyd Wright. *The Complete 1925 "Wendingen" series/Frank Lloyd Wright et al., with a new introduction by Donald Hoffmann*. New York: Dover Publications, 1992, p. 72. [© 2012 Frank Lloyd Wright Foundation, Scottsdale, AZ | Artist's Rights Society (ARS) NY.]

61 "When I speak of architecture as
organic I mean the great art of
structure coming back to its early
integrity: again *alive as a great
reality*." Cited in F.L. Wright, *Genius
and the Mobocracy*, New York, 1949,
p. 12.

views and so on. The architect cannot ignore these things without missing one of the essential requirements of construction, the necessities of the particular type of building under study, as a function of the lives and activities that will develop there. When building a hospital, the architect must consult with doctors and nurses; when building a factory, he must consult with engineers, administrators and workers; he must even consult with workers, businessmen and housewives when studying the location of a grocery store or school within a neighborhood.[117]

From School onwards, the student should use this direct method of investigation, so-called "first-hand" accounts, instead of resorting to manuals or, worse, to built examples which he knows only from magazines. These data, being well documented, would become part of a binder for the "Character of Buildings" course—if we still wish to use this name— which, if continually updated, will constitute the basis of his professional archive. A series of studies and critically informative literature on the theme would be the basis for a correct design. (Incidentally, in some cases, professors at the Faculty of Architecture at the University of São Paulo have undertaken research of this type, assigning student teams to specific tasks, yielding great results.)

When I say that "one should not go beyond the limits imposed by nature," I mean that one should stay in touch with *valid realities*. For the architect, this means all solutions within the limits of *real* possibility at its most current: achievable structures, plan organizations conceived according to a natural order, and not according to sterile desires based on ideological or literary suppositions. Here, I once again refer to the example of Wright studying the structure of a flower; transcribing his thoughts with respect to this, I hope that it is understood in the sense of a living reality, [61] and not overlaid with the now-fashionable concept of the "organic," which is already somewhat academic:

> But in Grecian art two flowers did find spiritual expression—the acanthus and the honeysuckle. In the art of Egypt—similarly we see the papyrus and the lotus. In Japan the chrysanthemum and many other flowers . . . But the true democrat will take the human plant as

This example from the "bourgeois-popular," home points to the problem of ideal assumptions on collective organization, which remained active throughout the nineteenth century and until the beginning of the First World War. The problem of housing is still far from solved, and the situation reported in Italy in 1941, and extending to almost all other countries, still exists, "But in urban areas under the most unrestrained and uncontrolled speculation, workers' housing is reduced to a purely restrictive expression, as organized with a total disregard of any thought of order and hygiene, in huge buildings that could well be named barracks." (I. Diotallevi and F. Marescotti, *Ordine e Destino della Casa Popolare Milano*, 1941, p. vi).

161 Project for a collective house, studied in Rome in 1912 by Giovanni Galli, builder, Raffaello Dini, accountant and Enrico De'Negri, professor of architectural design. This example of commercial "incorporation" has since been based by designers on economic-sociological assumptions that destined the bourgeois to bankruptcy in Rome at the beginning of the century. It is a kind of "phalanstery" à la Fourier, smoothed-over for the use of the so-called "middle class" (G. Galli, A.R. Dini and E. De'Negri, *La Nuova Casa*, Roma, 1912, pl. VII).

162 Illustration from the book above, representing the dining room of an apartment in the building.

it grows and—in the spirit of using the means at hand to put life into his conventionalization—preserve the individuality of the plant to protect the flower, which is its very life, getting from both a living expression of essential man—character fitted perfectly to a place in society with no loss of vital significance. Fine art is this flower of the man.[118]

By this I do not mean to suggest the concept of "imitation of nature" but, rather, a system of certification; no *valid* work goes beyond the scope of natural laws, even Roman and Gothic vaults and the skin-resistant structures of the newest concrete systems can easily be found in nature, in the veins of leaves, in the curvature of petals, in the stems of flowers.

To this purpose, I cite Nervi, who says that it is necessary for the architect to have intuitively "avere creato spontanei e fecondi collegamenti tra il proprio spirito e le divine leggi della natura"[119] ["created spontaneous and fruitful links between his own mind and the divine laws of nature"]. In the following definition, he synthesizes architectural work in a way that to purists and optimists may appear as a limitation:

L'avvicinarsi con animo modesto alle misteriose leggi di natura, lo sforzo di interpretarle e quel comandarle ubbidendo che è l'unico modo per portare la loro maestosa eternità a servizio dei nostri limitati e contingenti scopi, ha in sé una profonda poesia, che può tradursi in forme di una elevata espressività estetica e artistica.[120]

163 View of São Paulo from a terrace (Photo: Milko Javurek).

164 The monitoring of everyday life in the press may suggest to the architect a study of the reality of new issues (*The New York Times*, March, 1957, p. 25).

Is It a Plane, a Train, a Fort? Yes, and It's the Fantastic Village

Ever see the world upside down? They do it every day at Fantastic Village, the playground at Public School 130.

At the school at 156th Street and Prospect Avenue, in the Bronx, children—and their imagination—go soaring.

NEW PLAYGROUND LIVES UP TO NAME

Fantastic Village at P.S. 130 in Bronx Every Bit of That —More Planned in City

By LEONARD BUDER

There is a place called Fantastic Village in the southeast Bronx. It is not too difficult to find. It is near Serpentine Wall and Tunnel Maze.

Fantastic Village has a population of 450 children, ranging in age from 5 to 8, although perhaps no more than forty or fifty inhabit the place at any one time. When they are not in the village, they are very often—at least on weekdays—attending class at Public School 130, Prospect Avenue and 156th Street.

Fantastic Village, Serpentine Wall and Tunnel Maze are situated in the early childhood playground of the school. With its modernistic, unconventional forms, the playground seems somewhat out of place in the antiquated low-income area. But since its opening in September, when the school itself was opened, it has become a popular newcomer.

The children took to the playground at once. The teachers

The New York Times (by Arthur Brower)

A teacher reads a story for some of the pupils, while others turn roofless, marvelously obliging concrete structures into mountains, castles, forts, or just anything they like.

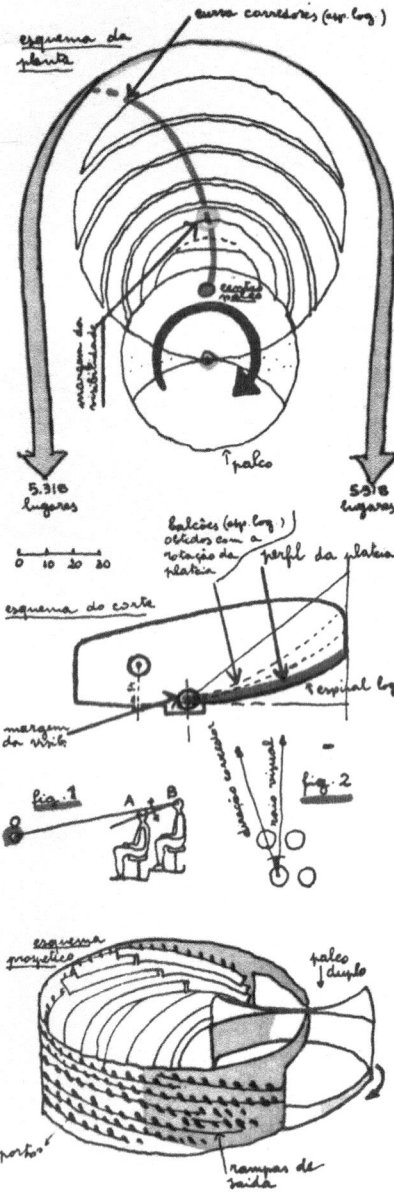

Example of a double-sided study card from "Caractères of Buildings."

Biog. Ciocca Gaetano. n. na Italia, em Garlasco (Pavia) em 1882; engenheiro industrial. Inventor genial, ocupou-se na 1ª guerra mundial com trabalhos militares. Esteve na Russia em 1930 para construir uma fabrica, e nos E.U. em 1934. Sempre tratou de problemas de estatística e pesquisa, e da casa popular prefabricada.

Bibl. No que concerne o "teatro popular de massas", o "total", etc. (problema muito discutido entre as duas guerras mundiais), cfr. além do teatro Ciocca, os de Gropius, Traugott Müller e Oscar Strnad, todos em Convegno di Lettere, tema: Il Teatro Drammatico, Roma, 1935 pag. 177 e segs, 154 e segs, 171 e 120. Sobre teatro em geral cfr. (mas um pouco superficiais) A. Cassi Ramelli, Edifici per gli Spettacoli, Milano, 1945, e Harold Burris-Meyer & Edward C. Cole, Theatres & Auditoriums, New York, 1949. Sôbre o teatro grego cfr. Carlo Anti, Teatri Greci Arcaici, Padova, 1947.

Nota

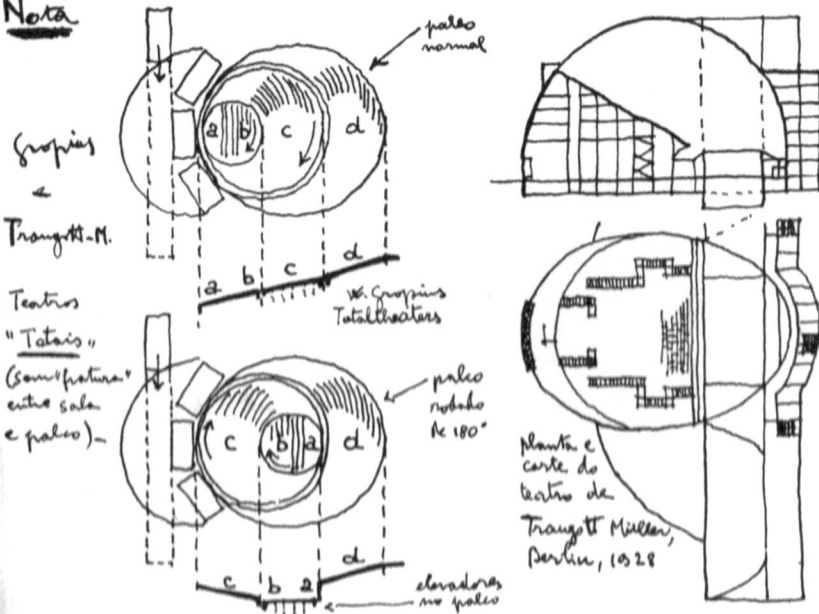

Gropius
e
Traugott-M.

Teatros
"Totais"
(sem "fratura" entre sala e palco) –

paleo normal

ↆ. Gropius
Totaltheaters

palco rodado de 180°

Planta e corte do teatro de Traugott Müller, Berlin, 1928

elevadores no palco

[A modest approach to the mysterious laws of nature, the effort to interpret and to obey their command, is the only way to bring their eternal majesty to our goals and our limited requirements, and is, in itself, a profound poem that can be translated in form to an elevated aesthetic and artistic expression.]

In order to confirm this point of view in a modern sense—I would have too much to consider were I inspired by Leonardo and the Humanists—I have reproduced the first drawing executed by Louis H. Sullivan at the École Nationale Supérieure des Beaux-arts in Paris in 1875, whose significance Wright interprets in the following terms: "In his every design a bit of Nature enters into building."[121]

Subordination of the drive towards a primarily aesthetic statement to the "purpose" of a work is the basis of architectural *sincerity* and another proof of its *validity*. Today, through the rapid means of production and advertising, works are quickly disseminated, solutions found, leaving nothing hidden, secret or obscure; this influence sometimes tyrannizes the student. It is precisely in this circumstance that the professor, while directing the student to exercise his own critical capacity, should analyze the factors that are resolved only through imitation, and focus on the "purpose" of the design, clarifying the essential requirements in order to permit the student to contribute personally to the work. The "purpose" is closely related to reason, matured by reflection and self-criticism; if the architect loses sight of this, he risks falling into sterility. Purposefulness is the result of a *compendium* of notions and the effort to prove, highlight, and focus all our energies towards their conceptualization, design and realization.

Architecture is brought to life through the art of Drawing. Nevertheless, it is wrong to think of architectural drawings simply as "drawings"; architectural drawings are not subject to artistic prescriptions, but must convey architectural requirements. I define "drawing" by the meaning attributed to it during the Renaissance, its mathematical

When nature is an architect.

165 *Salvia*, Charles ([Karl] Blossfeldt, *La Plante*, Berlin, n.d., [circa 1929] p. 101). [Blossfeldt, Karl. *Art Forms in Nature: examples from the plant world photographed direct from nature by Professor Karl Blossfeldt*, with an introduction by Karl Nierendorf. London: A. Zwemmer, 1929, p. 101, right. © 2013 Karl Blossfeldt Archiv/Ann u. Jürgen Wilde, Köln/Artist's Rights Society (ARS), NY.]

166 Egyptian columns, imitation of a bundle of roses; drawing dated to the Fourth Dynasty (engraving in Prissel d'Avenne, *Histoire de l'art égyptien*, cited in Viollet-le-Duc, *op. cit.*, vol. 2, pp. 181 and following).

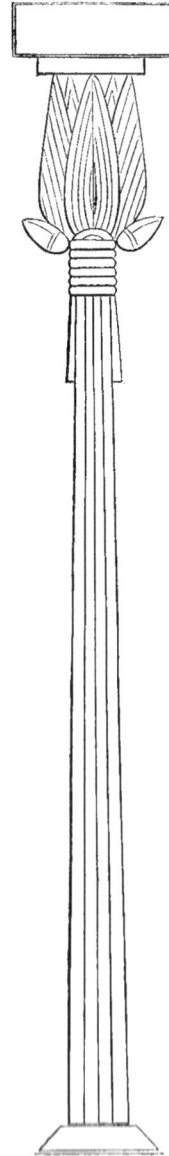

167 Drop of paraffin oil (D'Arcy Wentworth Thompson, *On Growth and Form*, Cambridge, 1952, vol. I, fig. 120). "The reasonings about the wonderful and intricate operations of Nature are so full of uncertainty, that, as the Wise-man truly observes, *hardly do we guess aright at the things that are upon the earth, and with labour do we find the things that are before us*" (Stephen Hales, *Vegetable Staticks*, 1727, Wentworth Thompson in *op. cit.*).

168 Detail design of Villard de Honnecourt for the Cathedral of Cambrai. The intimate connection between hand labor and architect allowed a limit to the "risk" of no detailing; the name *magister* can be translated as "master work," a wise master work, in effect. Villard de Honnecourt is the author of the famous "Livre de portraiture," a sort of treatise on proportions, which gave us the most reliable information about the organization and the traditions of the Gothic sites of the Middle Ages. The Villard's book established a kind of medieval doctrine of proportions, based on geometry. It was replaced by the rules of Vitruvius, rediscovered in the Renaissance.

meaning: [62] "il punto, la linea, la superfice, *il corpo esaltano i pregi dell'unità*"[122] ["the point, the line, the surface, *the body extol the virtues of unity*"] and not to the picturesque meaning that it assumed in the Baroque:

> jusqu'au temps de l'école de Lejay[123] les architectes se contentaient de tirer des lignes, et tout au plus de tracer des plans ... et l'on ne pouvoir juger l'effet de leur compositions. Dewailly,[124] au contraire, composa et exécuta ses dessin d'une manière large et pittoresque; aussi donna-t-il à son art un nouvel essor.[125]

> [Until the time of Lejay architects were content with drawing lines, and all the more, drawing plans ... and we cannot judge the effect of their compositions. Dewailly, however, composed and executed his drawings in a broad and picturesque manner; thus giving rise to a new art.]

Although it is true that laymen usually choose designs that have used scenographic perspective, architectural drawings should not be perceived as pictorial. First and foremost, we should understand these drawings in the same manner as Piero della Francesca.[126]

Le Corbusier, during his North American experience, expressed the following in one of his rich, if somewhat overstated, paradoxes: [63]

> Le dessin a tué l'architecture. C'est le dessin qu'on enseigne dans les écoles. A la tête de ces pratiques regrettables, règne dans l'équivoque même et parée d'une dignité que n'est que l'usurpation de l'esprit créateur des périodes antérieures, l'École des Beaux-arts de Paris. Siège du paradoxe le plus déconcertant, puisque, sous la férule des méthodes les plus conservatrices tout y est bonne volonté, travail acharné, foi. Le dilemme est au sein de l'École, institution qui se porte fort bien, comme le gui parasitaire s'empare de la sève des hautes et digne futaie, comme le cancer s'installe à l'aise autour du pylore d'un estomac ou autour du cœur. Le cancer se porte bien.[127]

> [Drawing killed architecture. It is drawing that we teach in the Schools. At the head of these regrettable practices, reigning in the midst of equivocation is the *École des Beaux-arts de Paris*, endowed with a dignity that is nothing more than a usurpation of the creative spirit of earlier periods. It is the seat of the most disconcerting paradox, since, under the rule of extremely conservative methods, everything there is goodwill, hard work, faith. The dilemma is at the heart of the School, an institution in excellent health, like the parasitical mistletoe, living off the sap of a tall and dignified grove, like a cancer which establishes itself comfortably around the pylorus of the stomach, or around the heart. *The cancer is in excellent health!*]

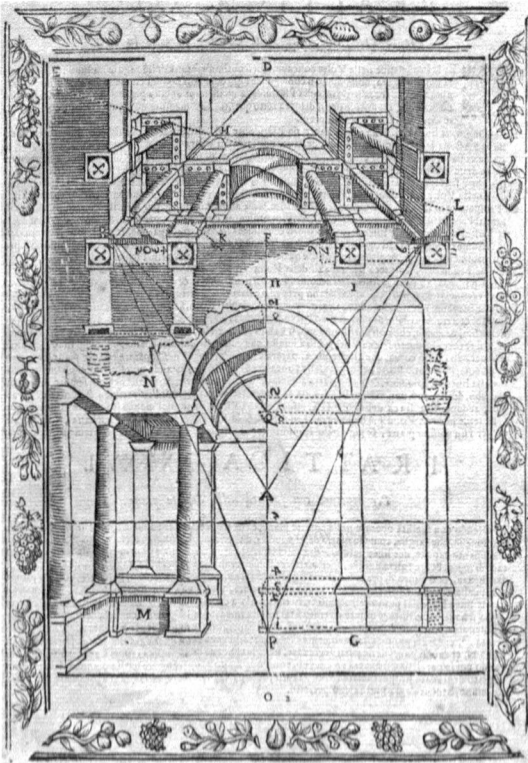

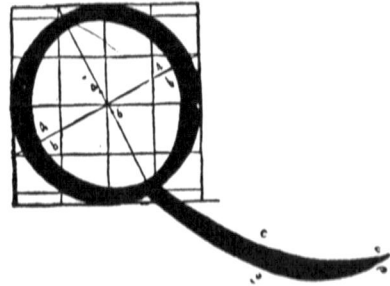

169 Perspective view from below (Troili, Giulio, called Il Pardosso. *Paradossi per pratticare la prospettiva senza saperla; fiori, per facultiare l'intelligenza; frutti, per non operare alla cieca. Cognitioni necessarie a pittori, scultori, architetti, ed a qualunque si diletta di Disegno; dat in luce da Giulio Troili da Spinlamberto, detto Paradosso.* Bologna: H.H. del Peri, 1672, p. 53, plate 54).

170 Page composed architecturally by Bodoni (*Orazione Funebre in morte di Ferdinando I, etc.*, Parma, MDCCCIII (1803), p. 16).

171 Geoffrey Tory, Proportional diagram of the letter Q. [from *Champ Fleury*. Paris: Par Maistre Geofroy Tory de Bourges . . . et par Giles Gourmont, 1529, in *Spazio 7*, Rome (December 1952–April 1953): 20.]

The architect has at his disposal, as a basis for executing ideas for a design proposal, the representative method of Monge. [64] However, external circumstances have made spectacular presentations the norm, ranging from perspectives *for the use of the client*, to models animated with little toys and photographs arranged into photo-montages, false images of reality. What should Schools do in the face of all this?

The student should learn to draw freehand (if he does not already know by the second year), with lines that are clean, coarse and analytical, just like those of an architect. Most students draw with lines like "lint," or if not that, in a shady, impressionistic manner that prevents any comprehension of the profound essence of each "form." I am reminded of a student whom I critiqued because of his confusing, impressionistic drawing, because it hid his lack of critical design clarity. When I advised him to draw in a "clear and synthetic" manner, he observed: "I understand: draw in the same manner as Steinberg"; to which I replied: "exactly in the same manner as Steinberg." Steinberg is an architect who was formed and educated in the school of coarse and analytical drawings. In order for students to acquire an essential analytical confidence in their architectural drawings, I have suggested to them what an old professor of "History of Styles" who possessed worthy didactic methods suggested to me: on large sheets of wrapping paper draw, in charcoal, dozens of bars similar to those drawn by children who are learning how to write; however, these bars must be at least one meter in length. Deep down, this system is quite rational, as it accustoms the hand to be analytically independent. This type of drawing trains the architect to capture the "caractères" of an architectural organism. Regarding "scenographic presentations," those that are most favored are drawn with absolute restraint, described as "drawing with the left hand" by the architect Giuseppe Pagano, of the Polytechnic School of Milan.

To summarize: the professor should exhibit, in a series of lectures illustrated by drawings, projections and, possibly, films, the most representative works of the history of architecture.

He should endeavor to convey to students the technical and ethical consciousness of the architect, and, above all, come up with a system, or a method by which the sequence of design can be made clear to the students. As I have observed, this method should be based on human measure, on the concept of "occupied space," on research, data collection and organizational schemes.

This quick overview, too short for so complex a subject, comes from years of direct experience. It seeks only to contribute to the teaching of a discipline that, if it is not apace with architecture, can effect delays that harm the education of future architects.

Naturally, students should learn all of the systems that are used to represent architecture; at School, models should be used for study

Dry and analytical drawing is the basic requirement of modern architecture; it eliminates all scenographical representation—the shading, blurriness and other factors which obscure the idea of the architecture. The "slight" drawing is almost a "non-drawing," one that does not compete with the work already built, as would happen with scenographic perspectives which, in a certain sense, overwhelmed architectural work by creating a sterile super-structure. Le Corbusier draws magnificently, with an "intellectual" style, and one can say that he was able to "describe" rather than draw; and Saul Steinberg, who is also an architect, can be taken as an example of an analytical synthesis which approaches a perfect documentation of a drawn architectural language.

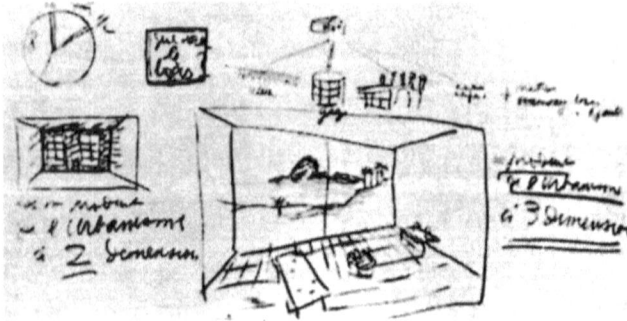

172 Original drawing by Le Corbusier, one of a series of lectures that the architect made in Rio de Janeiro, 1936 (author's collection). [© 2013 Artists Rights Society (ARS), New York/ADAGP, Paris/F.L.C.]

173 Saul Steinberg, *Untitled*, 1944. Ink on paper, 11¾ x 9 in. Beinecke Rare Book and Manuscript Library, Yale University [© The Saul Steinberg Foundation/Artist's Rights Society (ARS), New York].

65 The concluding paragraph of Focillon, *L'Eloge de la Main* (1934): "Nerval conte l'histoire d'une main maléfice qui, séparée de son corps, cours le monde pour y faire œuvre singulière. Je ne sépare la main ni du corps ni de l'esprit. Mais entre esprit et main les relations ne sont pas aussi simples que celles d'un chef obéi et d'un docile serviteur. L'esprit fait la main, la main fait l'esprit. Le geste qui ne crée pas, le geste sans lendemain provoque et définit l'état de conscience. Le geste qui crée exerce une action continue sur la vie intérieure. La main arrache le toucher à sa passivité réceptive, elle l'organise pour l'expérience et pour l'action. *Elle apprend à l'homme à posséder l'étendue, le poids, la densité, le nombre.* Créant un univers inédit, elle y laisse partout son empreinte. Elle se mesure avec la matière qu'elle métamorphose, avec la forme qu'elle transfigure. Éducatrice de l'homme, elle le multiplie dans l'espace et dans le temps."

["Nerval tells the story of an evil hand which, separated from its body, travels the world to create unique work. I do not separate the hand or the body or the mind. But between mind and hand relationships are not as simple as a leader obeyed and a docile servant. The spirit makes the hand, the hand makes the spirit. The gesture which does not create, the gesture without tomorrows provokes and sets the state of consciousness. The gesture that creates exercises a continuous action on the inner life. The hand pulls touch from its receptive passivity, organizes it for experience and action. *It teaches man to possess size, weight, density, number.* Creating a unique universe, it leaves its imprint everywhere. It measures itself by the matter it metamorphoses, with the form it transfigures. Educator of man, it multiplies him in space and in time."]

66 The photographers Alice Brill and Chico Albequerque are frequent contributors to Bo Bardi's magazine, *Habitat*.

67 Bo Bardi uses the English term here.

and should be executed with restraint regarding materials. Here we see an excellent way to give life to the beautiful idea that was defined by Focillon—after the severely Marxist propositions—in his tribute to the hand that "apprend à l'homme à posseder l'étendu, le poids, la densité, le nombre"[128] ["teaches man the command of size, weight, density, number"]. [65]

Representation has many practical problems. I cannot fail to consider, for example, the practice of photographic documentation, as it is a complex exercise not only with regard to the possibilities for organizing it into a photographic collection, but equally with regard to the manner in which architecture, both ancient and contemporary, should be photographed.

In archeological studies, as with medieval and modern architectures, documentary photography has already lost its interpretative value, and serves only as a testament to a "way of seeing" Architecture; observe the remarkable differences between the periods in which we see the appearance of the "pamphlet" by Rev. F.A.S. Marshall—*Photography: the importance of its applications in preserving pictorial records of the National Monuments of History and Art*, 1855[129] – and our own, in which we notice that Brazilian photographers see in a manner that is "different" from that of the past and from that adopted by European photographers, as they have themselves observed. [66]

On the other hand, how could I disallow the filming of Architecture, especially since film is the only method of representation able to capture a live image of our movement against the motionless construction? We should profit from all of the new methods of seeing, following them closely and updating them, so that we can move beyond all those things that have become outdated in practice. This is especially true when, on one hand, our period can be seen as one when "modern man is ancient," has enduring exigencies, and yet, new aspirations.

The ethical significance of the profession of architecture, in the context of its moral responsibility before society, transcends the value of what, in the fine arts, has been called "self-expression," [67] or "the expression" of oneself ("expression" here meaning *spirit without modesty*, or an artistic selfishness, as the expression of an artist is always implicit in his work). Gropius observes: "We now confirm that the social component is more valuable than the technical, economic and aesthetic components."[130] In effect, the architect must be fully conscious of his own responsibility as a "producer" of a real work, which *lasts* and is visible to everyone; work that will endure in the spiritual inheritance which every generation passes on to the next. The concept of "ethics" in the profession of architecture signifies a group of principles that begins with artistic modesty, the elimination of personal ambition and the desire to capture the limelight through frightening or surprising solutions, novelty or strangeness; a concern with the correctness of the structure, and a rigorous observation

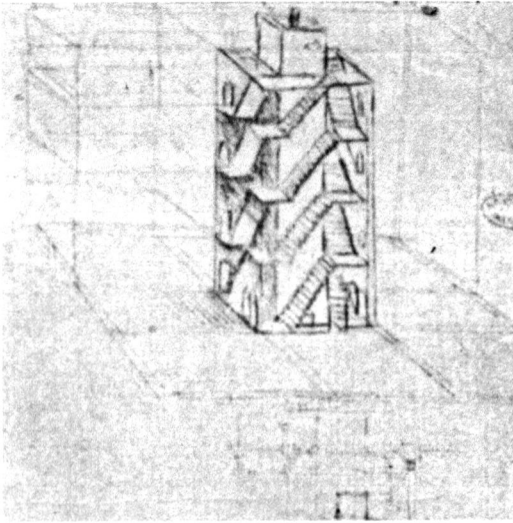

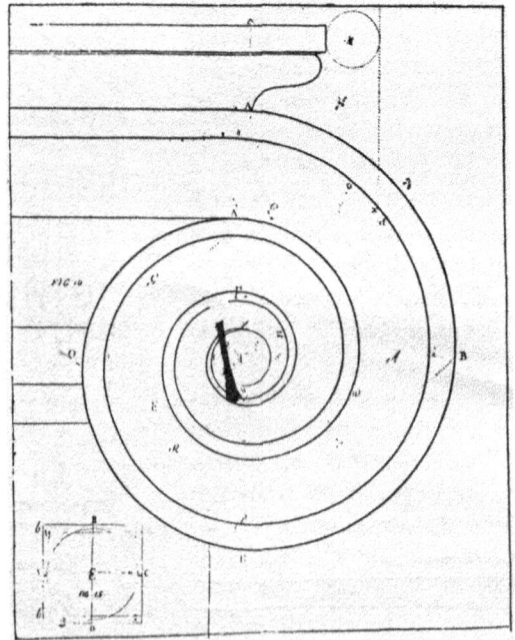

174 Leonardo da Vinci. Quadruple Staircase, a square plan (Manuscript B, Institut de France, Paris, folio 47 recto).

175 Volute of the Corinthian order (P.G. Piacenza, *Discussione ragionata di due questioni architettoniche tratte dal Libro terzo di Marco Vitruvio Pollione*, Milano, 1795, fig. 16).

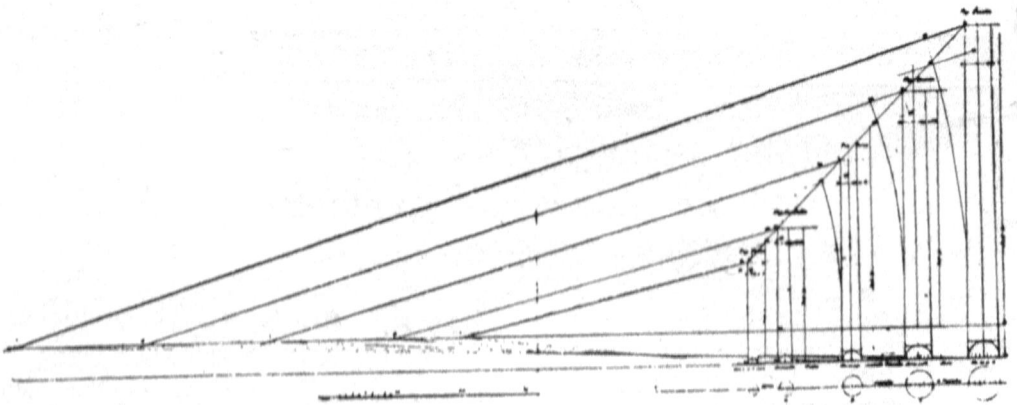

176 Schematic of a proposed approach to study the "foreshortening" of a column. (*La Rastremazione delle colonne secondo Vitruvio, etc. Opuscolo dell'architetto pittore scenico*, Paolo Landriani, Milano, 1833, plate V).

68 Latin, meaning, "in the wider sense."

69 Latin, meaning, "mindset/frame of mind."

70 Perhaps Bo Bardi means *magister fabrica*, Latin, meaning an official controlling the construction funds of a church.

of economic principles *lato sensu*, [68] above all in his relationship with the client. These principles are of fundamental didactic importance, above all in the case of "theory," because all of the elements that make up the complex activity that is architecture would break down if the ethical attitude of the architect were not impeccable. Here lies the benefit of establishing all of the responsibilities, especially those that arise from the relationship with the client.

The understandable eagerness to start building right away, the desire to get "a lot of work," can lead an architect, especially a recent graduate, to compromise and concede to what is known in North America as a "transaction between friends,"[131] rather than lose an "opportunity." Even today, the average client continues to regard the profession of architecture as a luxury: not completely indispensable, but only necessary for "embellishments," allowable if the construction company's financial resources have not been exhausted. It is extremely beneficial that, from School, the students be forewarned to this condition, this "inferiority complex" before the builder, a condition that will become apparent early on in their careers. As Wright says: "Regard it as just as desirable to build a chicken-house as to build a cathedral."[132] Nervi proposes:

> Per giustamente distribuire I meriti o I demeriti di una costruzione bisognerebbe affiancare al nome del progettista anche quello del proprietario, che ha scelto progettista e progetto e, inevitabilmente, influito alla sua realizzazione.[133]

> [To properly ascertain where to give credit or blame with regard to a building, the name of the owner, who implemented the project, should be considered with that of the designer, whom he selected.]

Another extremely sensitive topic is the relationship between the designer and the builder, in view of the financial conflict of interest, even when the designer is himself also the builder. The professor should also clarify for the student the issue of professional ethics regarding inter-relations among colleagues and collaborators, to develop the *forma mentis* [69] towards group work in a manner that does not "degrade" the architect but, rather, helps him to "distinguish himself" for his worthy contributions. The position of the architect as a *man of society* tends toward the figure of the *magister ad fabricam* [70] of the past, integrated with the lucidity and critical detachment that is indispensable to the modern spirit.

177 Eighteenth century engraving that compares six Renaissance palaces of Verona. Incising was for centuries the only means of representation: philologic and didactically inexact because – as the "effective" representation of architecture – it outweighed the personal interpretation of the draftsman, in the sense that just the "reliefs," and never the "engravings" serve as philological basis for the study of the architectural monuments of the past, reserving for prints, paintings, etc., only the role of historical documentation.

178 Palladio, Loggia del Capitano, Venice (Loukomski, *op.cit.*, XIII).

The contemporary tendency in the field of professional activities is specialization: the multitude of discoveries and the increasingly detailed investigations have made the division of work into professional sectors, as well as teamwork, indispensable. When talking about medicine or law, this is a consummated fact; however, where Architecture is concerned, such collaboration is beginning and, it could be said, already occurs, considering the fact that, in general, every architect refers to the engineer, especially in matters relating to the structure of the project or its [environmental] controls. The great architecture firms have been organized in this manner, and the design is no longer idealized and studied from an "artistic standpoint"—as it would have been at the time of Sangallo, the first architect to introduce this standard of work, even if his formulation was based on strict military hierarchy—but instead in technical collaboration, as illustrated by Mies van der Rohe and Wright. More than any other professional, the architect must participate in the fight against prejudices by aligning himself with another professional that is in close contact with his fellow man: the doctor. This had already been observed by Alberti,[134] who, during the Renaissance, had synthesized Greek wisdom and the School of Salerno. Therefore, we would expect the architect to have the desire to participate in every endeavor that aims to improve health or save humanity, dedicating himself to works that are destined to help those who need to be taken care of and cured. The job of designing a prison will be as important as that of designing a small cottage, or a monumental building in the manner of Ledoux.

Today, I worry about the satisfaction and confidence that accompanies the design and execution of buildings that, though they are considered great successes, are based on the most elementary of theories, often the product of compromises that the architect is obliged to honor. These constructions begin as soon as a single line is drawn, leading the architect to hurriedly transform a single scratch into a technical drawing, with the improvised collaboration of suppliers. These projects take shape amidst many others, all of them produced by the most imprudent self-sufficiency. One of the main problems of contemporary architecture, common to every country in the world, results from the absence of "doubt" and critical sense—or the examination of one's conscience in order to analyze if any theory was followed, even if integrated by a few essential points. The absence of this doubt in the minds of the most prominent architects of our time is a problem. I am not referring to the few architects who represent the unique aesthetics of an era, but instead to the characteristic success of those responsible for an inauthentic aesthetics, who are pleased with the aforementioned frivolity.[135]

179 New York, professional placards indicating the respective construction sites of the Guggenheim Museum, by Wright, and a skyscraper on Park Avenue, by Mies van der Rohe and Philip Johnson.

180 Bauhaus, Dessau, 1925: A studio (Herbert Bayer, Walter Gropius and Ise Gropius (eds), *Bauhaus 1919–1928*, New York: The Museum of Modern Art, 1938, p. 160).

181 Barracks to guard rural Maupertuis; Ledoux, architect. "L'artiste démontre son caractère dans ses ouvrages; les grands intérêts le développent: les évènements, suivant la manière dont il en est affecte, l'exaltent ou l'anéantissent" (Marcel Hubert Raval, *Claude-Nicolas Ledoux, 1736–1806; commentaires, cartes et croquis de J.-Ch. Moreux*, Paris: Arts et métiers graphiques, 1945, p. 128, fig. 102).

In France, one of the richest countries in the history of aesthetics, it is the "beaux-arts" architects who are currently responsible for 99 percent of the country's building projects. In Italy, the architects of scenographic "Neo-Romanticism" can, with impunity, ruin the plaza of a historic city with an edifice lacking both harmony and character, and this in a country which possesses, in some archive, a letter from Raphael to Baldassare Castiglione, in which he observes that the Pope "con l'onorarmi m'ha messo un gran peso sopra le spalle; questo é la cura della Fabbrica di S. Pietro" ["has honored me with a great weight on my shoulders; this is the responsibility to build St. Peter's"]; and concludes: "io mi servo di certa idea, che mi viene alla mente. Se questa in se ha alcuna eccellenza d'arte, io non so: ben mi affatico di averla"[136] ["I am the servant of an idea that has come into my mind. If it is art, I do not know: I work hard for it."]

With the aim of reaching a conclusion, even when considering the inexhaustible nature of this topic, I must return to the starting-point, as constituted by history, and to my recent affirmations, in order to contribute to the clarification of the tasks that originate from history itself and from yesterday's chronicle, so to speak.

In order to eliminate the schism between the present and the past, it is necessary to consider the historical process that has led to the architecture of today. While accepting a historical continuity, it would behoove the professor to proceed with extreme caution. Historical development does not imply "reconciliation"; instead, in the case of architecture, it means a profound and always present critical examination—indispensable to avoid falling into formalist abstractions. The position of the avant-garde has long been surpassed and modern architecture has reached a comfortable formalism that it is generally accepted in cities; therefore, it is necessary— and the School's most important task—to clearly explain to students that historical impartiality is not "reconciliation," that "avant-gardism" has arrived in academia, that internationalism does not mean cosmopolitanism, that an abstract international language cannot solve problems. Rather, a rigorous *method* is necessary to consider the problems of different countries, real problems that must be solved through the use of *effective* means and not with abstract criticism, whether or not it deals with the interpretation of space or form. Furthermore, it is equally necessary to clarify to the student that the "beautiful plastic solution" of an architect—even if he is a great artist—will not relieve us of the existence of sad country homes, favelas and shacks. The graduating architect has a moral responsibility to society—as an urbanist and a builder—to base his work on effective investigation and on the real needs of each country.

182 Tower of the Church of S. Gaudenzio in Novara; Alessandro Antonelli, architect. (Arialdo Daverio, *La Cupola di S.Gaudenzio*, Novara, 1940, n.p.).

183 [Internal] Brick structure of the cupola of the Church of S. Gaudenzio in Novara; Alessandro Antonelli, architect *(ibid.)*.

It is obvious that a theory cannot be applied to indeterminate space but must, on the contrary, limit itself to defined spaces whose environmental, moral and social conditions correspond to and favor its realization. It would be interesting to pinpoint which theories have prevailed in the development of Brazilian architecture throughout the past four centuries, inquiring which and how many local contributions have affirmed themselves and have remained at the core of a theory since its inception.

The true meaning of the term "national" is that which, deprived of empty political–nationalist meanings, will lead to international collaboration, an effective and vital contribution of specific activities that will satisfy the spiritual and material needs of each country. The sum of these contributions, synthesized in an international language, will be the basis of a new culture that will no longer be "European" or "American" but, yes, a global culture. This language will be neither that of an abstract and vague "cosmopolitanism" nor that of "national" claims of an aesthetic–ideological character.[137]

After having examined many historically inspired aspects of Architecture, we have reached the obvious conclusion that, in order to obtain a concrete architectonic conscience, one must not resort to scant interpretations; instead, one must concentrate all of his efforts in the acquisition of a *method*. Gropius, who dedicated all of his life to teaching, envisioning the architect as a creator of culture, affirmed this same idea in his writing. Recently, confirming what Leslie Martin had already perfectly defined, he reaffirmed that the objective of his work as an architect and educator is to dedicate his life to the search for a *method*.[138]

There was a time when the architectural apprentice could allow himself to proceed unilaterally, using a simple manual in order to create architecture; today, his problem has completely changed.

It is necessary to open a wider horizon for students, and not to oblige them to look in a single direction, in a unilateral way. On the contrary, by indicating the scope and the interpretations of a concept, without digressions, as well as its spatial spirit, it is possible to stimulate the interest of the student and to work alongside him.

184 Detail of the residential complex at Parque Guinle,
Rio de Janeiro; Lucio Costa, architect.

Lúcio Costa is an interpreter and defender of national "caractères" (I have said in
what sense the word is understood) of Brazilian architecture. In his realizations
we indeed find such "caractères," as in the well-known Conjuncto Guinle park, in
Rio, which is reproduced here in detail. He traces the origins of Brazilian
architecture and discovers its character not in the authentic architecture of the
"official" Portuguese, but the "popular," transferred to our land in the person of
the "uneducated", the old masters and masons. He thinks this early greatness is
what gave Brazilian architecture "This unassuming air and purity that it has
maintained, despite the hardships it underwent, until the mid-nineteenth
century." And again: "Our home is presented well, almost always poor, compared
to the opulence of the 'palazzi' and the Italian 'villas,' the castles of France and
the English 'mansions' of the same era, or the rich appearance and pride of the
'solârs' of the Hispanic Americans, or even the appearance of certain coquettish
palaces and Portuguese noble residences." And it is this "caracter" of domesticity
and modesty, so clearly focused, and practically recommended, which we find
wholly intact in the early architecture of Oscar Niemeyer and his contemporaries.
It is to this that we owe the success of Brazilian architecture, which suddenly
appeared to the world as an invitation towards honesty and a joyful life, leaving
behind the bloody experience of the war against rhetoric (see L. Costa, *op. cit.*, pp.
23 and following).

185 J.G. Heck, *Bilder Atlas zum Conversations-Lexikon, etc. . . .*, Leipzig, 1849, plate VII.

186 "Charge" by Robert
Osborn from the book
Architecturally Speaking by
Eugene Raskin, New York,
Reinhold Publishing
Corporation, 1954 (p. 104).

NOTES

by Lina Bo Bardi to Propaedeutic Contribution to the Teaching of Architecture Theory

Chapter 1

1   Cited in dr. G.P. Ricci, *Antonio Jannuzzi, Irmão e Cia. na Exposição Nacional*, Rio de Janeiro, 1908, p. 35.

2   The importance of teaching theory and aesthetics in general was so little appreciated in the nineteenth century that Theodore Vischer had to relinquish his course at the Polytechnic in Zurich "per mancanza di uditori" ["due to lack of audience"] (according to a letter from Francesco de Sanctis, April 13, 1856, to Angelo De Meis, published in *Lettere dall'esilio (1853–1860) raccolte e annotate da B. Croce*, Bari, 1938, p. 53). It is also interesting to observe that in the nineteenth century, amidst the cultural-historicist confusion surrounding the teaching of Architecture, theory appears under different labels; for example, at the Royal Technical Institute of Berlin, the third- and fourth-year course was named, "On the most important kinds

187 Visconde do Guahy Palace, Rio de Janeiro; Januzzi, contractor. "Fioravente Januzzi . . . was one of those old masters who, even without university studies, managed his humble instruments in partnership with all the exigent demands of the static materials of construction, taking advantage of the knowledge gained through practice with a trained engineer."

of private and public buildings, and city plans" (Syllabus in Vittorio Treves, *L'Architettura d'oggi–Gli architetti e le Scuole d'A. in Italia*, Torino, 1890, p. 33).

3   Leon Battista Alberti, *Della Architettura, Libre Dieci*, translation by Cosimo Bartoli, Milano, 1833; Book IV, chap. II, p. 183. *De re aedificatoria*, c. 1450.

4   R.G. Collingwood, *Autobiographia*, Italian trans. by Giampaolo Gandolfi, Venice, 1955, p. 88. Original title: *An Autobiography*, London, 1938.

5   Geoffrey Scott, *The Architecture of Humanism: A Study in the History of Taste*, Garden City, NY, 1954 (but first edition, 1914), p. 179. Scott, a student of Bernard Berenson, applied the system of pure visibility to the criticism of Architecture.

6   It is necessary to clarify that I use the term "humanism" in its broad sense, and in reference to that specific historical movement that developed, primarily in Italy, in the fifteenth and sixteenth centuries, or in the seventeenth-century Counter-Reformation; the new humanism to which I allude is not that of the pseudo-humanist "transcendentals" of the Counter-Reformation, but proper to the fundamental exigencies which animated the first Italian humanists—that is, to discover *in man* his true sense of measure and dignity.

7   Scott, *op. cit.*, p. 179.

8   Some might have thought it suitable to first define the concept of "theory." However, this would risk establishing a vicious circle, since by "theoretically" defining "theory" we would remain within its sphere. Certainly, every specific and determinate investigation—as is mine—cannot refrain from departing from particular methodological presumptions that delimit its specific field. At the same time, and for this reason, one cannot take these same presumptions as the object of research, because that would lead the research away from "science" and towards "philosophy"—or the study of the conditions of science's possibilities while conducting a specific and determinate investigation. Nonetheless, in the hopes of clarifying some aspects of my position, which I consider essential, I could distinguish between a concept of "theory" designated as *formal* and which refers to its *essence*, and the concept of its process, its development. Regarding the former, it is essential to observe that it concerns the role played by "theory" relative to "reality." To exemplify the problems associated with this, I remind the readers of Benedetto Croce, for whom the totality or the spirit has two essential and distinct forms: the *theoretical* form and the *practical* form, or *knowledge* and *volition*, *contemplation* and *action*; and of Giovanni Gentile, for whom there was an essential identity between *theory* and *practice*, conceiving that knowledge, as a spiritual act, is simultaneously volition and vice versa. Regarding the second point, I would like to emphasize that "theory," precisely because of its development in a broad sense, is just as infinite as the historical process through which its development occurs. It is therefore wrong to treat any of its historical moments as absolute and, consequently, to speak of a *theory* (in our case, "theory of Architecture") that is valid in and of itself. *In this sense*, an absolutely valid formal and abstract "theory" of Architecture does not exist. It is its history that gives the "theory" its character and that, at the same time, surpasses it.

9   Talbot Hamlin, *Forms and Functions of Twentieth-Century Architecture*, vol. 4, New York, 1952.

10 Sebastiano Serlio, *Sette Libri dell'Architettura*, Venetia, 1537.

11 Carl W. Condit, *The Rise of the Skyscraper*, Chicago, 1952, p. 42.

188 Country house of the Conde de Barca, Rio de Janeiro Thomas Ender, *O velho Rio de Janeiro, através das gravuras de Thomas Ender.* São Paulo: Edições Melhoramentos, 1956, p. 112.

189 A renovation on Park Avenue in New York: a skyscraper next to an old house that will be demolished [*sic*].

12   Viollet-le-Duc, *Entretiens sur l'Architecture*, Paris, vol. II, p. 65, fig.4.
     [(2 vols), Paris, 1863–72.]

13   André Lurçat, *Formes, Compositions et Lois d'Harmonie—Eléments d'une science
     de l'esthétique architectural,* Paris, n.d. but 1953; vol. 3.

14   Failing to cite the "literature" is sometimes the mark of a polemical
     attitude, which reveals a flawed sense of history, because an idea about the
     development of a prevalent cultural spirit has been put in its midst.
     Remember, to give just one example, the observations of Richard Benz (*Die
     Deutsche Romantik*, Stuttgart, 5th edn, 1956, p. 8) who claims not to rely
     on "literature" because it is always the result of an image or representation
     of Romanticism (in his case) which has been *provided*, when, in reality, he
     believes that one should personally *relive* (*Einfühlung*) the spirit of the
     period that one is representing. It is as if it was possible to erase all that
     stands between the chosen period (or any period) and us (in this case, the
     Author), necessarily conditioning us and our interpretation. As if, other
     than the one provided by "literature," the concept of a particular period
     now enters it and us. That is, when that term need not be the result of
     interpretations that have emerged in that same period. The result is a total
     absence of historiographical sense.

15   André Gutton, *Conversation sur l'Architecture: cours de théorie de l'architecture
     professé à École Nationale Supérieur des Beaux-Arts*, Paris, vol. I 1949, II 1954,
     III 1956.

16   "Anche a non essere filosofi, non ci si può non guardare attorno, ed assistere
     al tramonto della sistemazione romantica del pensiero, all'imporsi d'una
     rinnovata problematica in tutti I campi—della profonda rivoluzione formale
     dell'arte, alla crisi delle scienze fisiche dopo la relatività e il quantissmo,
     alle nuove impostazioni della biologia, ecc.—né ci si può sottrarre all'allarme
     degli inquieti movimenti filosofici che urgono da ogni parte: dalla ripresa
     della fenomenologia husserliana all'esistenzialismo, al neopositivismo logico,
     al razionalismo critico, al materialismo dialettico, ecc. E, qualunque sia
     l'orientamento personale di chi oggi è veramente vivo, par dubbio si possa
     ancora presentare come pacifica l'illusione romantica che la filosofia sia un
     sapere assoluto nel senso di un sapere di contenuti razionalmente assoluti;
     peggio che si possa ancora pretendere di riassumere e "liquidare" la problem-
     atica dell'arte con enunciati che, per la mancanza di interno movimento
     dialettico, non possono che cadere fuori della cultura e della vita: in un
     vacuo dogmatismo, in una morta astrazione." [Even if you don't call yourself
     a philosopher, you really can't avoid looking around and you can't passively
     witness the end of the romantic school of thought, and the dawn of new
     approaches in all fields—from the powerful revolution of formalism in art,
     to the crisis of physics after relativity and the quantum theory, to the new
     configurations of biology, etc.—neither you can pretend not to notice the
     signs of alarm coming from restless philosophical movements calling from
     all sides: from the rebirth of Husserl's Phenomenology to existentialism,
     logical neo-positivism, critical rationalism, dialectic materialism, etc. And,
     whatever might be the personal point of view of those who are truly alive
     today, I doubt that anybody can reaffirm the innocence of that romantic
     delusion according to which Philosophy would be an absolute form of
     knowledge, in the sense that Philosophy is described as a form of knowledge
     the contents of which are rationally absolute. Most importantly, you cannot
     expect to summarize, and simply get rid of, all the problematic issues
     surrounding art with theories that, because they lack an internal dialectic

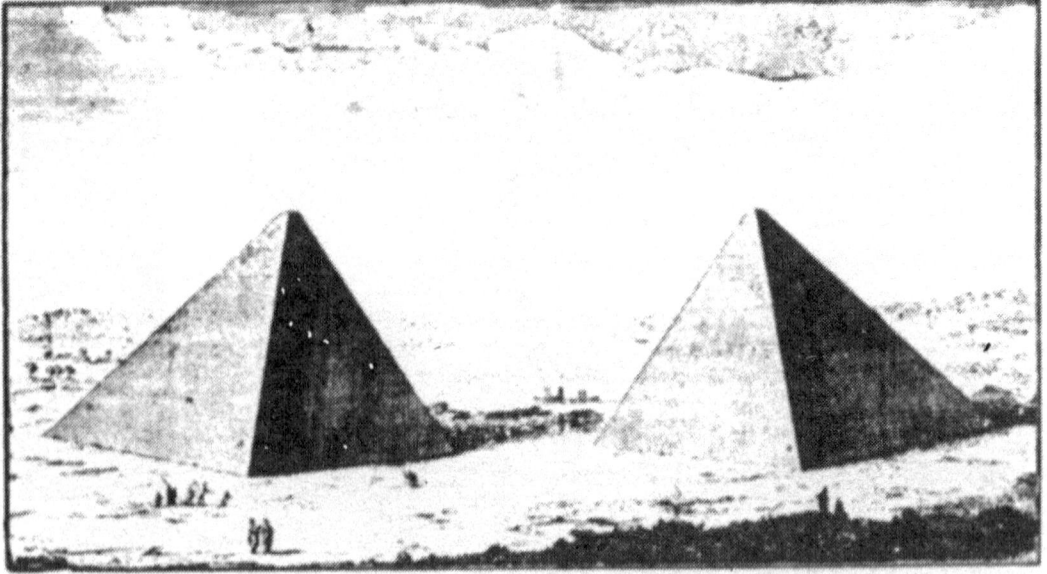

190 Pyramid, engraving from the eighteenth century
(author's collection).

191 Cupola of the Church of Santa Maria del Fiore,
Florence, by Filippo Brunelleschi.

"Signori operai, e non e dubbio che le cose grandi hanno sempre nel condursi difficoltà; e se niuna n'ebbe mai, questa vostra l´ha maggiore che voi per avventura non avvisate, perciocché io non so che anco gli antichi voltassero mai una volta si terribile come ara questa . . . e mi sbigottisce non meno la larghezza che l'altezza dell'edificio, perciocché se ella si potessi girar tonda, si potrebbe tenere il modo che tennero i Romani nel voltare il Panteon di Roma cioè la Ritonda; ma qui bisogna seguitare L'otto facce, ed entrare in catene ed in morse di pietre, che sarà cosa molto difficile." Thus spoke Brunelleschi: "L'uffizio degli operai di S. Maria del Fiore ed i consoli dell'Arte della Lana . . .", frisando a dificuldade do enxerto de uma cobertura "classica" sobre um organismo "gótico". (Giorgio Vasari, *Le Vite dei più eccellenti pittori, scultori e architetti*, edited by C.L. Ragghianti, Milano 1942, vol. I, pp. 601 and following). Five centuries later, P.L. Nervi, studying the cracks in the masterpiece of the Renaissance architect, concluded: "Ne, per un complesso di considerazioni dedotte dall'andamento delle lesioni, dall'esame dei pilastrini di sostegno e di tutto il fabbricato, ritengo si debba pensare a cedimento di fondazioni . . . E evidente, quindi, che non si può spiegare la presenza di cosi imponenti e, quel che e peggio, progressive lesioni, se non attribuendole ad un fatto interno, dovuto ad una specie di vitalità dei muri e delle pietre, in qualche modo analoga alla vitalità delle piante e degli animali" (P.L. Nervi, *Scienza o arte del Costruire?* cit., p. 16). A demonstration of curiosity and humility concerning the real masters of the imponderable, we could say, almost, the "irrational," in architectural works.

movement, end up falling out of the realm of culture and life: in a place of empty dogmatism and dead abstraction.] Sergio Bettini's response to G. Nicco Fasola's letter regarding Borissavliévitch (from the journal *Arte Veneta*, no. 13–16, 1950, pp. 158 and following.

17   "...Necesità di un nuovo instituto, perché non resti imprigionata l'architettura civile nelle fasi, né membri, né compositi, e né termini stessi architettonici finora usati..." [In the Appendix of his 1981 dissertation, "Sortes architectii in the eighteenth-century Veneto," University of Pennsylvania, Philadelphia, Marco Frascari translates this as follows: "the need for new norms, so that architecture shall not remain confined by the appearances, the memberings, the compositions and the terminologies, that have been usual up to now,"] in *Elementi dell'Architettura Lodoliana ossia L'arte del Fabbricare con solidità scientifica e con eleganza non capricciosa*, by Andrea Memmo, Zara, 1834, vol. 2, p. 52.

18   Julien Guadet, *Éléments et Théorie de l'Architecture, Cours professé à l'École Nationale et Spéciale des Beaux-Arts. Paris*, 1909, 5th edn, vol. 4. In order to emphasize the importance of this treatise, I note the fact that Georges Gromort starts his famous *Essai sur la Théorie de l'Architecture, Cours professé à l'École Nationale Supérieure des Beaux-Arts, de 1937 à 1940* (Paris, 1946, p. 9) with these words: "J'ai, pour ma part, une telle estime pour le grand ouvrage de Guadet que je me sens Presque tenté de m'excuser de ce que ce livre ressemble si peu au sien ... Ses *Éléments* ... n'ont rien perdu de leur valeur." ["I hold the work of Guadet in such high regard that I am tempted to apologize for the fact that this book bears so little resemblance to his, ... The *Éléments* ... has lost nothing of its value."] In his didactic explanation, Gromort frequently refers to his predecessor and, to a certain extent, continues his lesson. Nonetheless, it is interesting to note that in this lesson Gromort totally excludes all of this century's great architects, as if history had ended with the venerable Guadet.

19   Guadet, *op. cit.*, vol. IV, p. 651.

20   *Ibidem*, p. 653.

21   *Ibidem*, p. 654.

22   "... siccome il fine di ogni scienza ... si è il ritrovamento della verità, delle cose... così il fine di ogni arte è il non fare errore nell'operare, non partendosi giammai dalla diritta ragione della pratica sua ..." ["... since the aim of all science ... was the discovery of the truth of things ... so the aim of all art is to not err in making, nor ever depart from the straight practice of reason ..."], *Trattato di Teofilo Gallaccini sopra gli errori degli Architetti ora per primia volta pubblicato*, Venezia, 1762, p. 3. This treatise was written in 1641. See also: *Osservazioni di Antonio Viscentini architetto Veneto che servono di continuazione al Trattato di T.G. etc.*, Venezia, 1771. The purists' controversy continues to be a preparation for Neo-Classicism.

23   Vitruvio, *De Architectura Libri*, trans. (with preface) by Ugo Fleres, Villasanta, Milan, 1933. The first translator, and cinquecentist commentator, of Vitruvius said "l'Architettura é nome greco, di due voci composto, delle quali la prima significa principale e capo: la seconda fabro o artefice, e chi volesse bene volgarmente esprimere la forza del detto nome direbbe capomaestra. Et perciò dice Platone, che l'Architetto non fá mestiere alcuno, ma é soprastante a quelli, che usano i mestieri: là dove potremo dire l'architetto non essere fabro non maestro di legnami, non muratore, non separatamente certo, e terminatoartefice, ma capo, soprastante, e regolatore di tutti l'Artefici." ["Architecture is a Greek word, composed of two parts,

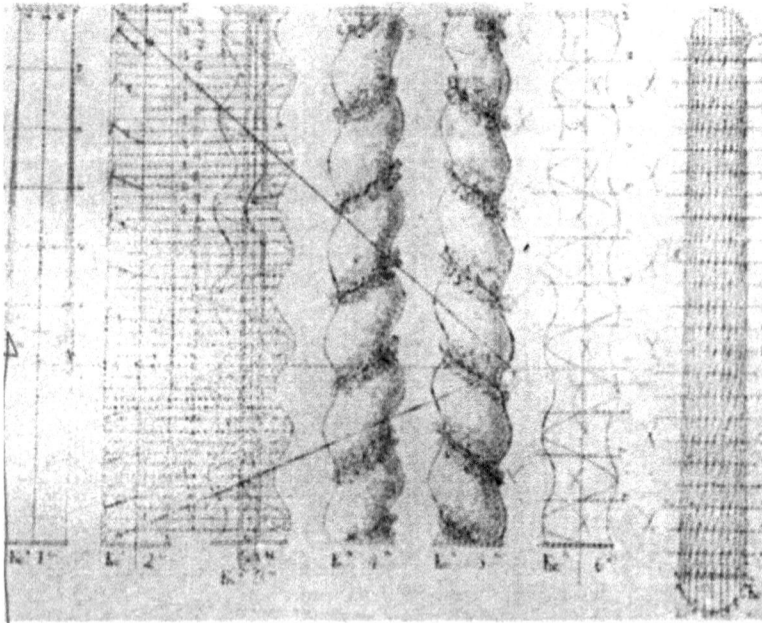

192 Twisted columns from a plate by Bibiena (Ferdinando Galli Bibiena, etc. *L'Architettura civile preparata su la Geometria etc.*, Parma, MDCCXI (1711), plate 37).

Twisted columns deserve the anathema of a "moral" Architecture, Francesco Milizia, who, with Lodoli, and Gallaccini anticipated functionalism during the Baroque Period: "Pessime sono le colonne torse, cioè spirali ed attortigliate. E chi non vede che una tal forma rappresenta un sostegno piegante sotto la gravezza del carico? . . . Pure si fatta stranezza ha avuto voga per la sua stranezza stessa, e per la difficolta del lavoro. Il sontuoso e grande altare di S. Pietro diede corso a questa bizzarria . . . Taluno ha tentato di introdurre in architettura colonne curve sedenti, a guisa di gambe de'cani . . . Per buona sorte tanto delirio e stato conosciuto per delirio".

[Twisted columns are very bad, for example, spirals and twists, And who does not see that such forms represent buckling under the force of gravity? . . . purity is made strange, for the pure sake of it, and due to the difficulty of the work, the great and sumptuous altar of St. Peter's succumbed to this strangeness . . . someone has even attempted to introduce columns that curve like canine teeth . . . fortunately this kind of delirium is well understood to be delirium.] (Milzia, *Principi di Architettura, op. cit.*, p. 23).

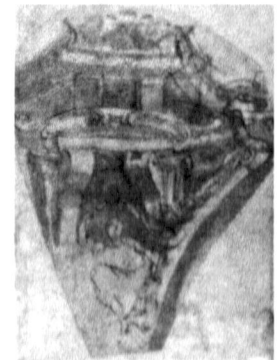

193 S. Peter's, Rome, Bernini's colonnade; view from the cupola of the Basilica.

194 Project for a scroll: anonymous seventeenth-century Italian architect XVII; original drawing.

of which the first means the first or principal: the second means fabricator or artisan, and he who likes can express the force of that term simply as master builder. And so Plato says, that the Architect is not a tradesman, but above all trades, we must say, not simply a fabricator, master carpenter, builder, alone, but the final artisan, the head, above all and regulator of all trades."] (Vitruvio, *De Architectura*, Italian trans. of Mons. Daniele Barbaro, Venezia, 1556, Introduction.)

24   Fransesco Pellati, *Vitruvio*, Rome, 1938, p. 64. [From Quintilian, *De institutione oratoria, Libre duodecim*, vol. 1.]

25   *Sulle Forme e caratteri dell'Architettura civile e sulle cause delle loro variazione.* Memoria di Romolo Burri, architect-engineer, Rome, 1873, p. 5. (Winning memoir of the first Poletti competition promoted by the San Luca Academy in Rome.)

26   Verses usually attributed to Carlo Lodoli. Notice the inscription in his portrait (by Antonio Longhi) in *Elementi, etc.* Roma, 1786, vol. I, facing p. 1.

27   Francesco Milizia, *Principi di architettura civile.* Opera curata ed illustrate da Giovanni Antolini, Milano, 1847, p. 3.

28   Francesco Milizia, *Dell'arte di vedere nelle belle arti del Disegno segundo i principe di Sulzer e di Mengs*, Genoa, 1786, p. 95. [Venice: presso G. Pasquali,1781; 1792; 1798; 1813; Alvisopoli, 1823.]

29   Francesco Algarotti, *Saggio Sull'Architettura e sulla Pittura*, Milano, n.d. Essay from 1756, p. 17.

30   *Cours d'architecture enseigné dans l'Académie Royale d'Architecture. Première partie où sont expliquez les termes, l'origine & les Principes d'Architecture & les pratiques des cinq Ordres suivant la doctrine de Vitruve & de ses principaux Sectateurs & suivant celle des trois plus habiles Architectes que ayant écrit entre les Modernes, qui sont Vignole, Palladio & Scamozzi. Dédié au Roy par M. François Blondel de l'Académie Royale des Sciences . . . Seconde Edition, augmentée & corrigée.* À Paris, chez L'AUTEUR. Et se Vend À Amsterdam, Chez Pierre Mortier, Libraire sur le Vygendam. M.DC.XCVIII. [1698] I provide the complete title of this famous work in order to demonstrate that Blondel, in an attempted revival, religiously follows all of Vitruvius' measures, to the extent that he modifies those of the other masters. Vitruvius' legacy is the greatest chapter in the history of Architecture. There was even a Vitruvius Britannicus, and it is known that Hegemann and Peets' manual is titled *The American Vitruvius*. Vitruvius also arrived in America with the Missions: priests, who also worked as architects, when searching for architectural models and ideas, could find only Vitruvius' treatise in the library of their monasteries. An example of this is provided by the façade of the Church of the Mission of Santa Barbara, California, 1785–1795, which was considered by the Europeans as a marvel, as it had been built "by ignorant Indians under the direction of a priest" (Duhaut-Cilly, *Viaggio intorno al Globo*, vol. I, pp. 270–80). In order to draw the façade, the builder (Father Antonio Ripoll) copied Plate X of a Spanish "Vitruvius," only modifying the spaces and adding two columns; the windows, however, followed the Moorish style. (Newcomb, *The Old Mission Churches etc.*, Philadelphia, 1925, p. 220 and the subsequent figures on p. 221).

31   Carlo A. Ragghianti, *Il Pungolo dell'Arte*, Venezia, 1956, p. 280. The author defines urbanism as: "L'oggetto dell'urbanistica è il rilevamento di una situazione storica data, al fine di operare la trasformazione attuale e future second principia, credenze, convinzioni, idée motrici, direttive e programmi,

195 Allegory of Architecture. François Blondel, *Cours d'architecture [enseigné dans l'Academie royale d'architecture . . . par m. François Blondel. 2. ed., augm. & cor.*, Paris: Chez l'auteur, 1698, p. 313.]

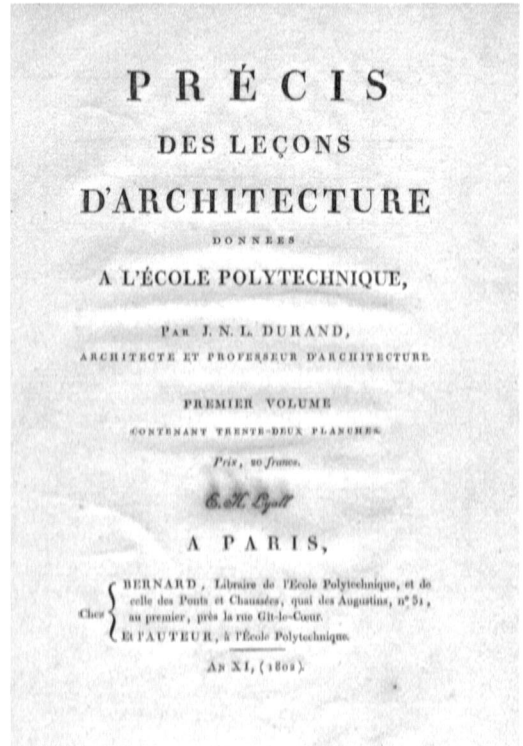

196 Frontispiece from Volume 1 of [Jean-Nicolas-Louis Durand, *Preçis des leçons d'architecture données à l'École polytechnique, par J.N.L. Durand*, Paris: Chez l'Auteur, 1802.]

quali che questi siano. E allora per evitare equivoci o confusioni, credo che questo fondamentale lavoro dovrebbe essere identificato e definito per ciò che veramente è con una designazione sua propria e distinta. Nessuna, in questo senso, mi sembra più esplicita e rispondente di questa: *pianificazione*." ["The goal of urbanism is the survey of a given historical situation so as to perform its current and future transformation according to principles, beliefs, convictions, motives, directives and programs, whatever they might be. So to avoid ambiguity or confusion, I believe that this fundamental work should be identified and defined for what it really is with its own distinct designation. Nothing, in this sense, seems more explicit and satisfying than this: *planning*."] (p. 275).

32   Thomas Jefferson, *Architect-Original Designs in the Collection of T.J. Boston*, 1916. Cf. in general the ample literature about the "Greek Revival" in North America.

33   ". . . uno de grandi avvenimenti per chi dee costruire fosse pure il maggior re del mondo è quello di non prodigalizzare la material" [". . . one of the great tenets for those who build, even if it is for the greatest king of the world, is not to extravagantly waste material"] (Lodoli, *op cit.*, ed. Zara, vol. I, p. 174).

34   "Riguardo poi ai ricchi privati offuscherebbero eglino il loro splendore, se invece delle micidiali mense di tante sofisticatezze per chincagliere e per insulsi sfarzi, e in vece di togliere tanta gente all'agricoltura e ai mestieri più sodi, impiegassero i loro denaro, dopo essersi provveduti di belle e propri abitazioni in città e campagna, a costruir ponti, a prosciugar marassi, a lastricare strade, a far acquedotti, a slargar cloache, e a conferire in vari altri modi alla pubblica felicità?" ["If we want to talk about wealthy citizens, then do you think they would harm their greatness if, instead of the fatal quantity of money they pour into fancy junk and useless pomp, and instead of taking so many people away from agriculture and other more sensible jobs, they would invest their money, after having provided themselves with beautiful and proper abodes both in the city and in the countryside, in the construction of bridges, in the draining of salt marshes, in the paving of streets, in the making of aqueducts, in the widening of sewers, and in contributing in many other ways to the public good?"] (Milizia, *op. cit.*, p. 574).

35   Cf.: "All judgment of Art is founded on the knowledge of Nature" (John Ruskin, *The Stones of Venice*, London, 1895, vol. III, p. 54). Cf. William White, *The Principles of Art . . . in the Ruskin Museum*, London, 1895, p. 504 and following.

36   Treated here, obviously, is "nature" in the broadest sense, for example as in Frederick J.E. Woodbridge, *Saggio Sulla Natura*, translated to Italian by Francesco Tató, Milano, 1956, especially the first chapter.

37   Information in the article: *O Homen Anti-Natureza?* [Anti-Nature Man?] (HABITAT 15, São Paulo, p. 56).

38   "Si la naturaleza se opone, lucharemos contra ella, y la venceremos." ["If Nature opposes, we shall conquer."]. This reminds me of Socrates when he speaks to Phaedrus in Valéry's *Eupalinos:* "Je pense invinciblement à un homme que voudrait grimper sur ses propres épaules!" ["I think about the invincible difficulty of a man who wants to climb on his own shoulders!] (Paul Valéry, *Eupalinos ou L'Architecte . . .* Paris, 1924, p. 98).

39   Taddeus Zielinsky, *L'Antico e Noi*, trans. various, edited by P.E. Pavolini, Firenze, 1915, p. 89. The work is, however, from 1903. I mention this work because it refers to the pedagogical teaching of the "Ancients."

197 Church of Santa Barbara, California, eighteenth century (Rexford Newcomb, *The Old Mission Churches and Historic Houses of California: Their History, Architecture, Art and Lore*, Philadelphia: J.B. Lippincott Company, 1925, p. 221, top).

198 Plate X of Vitruvius, Spanish edition, no publication details (author's collection).

199 Basilica of Constantine, Rome, also called the Temple of Peace, sixteenth century (Cosmo Medici Duci etc., Joanne Antonio Dosio. Rome, MDLXIX (1569), plate 8). [Dosio, Giovanni Antonio. Vrbis Romae aedificiorum illustriumquae supersunt reliquiae/summa cum diligentia a Ioanne Antonio Dosio stilo ferreo ut hodie cernuntur descriptae et a Io. Baptista de Cavaleris aeneis tabulis incisis repraesentatae. [Rome : s.n.], MDLXIX kal Mai [1569]. plate 8.]

40   Note that when I speak of "Romanticism," I am using the term in a sense limited to the specific context of architecture and its history. As a matter of fact, the concept itself is extremely complex, and a definition of Romanticism is extremely difficult in light of its indefinite and even (forgive the necessary paradox) consciously vague and contradictory aspects. This is so even when Romanticism is considered as the historical–cultural movement in Germany at the end of the eighteenth century which also gained strength in other countries, and lasted more or less until the first half of the following century, and not as the term is regularly used, to refer to the big spiritual category in history which alternates for some with the "Classical." It is true that a romantic "activism" also exists, especially if we consider some of the movement's philosophical presumptions, such as Fichte's philosophy and his influence on such romantics as Novalis. However, this is another problem that does not necessarily contradict the aspect which I have referenced above.

41   *Il Quattro Libri dell'Architettura Di Andrea Palladio, etc.* Venice, 1570, Book IV, Proemio a i Lettori, p. 3.

42   In order to clarify what we understand as the "deification of man," we present the words of Grita, who criticized Giuseppe Sacconi's claim that a spirit had inspired the famous monument honoring Vittorio Emanuel II in Rome: "Per ingrandire ed arricchire un monumento . . . non vi sono che due mezzi: l'esagerazione delle dimensioni e la molteplicità delle figure . . . La colossalità è un mezzo ormai troppo vecchio; rimandiamolo all'antico Egitto . . ." ["To enlarge and enrich a monument . . . there are only two means: the exaggeration of the size and the multiplicity of figures . . . the colossal is a means that is too old; let us leave it to the ancient Egyptians."] (Salvatore Grita, *Polemiche Artistiche*, Roma, 1884, p. 237).

43   Luca Pacioli, *De Divina Proportione*, Venice, 1509. Cited in Julius Schlosser-Magnino, *La letteratura artistica—Manuale delle fonti della storia dell'arte moderna*, translated by Fillipo Rossi, Firenze, n.d., but 1922, pp. 123 and following.

44   "Diceva che spettava alle spalle di dar forma alle spalliere delle sedie, ed al deretano la forma del sedere delle medesime." (Lodoli, *op. cit.*, ed. Zara, vol. I, p. 84). ["He said that it was up to the shoulders to give form to the back of the chairs and up to the behind to give form to the seat."]

45   *Lettere di XIII Huomini illustri*, Venice, 1560, p. 280. (One of the editions of the notebooks of Dionigi Atanagi.)

46   Cf.: Enrico Calandra, *Breve storia della Architettura in Sicilia*, Bari, 1938. This essay is an excellent example of historical research, of criticism and a fair assessment of contemporary Architecture.

47   Gio Paolo Lomazzo, Pittore del XVI Secolo sixteenth-century painter, *Trattato dell'Arte della Pittura Scultura e Architettura*, Roma, 1844, vol. I, p. 155.

48   Hermann Weyl, *Symmetry*, Princeton, N.J., 1952, p. 5.

49   Vitruvius, *op. cit.*, I, chapter 2.

50   Viollet-le-Duc, *Dictionnaire raisonné de l'architecture française du XIe au XVIe siècle*, B. Bance, Paris, MDCCCLXVI (1866), vol. VIII, p. 517.

51   Vignola's treatise was, for four centuries, the so-called bible for schools of Architecture. In the IX International Conference of Architects (October 1911) the following vote, authored by the architect Leonardo Paterna

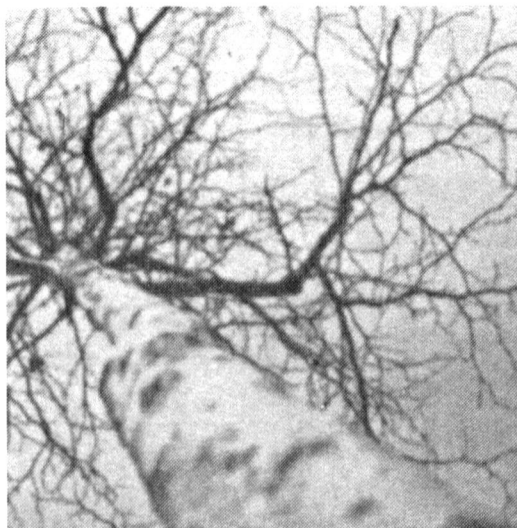

200 Tree, compare the term to that of Quatremère de Quincy: ". . . I due versi di Ovidio che esprimono la metamorfosi della casa de Filemone e Bauci sono l'epigrafe a quella teoria: Illa vetus dominis quondam casa parva duobus/Vertitur in templum, furcas subiere columnae. Ecco l'espressione incontrastabile della metamorfosi reale che ha subito l'architettura, ed ecco come gli alberi sono divenuti colonne" (*Dizionario storico di architettura etc. di Quatemère de Quincy*, tr. Antonio Mainardi etc., Mantua, 1842, vol. I, p. 50).

201 *Anémone de mer*, Jean Painlevé ©Les documents cinématographiques, Paris

202 *Panache respiratoire du ver spirographe*, c.1929, Jean Painlevé ©Les documents cinématographiques, Paris].

Baldizzi, was proposed: "Le Congrès International des Architectes à Rome en 1911, trouve insuffisant le *Traité des Cinq ordres d'Architecture* de Vignola pour server à l'enseignement de cette matière et demande que dans toutes les écoles de Dessin architectonique, on reconduise l'enseignement aux origines de l'Art, que l'on donne connaissance de tout le développement que les premiers éléments ont subi durant les diverses périodes et surtout pendant la période pré-hellénique grecque et greco-romaine pour former le gout des élèves aux plus belles proportions qui seront adoptées ensuite dans les périodes successives pour les constructions de divers styles, tout en laissant aux élèves dans les exercices graphiques la liberté de s'arrêter aux manifestations artistiques en harmonie avec l'inclination individuelle ou avec l'endroit où se trouve l'école et les diriger ainsi ver la recherche de formes nouvelles et le plus conformes au matériel de construction qui doit les revêtir d'une façon solide et convenable." ["The International Congress of Architects in Rome, 1911, found Vignola's *Treatise on the Five Orders of Architecture* insufficient to serve as the basis for the teaching of this material and demanded that in all schools of Architectural drawing the teaching be redirected to the origins of art, to give knowledge of the complete development of these first elements during the diverse pre-Hellenic and Greco-Roman period in order to cultivate the taste of the students to the most beautiful proportions which will be later adopted in subsequent periods for constructions in diverse styles, always leaving to students the freedom, in the graphic exercises, to stop at the artistic manifestations in harmony with either their individual inclinations or the geographic location of their school and to guide them towards research into new forms and those that conform best to the material of construction with which they must be clad in a solid and suitable fashion."]

52   "In modo che non humane: ma divine negli occhi nostri s'appresentano." ["In a way not human, but divine eyes present themselves to us."] (L.P., *Summa Arithmeticae*, Venice, 1494—maybe in Epistola a Guidobalo d'Urbino—Schlosser, *op. cit.*, p. 124).

53   Le Corbusier, *Modulor 2*, Paris, 1954, p. 13.

54   Guadet, *op. cit.*, Vol. I, pp. 138 and following.

55   Conrad Fiedler, *On Judging Works of Visual Art*, trans. H. Schaefer-Simmern and Fulmer Mood, Berkeley, 1949, pp. 57 and following.

56   *Quadrante* magazine, Milan, 1933, no. 5, p. 20. Issue dedicated to the conference in Athens.

57   Pier Luigi Nervi, *Costuire Corretamente: Caratteristiche e possibilità delle strutture cementizie armate*, Milano: Ulrico Hoepli, 1955, p. 1.

58   Enrico [Heinrich] Wölfflin, *L'Arte classica nel Rinascimento*, trans. Rodolfo Paoli, Firenze, 1941, p. 251.

59   Fiedler, *op. cit.*, p. 1.

60   Prelezione al Corso di Storia architettonica per gli ingegneri laureati che assolvono gli studi architettonici nell'(Imperiale) R(egia) Accademia di Belle Arti in Venezia, dated 15 gennaio 1856, in *Scritti d'Arte di Pietro Estense Selvatico*, Firenze, 1859, p. 291 and following.

61   See: George Santayana, *The Life of Reason*, New York, 1954, chap. IV, Reason in Art, pp. 301 and following.

62   Jacopo da Vignola, *Gli ordini d'architettura civile corredati delle aggiunte fattevi dagli architetti G.B. Spampani e Carlo Antononi ed ombreggiati secondo il recente metodo delle R. Academie di Belle Arti del Regno etc.*, Milano, 1832.

203 Façade of Cologne cathedral
(*Kunstgeschichte in Bildern Abt.2, Das Mittelalter*. Leipzig: Seemann, 1902, vol. II, plate 57).

204 Section of the nave of Chartres Cathedral (*ibid.*, plate 44).

63   Bruno Hessling, *Dekorative Malerei und Flachenverzierung*, G.M.B.H. Buchandlung für Architektur und Kunstgewerbe, Berlin–New York. Architecture Catalog, 1900.

64   See, for example, the observations of K. Everett Gilbert and H. Kuhn. *A History of Esthetics*, New York, 1939, p. 416, about the pedagogical function that must regulate civil taste and the inclinations, which Aristotle refers to in *Politics*. Ruskin seconds (*Stones of Venice*, II, 3 and IX, 62, note).

65   Cicero, *De Oratore*, trans. H. Bornecque and E. Courband, Paris, 1956, Book III, LI. 197, pp. 81 and following.

66   Urbano Vitry, *Il proprietario architetto contenente modelli di abitazioni, etc.* Venice, 1832, pp. V, 22 and following.

67   Un jour, Napoléon III dit: "Ça ne peut plus durer, c'est trop dangereux, nettoyez-moi cela, sectionnez-moi ce maquis inaccessible, ouvrez des trajectoires aux boulets de mes canons; on verra bien si la révolte pourra surgir encore." Ce fut Haussmann. Les boulets de canon instauraient une nouvelle vitesse dans la vie des villes. Soixante-dix années plus tarde—aujourd'hui—l'âge de l'automobile se doit d'élever un monument de connaissance à Napoléon—Haussmann." [One day, Napoleon III said: "This cannot go on, it's too dangerous, clean this up for me, cut this inaccessible morass, open up trajectories for my bullets and cannons; we will see if this revolt can still survive." It was Haussmann. Bullets and cannon established a new speed in the life of cities. Seventy years later—today—the age of the automobile should raise a monument to the wisdom of Napoleon and Haussmann.] In Le Corbusier, "Mort de la Rue," *Plans*, no. 5, May 1931, Paris; notebook page following p. 48.

68   Problem treated by Moholy-Nagy (L.M.N., *Vision in Motion*, Chicago, 1947, p. 29) in reference to the aesthetic interferences of the dictator–amateur artist. Exhaustively developed in A. Philip McMahon, *Preface to an American Philosophy of Art*, Chicago, 1945, all of chap. V—"The Absolute Artist of Romantic Idealism." With respect to Italian law, see: Giuseppe Bottai, *La legge per le arti*, in the review *Stile*, Milan, July–August, 1942, pp. 1 and following.

69   Blondel, *op. cit.*, intro.

70   The Charter of Athens-CIAM (Congrès internationale d'architecture moderne). Center of Folkloric studies of Grémio of the Faculty of Architecture and Urbanism, São Paulo, 1950, n. 5. Unique and well translated into Portuguese, mimeograph.

71   *Memoratório de Mercede Comacinorum* (encoded manuscript, monastery at Cava dei Tirreni, Italy) was remembered for the first time by Pietro Giannone in *Storia Civile del Regno di Napoli*, and reviewed in Giuseppe Merzario, *Il Maestri Comacini-Storia artistica di Mille duecento anni (600–1800)*, Milan,1893, vol. I, pp. 39 and following.

72   Cf.: Antonello Gerbi, *La politica del Romanticismo*, Bari, 1932. Above all in what concerns the Romanticist inspiration to historicism, as illustrated especially by figures such as the young Goethe, Herder, Justus Möser, etc.

73   Here is a document that demonstrates the Romanticists' most declared reverence to the "Ancient" *sub specie architecturae*, justly defined as a problem by Hopkins, in order to explain the "adventitious beauty" that Emerson discovered in his pilgrimage to the old Europe. (Vivian C. Hopkins, *Spires of Form, a Study of Emerson's Aesthetic Theory*, Cambridge, 1951, pp. 82 and following; note no. 24, p. 239).

205 Façade of the studio-house of the sculptor Ettore Ximenes, Rome, c. 1900; Leonardo Paterna Baldizzi, architect (*L.P.B., Non Omnis Moriar*, Roma, 1943, fig. 75).

206 Church of the Sagrada Familia, Barcelona; Antonia Gaudi, Architect.

The Academy of the Villa Medici, the first school established in Rome for the study of the classical canon, founded the "Prix de Rome," the usefulness of which is much discussed. Here is the answer of Emile Galle Maurice Le Blond, author of an inquiry into the said Award: "L'artiste a besoin que le spectacle changeante de la vie et les chaleureux contacts de la nature viennent ébranler ses facultés d'émotion esthétique, afin qu'il éprouve l'irrésistible désir de communiquer a d'autres hommes, par ses ouvres, son admiration et son poignant émoi. Si utile, si instructive que soit, pour l'éducation de l'artiste, la connaissance des chefs-d'oeuvre de ses devanciers, elle ne saurait point, sans danger, anéantir la personnalité de l'artiste et son génie, se substituer a cette école, a cette galerie de chefs-d'oeuvre qui s'appelle la vie" (Emile Galle, *Ecrits pour l'Art*, Paris, 1908, p. 282).

74   Ralph Waldo Emerson, *Journal*, 1840.

75   Emerson, *Problem of the creative artist*. Manuscript cited by Hopkins, *op. cit.*, p. 87.

76   Cf.: Edward Garbett, *Rudimentary Treatise on the Principles of Design in Architecture*, (*Ibidem*, p. 91).

77   Cf.: Horacio Greenough, who defines the function of Architecture in this manner: "The external expression of the inward function of the building–adaptation of its features and their gradation to its dignity and importance." Emerson presented the idea of G. in this manner: "A scientific arrangement of spaces and forms to functions and to site; an emphasis of feature proportioned to their *graduated* importance in function; color and ornament to be decided and arranged and varied by strictly organic laws, having a distinct reason for each decision; the entire and immediate banishment of all make-shift and make-believe." (*Ibidem*, p. 90).

78   Cf.: *Ibidem*, p. 91.

79   "Oui, messieurs, donnez-moi la carte d'un pays, sa configuration, son climat, ses eaux, ses vents et toute sa géographie physique; donnez-moi ses production naturelles, sa flore, sa zoologie, etc. et je me charge de vous dire a priori quel sera l'homme de ce pays et quel rôle ce pays jouera dans l'histoire, non pas accidentellement, mais nécessairement, non pas à telle époque, mais dans toutes, enfin l'idée qu'il est appelé à représenter." ["Yes, gentlemen, give me the map of a country, its configuration, its climate, its waters, winds and all its physical geography; give me its natural products, its flora and fauna, etc. and I will tell you a priori what the man in this country will be and what role this country will play in history, not accidentally, but necessarily, not only in a given time, but for all time, finally, the idea that he is called upon to represent."] (Victor Cousin, "Introduction à l'Histoire de la philosophie," in *Oeuvres complètes*, Paris, 1840, vol. I, p. 63).

Chapter 2

80   "I. Ciclo—Semiarti—Giardinaggio—Mimica, Danza, Pantomimica—Ornamentistica. II. Ciclo—Arti compiute—Architettura—Scultura, Pittura, Poesia-Musica. III. Ciclo—Arti evanescenti—Declamatoria—Oratoria—Dialética." Antonio Tari, *Del Sistema delle Arti*, Naples, 1864; reprinted in *Saggi di Estetica e Metafisica*, ed. Benedetto Croce, Bari, 1911, p. 35.

81   The need for a "flexibility" that is especially particular to contemporary architecture is opposed to a solely formal and abstract criterion that we could identify with "metric rule." This is similar, to a certain extent, to the dialectic posed by Aristotle, in *Nichomachean Ethics*, between "equity" and "legal" Justice. Only by identifying the former as a "lesbian rule," possessed of the quality of adaptation and plasticity to the anfractuosities of rocks used in constructions, can human needs be better met.

82   "Ce que je rapporte pour confirmer ce que j'ay dit tant de fois, que le Génie feul ne suffit pas pour faire un Architecte, & qu'il faut que par l'étude, l'application, le long usage & l'expérience, il s'acquière une connaissance parfaite des règles de son Art & des proportions, & qu'il ait la science d'en faire le discernement & le choi afin de s'en pouvoir servir à propos & les mettre utilement en pratique en toutes fortes d'occasions". ["This is what I maintain and what I have said many times, that Genius is not enough to create an Architect, and what is required is study, practice, experience, such

207 A building imitating a medieval castle, between Park Avenue and 34th Street in New York, c. 1898 (Photo A. Wittemann).

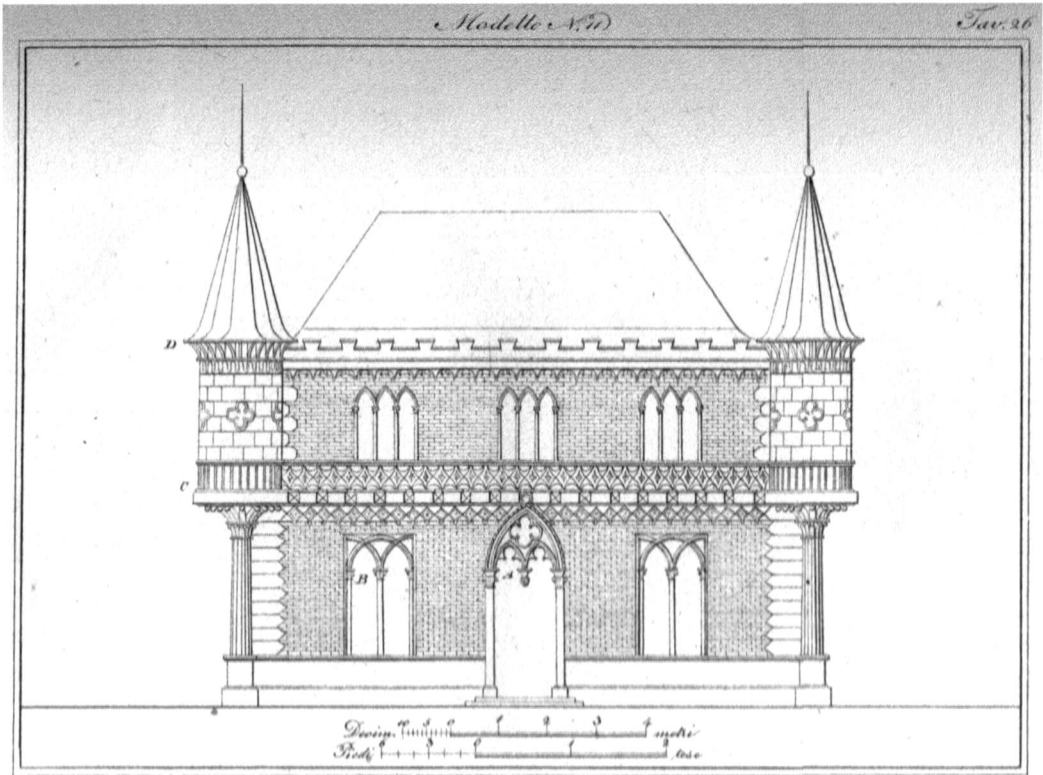

208 Façade of a "Gothic" house (Vitry, Urbain. *Il Proprietario Architetto, contenente modelli di abitazioni di città e di campagna, di poderi, conservatoi per agrumi, porte, pozzi, fontane, etc . . . opera utile agli architetti, ingegneri, imprenditori . . ./disegnata e composta da Urbano Vitry.* Venezia: G. Antonelli, 1832.], *cit.*, plate XXVI).

Balmoral Castle III, Ballater, Fifeshire; William Smith of Aberdeen, architect, constructed in collaboration with Queen Victoria and Prince Albert (1853–55), exercised a certain influence in America. Even today, for example, vestiges of its influence are to be seen in New York.

that he will master the rules of his art and of proportion and have the scientific discernment to use them and to put them to good use on all sorts of occasions."] Blondel, *op. cit.*, Book V., chap. XX, p. 787.

83   *Bâtir, Bulletin mensuel de la Masse de l'Ecole spéciale d'Architecture*, Paris, 1932, no. 1.

84   When the first two volumes of the *History of Italian Architecture* appeared in Adolfo Venturi's masterpiece *Storia dell'Arte Italiana* (Milano, [U. Hoepli], 1901–1940), the "tecnicos" [engineers] soon reacted against the way in which the history of architecture had been reduced to a pure architectonic–literary aesthetic. Giovannoni was the main opponent, creating a movement that, following the Morellian method in painting (Giovanni Morelli, *Della Pittura Italiana*, Milano, 1897), made an appeal to [formal] analysis and to the use of more detailed sources through a comparative examination of the forms, as a way to access the "evolutionary laws (of the mind and hand of artifice) of which the forms are just the means, the alphabet of architecture," such that it would be made visible to engineers. "La scissione dell'architettura—says Stefano Bottari (S.B., *La critica figurativa e l'estetica moderna*, Bari, 1935, p. 77)—dal gruppo di quelle arti che si dicono 'figurative' si è sempre più venuta accentuando al punto da sembrare acquisito che di essa non possano parlare che i tecnici." ["The split of architecture from the group of so-called 'figurative' arts seems to emphasize, almost to the point of admission, the fact that it cannot speak to engineers."]

85   Concerning one of Bramante's works that was restored by Baldassare Peruzzi, Serlio observes "che l'Architetto esser dovrebbe piuttosto timido che animoso; e cosi fare le sue cose consideratamente, e con consigli etiam de' minore di se, da' quali spesse fiate s'impara; ma se sarà troppo animoso, e si confidi troppo nel suo sapere, spesse volte perirà; cioè che le sue cose gli riusciran male." ["the architect ought to be timid rather than courageous, and make his work with care, even the small work, but if he is courageous and over-confident in his wisdom, then his work will succeed badly."] Cited in: *Investigazioni preliminari per la scienza dell'architettura civile di Nicola d'Apuzzo architetto*, Napoli, 1844, p. 119.

86   ". . . del resto nella 'Universitas litterarum' non è mai possibile divider nettamente I bisogni dei giovani che cominciano da quelli degli studiosi 'maturi'. Dobbiamo infatti tutti ricominciare ogni giorno ad imparare di nuovo *ex fundamentis*". [. . .in the rest of the 'Universitas litterarum' it is no longer possible to clearly divide the needs of the young people from those of the 'mature' students. Thus we have to start to learn again the *ex fundamentis*."] (K. Lehmann-Hartleben in the archaeological commentary *Lettere Scelte di Plinio il Giovane*, Firenze, 1936, p. vii.)

87   Miloutine Borissavliévitch, *Les Théories de l'Architecture*, Paris, 1952 (in Bibl: Eduard von Hartmann, *Philosophie des Schoenen*, Berlin, 1887; Friedrich Ostendorf, *Sechs Buecher vom Bauen*, Berlin, W. Ernst u. Sohn, 1914; August Schmarsow, *Grundbegriffe der Kunstwissenschaften*, Leipzig and Berlin, 1905. All are mentioned in the chapter 'Introduction', page 1 and following pages). The author sustains a positivistic theory, optical–physiological, elucidated in his *Traité d'Esthétique Scientifique de l'Architecture*, Paris, 1954. These volumes provide a good orientation to the subject indicated.

88   Wotton translated the "triad" in the following manner: "Commoditie, Firmness, and Delight." (*The Elements of Architecture collected by Henry Wotton from the Best Authors and Examples*, London, 1803, p. 1. Reproduction of the book published in London, 1624).

209 View of the area of the Île de France, Paris (*Wasmuths Lexikon der Baukunst*, vol. 4, Berlin: E. Wasmuth, a.g. [c.1929– c.1937], facing p. 32).

210 Place de l'Etoile, Paris, the plan of which was the consequence of a monument, the Arc de Triomphe, 1806.

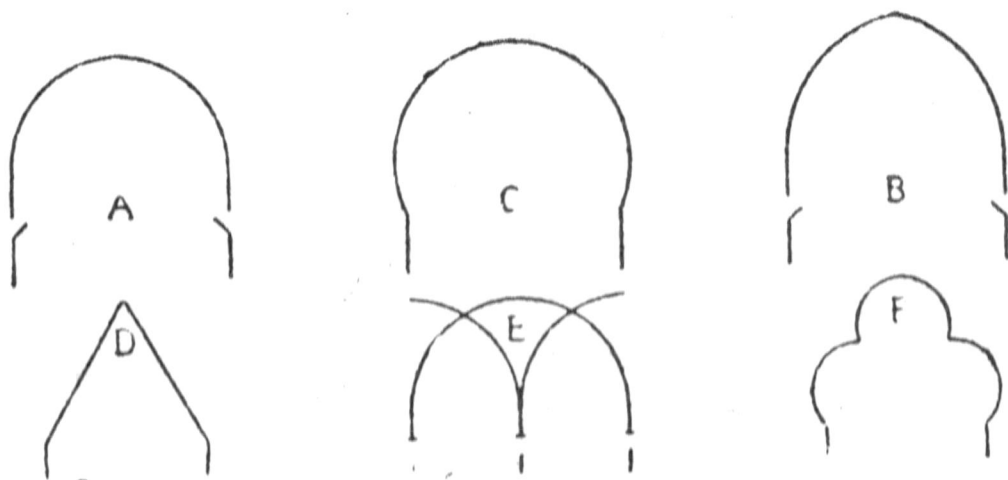

211 Examples of vaults used in the twelfth century (Auguste Choisy, *Histoire de l'architecture*, Paris: Rouveyre, 1903, p. 165, top).

89   Pietro Valente, *Dell'Essenza e Dignità dell'architettura, e de Doveri dell'Architetto, Discorso etc. . . .* Napoli, 1836, pp. 11 and following.

90   Henri Focillon, *Vie des Formes, suivi de Éloge de la main*, Paris, 1955, p. 36. The essay is from 1934.

91   Scott, *op. cit.*, p. 168.

92   Bruno Zevi, *Saper vedere l'Architettura*, Torino, 1948, p. 148.

93   "L'architettura è 1. Come la base e la regolatrice di tutte le alter arti. 2. Ella forma il legame della società civile. 3. Produce e aumenta il commercio. 4. Impiega le pubbliche e private ricchezze in beneficio e decoro dello Stato, de proprietari e de posteri. 5. Difende la vita, i beni, la libertà de cittadini." ["Architecture is 1. The base and the regulator of all other arts. 2. It forms the links of civil society. 3. Produces and augments commerce. 4. Employs public and private riches in the profit and decoration of the State, proprietors and the future. 5. Defends life, the goods, the freedom of citizens."] (Milizia, *op. cit.*, p. 2).

94   Pier Luigi Nervi, *op. cit.*, p. 1.

95   "On peut y joindre cet art né de la nécessité, et perfectionné par le luxe, l'Architecture, qui s'étant élevé par degrés des chaumières aux palais, n'est aux yeux du Philosophe, si l'on peut parler ainsi, que la masque embelli d'un de nos plus grandes besoins." [Jean Le Rond d'Alembert] (*Discours Préliminaire de l'Encyclopédie*, cited by Algarotti, *op. cit.*, p. 32.). ["We could add that this art, Architecture, born of necessity and perfected by luxury, which has lifted itself, by degrees, from thatched cottages to palaces, is nothing more to Philosophers, if we can speak of it this way, than the embellished mask of one of our greatest needs."]

96   In his treatise, Vitruvius writes that the architect must be a man of letters, good at drawing, learned in geometry, a connoisseur of optics and history, versed in the science of numbers and should also have learned philosophy, know music, be aware of medicine, be knowledgeable of law and, finally, comprehend the movement of the heavenly bodies. (Vitruvius, *op. cit.*, Book I, p. 75).

97   F.L. Wright, *The Future of Architecture*, London, 1955, p. 92.

98   *Ibidem*, pp. 180 and following.

99   Giovannoni, Gustavo, *Corso di architettura*, Roma, 1932, vol. 2.

100 Hamlin, *op. cit.* p. xi.

101 The controversy surrounding "monumentalism" probably first emerged in Italy because of Mário Morasso (*L'imperialismo artistico*, Torino, 1903), who saw monuments as "colossi di pietra" ["stone giants"] overcome by time, invoking for the "arti che oltre al rappresentare edificano e costruiscono in realtà come la natura" ["arts to be edified and built into reality as nature"] and said: "la macchina è il solo e vero monumento moderno, che nulla ha che vedere con tutti quelli passati, e in cui persino la materia è nuova; non più la pietra ma il ferro" ["the machine is the only true modern monument, which has nothing to do with all those past, and where even the materials are new, no longer stone, but iron"] (p. 204). Moraso saw, in the obstinacy of keeping architecture in its courtly phase, his own decadence: "l'arte grandiose e costosa, quella che presuppone una più intensa idealità a cui servire ed una quantità più ingente di energie cui valersi fu appunto quella che nel presente regime democratico utilitario decadde . . ." [The most magnificent and expensive art, one that requires a more intense idealism and a great deal more energy relies precisely on those things that we must decline in the present utilitarian democratic regime . . ."] (p. 211).

212 Room with retractable beds and tables; Luckhardt brothers, architects (Diotallevi and Marescotti, *Ordine e Destino della Casa Popolare Milano*, 1941, p. 25. This book has the following inscription in the frontispiece. "Le fabbriche dei poveri siano per la loro facoltà a quelle dei ricchi simili.— Leon Battista Alberti").

213 Utilization of space in a kitchen (Bruno Taut, *Ein Wohnhaus, cit.*, p. 56).

102   In another one of his books, Hamlin writes of this Capitol, whose plan is
       reproduced: "a plan of superb and logical formality, where every element
       in the arrangement is designed for a specific purpose and in close accordance
       with the structural system. In this building the integration of use,
       construction, and effect is well-nigh perfect." (Talbot Hamlin, *Architecture:
       An Art for all Men,* New York, 1947, p. 51.) The image of the plan has been
       reproduced from T.H. *op. cit.*, vol. I, n. 10, p. 15.

103   "Parmi les dépendances des chambres, il faut classer encore le cabinet
       d'aisances. Cela vous parait indispensable, et vous avez raison. Et cependant,
       pendant bien longtemps on s'en est passé, et maintenant encore, en France
       même, vous rencontrerez des répugnances routinières à tolérer dans la
       maison cet accessoire indispensable." ["Amongst the dependencies of the
       rooms, we must include the sanitary facility. This would seem indispensable,
       and with good reason. However long ago this was, we continue, even in
       France, to routinely encounter repugnance to having this essential accessory
       in the house."] Guadet, *op. cit.*, vol. II, p. 61.

104   Hamlin, *op. cit.*, vol. I, p. 68.

105   "On sépare trop souvent l'étude de la construction et celle de la décoration,
       et dans notre société moderne où les spécialisations tiennent tant de place,
       on a créé deux nouveautés: l'art dit décoratif, et la profession de décorateurs
       . . . Construction, décoration, tout cela c'est une seule chose, c'est l'archi-
       tecture." ["Too often, we separate the study of construction from the study
       of decoration, and in our modern society where specializations dominate,
       we have created two novelties: so-called decorative art, and the profession
       of decorator . . . Construction, decoration, it is all one thing, it is archi-
       tecture."] Guadet, *op. cit.*, vol. I, p. 556.

106   Università degli Studi di Roma, Facoltà di Architettura, Ordine degli
       Studi 1956–57. [University of Rome, Faculty of Architecture, Order of
       Studies, 1956–57.] Roma, 1956.

107   Francesco Milizia, *Memorie degli Architetti antichi e moderni,* Bassano, 1795,
       p. xv.

108   Armando Melis, *Degli edifici-distribuzione proporziona mento organizzazione
       degli edifici tipici-schemi funzionali*, Torino, 1947.

109   Ernst Neufert, *Encyclopedia pratica per progettare e costruire etc.*, first Italian
       edition edited by Luigi Lenzi, Milano, 1949. First German edition under
       the care of the Germanic Committee for Unification, Berlin, 1936.

110   *Manuale dell'architetto compilato a cura del consiglio nazionale delle Ricerche,
       pubblicato dall'ufficio informazioni Stati Uniti in Roma*, 1946. This manual
       was organized by Bruno Zevi.

111   According to Louis Hautecoeur (*L'architecture française.* Paris, 1950, p. 184),
       the divorce between the architect—the Vitruvian—and the engineer of the
       ingenium, of the bellicose machine, professions that were often exercised by
       a single person, dates back to the creation of the corps of military and
       bridge engineers by Louis XIV. The profession of the architect became
       linked with decorative work; despite the settlements reached in various
       European states, resentments still exist, thus necessitating clarification. In
       the nineteenth century, with the growing autonomy and clearer definition
       of the engineering profession, those who called for the creation of schools
       of architecture made a mistake when establishing its objectives. Tullo
       Massarani asked the Italian Senate for the establishment of schools of
       architecture, distinguishing between science and art, and claiming "artistic
       rights" so that the architect–artist imprinted on his works "quel suggello

214 Expandable ladder system used in Rome for putting ornaments in buildings. (*Castelli e Ponti di Maestro Niccola Zabaglia etc. e con la descrizione del trasporto dell'obelisco vaticano etc., del Cavaliere Domenico Fontana*, Roma, MDCCXLIII (1743), plate IX).

Hoisting the Ribs for the Transept Roof.

215 Mounting a metallic part of the dome of the Crystal Palace (Berlyn, *The Crystal Palace, Op. cit.*, facing p. 75).

di eleganza, di vetustà, di maestosa e virile grandezza che fa ammirati ed ammirandi gli edifice dei tempo migliori." ["that imprint of elegance, of antiquity, of regal and virile greatness that makes us admire those buildings from better times and makes them admirable."] (*Delle Scuole d'Architettura, parole dette in Senato da T.M.*, Roma, 1890, p. 14). Even with the controversy raised by Viollet-le-Duc and the rest—including Nervi—who, in the course of a century, have become interested in the problem, the distinction between civil engineering and architecture remains senseless.

112   Nervi, *op. cit.*, p. 6.

113   Viollet-le-Duc, *Dictionnaire, Op. cit.*, vol. I, p. 116.

114   Walter Gropius, *Scope of Total Architecture*, New York, 1943, pp. 45 and following.

115   For example: "Un monument à la gloire de l'Independence d'un grand pays" ["A monument to the glory of the independence of a great country"], theme of the 1911 Rome Grand Prix. The young contenders were asked to monumentalize the glory of independence in an imaginary country that, although "great," could be found in any continent; if this country was hypothetically European, it could commemorate its independence as if it had been achieved through the "Magna Carta," or the seizure of Rome of 1870, facts that are disconnected from language, spirit or history. The program recommended the following architectural–decorative criteria: "Groupes allégoriques, bas reliefs, inscriptions relatant les principaux épisodes ayant précède ou suivi la déclaration de l'Independence" ["Allegorical figures, bas reliefs, inscriptions relating to the episodes that preceded or followed the declaration of independence"], besides fountains, water effects, etc. The winner, René Milard, was awarded the prize—mostly by virtue of his creativity—for creating statues of non-existent "grandes hommes." What is incredible is that the plan was included in a book titled, *Philosophie de la composition architecturale* by Albert Ferran, Prix de Rome, Paris, 1955, pp. 60 and following.

116   "If the emphasis today is on the plain human being, not on the Caesars, we have to study man's basic biology, his way of seeing, his perception of distance, in order to grasp what scale will fit him. Buildings should serve his physical and emotional needs, not dictate to him. Their design should avoid all arbitrary physical and psychological barriers. Buildings ought to be means to an end, not ends in themselves; then their scale will be human. This does not limit the greatness of conception nor the dignity of expression; it seeks merely to define the mental tools of the designer. When we perceive space, the size of our body—of which we are permanently conscious— serves as our yardstick or module; that is, our search for the human scale is a search for a finite framework of relationships within infinite space." (Walter Gropius, "In search of a common denominator", in *Building for Modern Man—A symposium*, edited by Thomas H. Creighton, Princeton University Press, 1949, p. 171).

117   During the Congress for Civil Reconstruction in Italy, the group from the Movimento Studi Architettura, of which I was a founding participant, proposed that a housewife and an inhabitant of the neighborhood that was to be planned be included in the "Urbanistic Councils," so that we could combine the architects' theoretical knowledge with the knowledge of everyday problems that Architecture was meant to solve. (*Rassegna del 1° Convegno nazionale per la ricostruzione edilizia.* Milano, December 14–16, 1945).

118   Wright, *op. cit.*, pp. 87 and 89.

216 Design of a church, according to a scheme with the symmetrical elements of the "classical baroque," after the common Neo-Classicism. Original drawing, nineteenth century (author's collection).

217 Church of Santa Teresa, Montmagny, Seine-et-Oise, 1925; August Perret, architect Jamot, Paul, [August Perret, and Gustave Perret.] *A. G. Perret et l'Architecture du Béton Armé.* [Paris & Bruxelles: G. Vanoest,] 1927, facing p. 50, [plate XXVII.]

119   Pier Luigi Nervi, *Scienza o Arte del costruire?* Roma, 1945, p. 31.

120   *Ibidem*, p. 72.

121   Frank Lloyd Wright, *Genius and the Mobocracy*, New York, 1949, p. 3.

122   Giovanni Salutati, *Epistolario a cura di Francesco Novati*, Roma, 1905, vol. IV, p. 322.

123   Incorrect spelling: Jean-Laurent Le Geay, French architect who was influenced by Piranesi.

124   Charles Dewailly, eighteenth-century French architect.

125   *Notice sur la vie et les travaux de Charles Dewailly, in Memoire de l'Institut National*, III, Histoire, p. 39.

126   See transcript and commentary of G. Nicco Fasola in *Piero della Francesca, De prospectiva pingendi, in Raccolta di fonti per la storia dell'arte*, Firenze, 1942.

127   Le Corbusier, *Quand les Cathédrales étaient blanches*, Paris, 1937, p. 171.

128   Focillon, *op. cit.*, p. 121.

129   Cited in Helmut Gernskeim, *Focus on Architecture and Sculpture, etc.*, Preface by Nicholas Pevsner, London, 1949, p. 21.

130   Walter Gropius, "O arquiteto na sociedad industrial, conferencia proferida em São Paulo," ["The architect within our industrial society, conference held in São Paulo"] in *Habitat*, no.14 [January–February 1954], São Paulo, p. 25. [Translation in Walter Gropius, *Scope of Total Architecture*, Collier Books, New York, 1962, pp. 71–82. Originally published in, "Gropius Appraises Today's Architect," *Architectural Forum*, New York, May 1952.]

131   C. Matlack Price, *The Practical Book of Architecture*, Philadelphia and London, 1916, p. 244.

132   Frank Lloyd Wright, *The Future of Architecture*, p. 218.

133   Pier Luigi Nervi, *Scienza o Arte del construire*? p. 57.

134   Alberti, *op. cit.*, Book I, chap. IX, pp. 20–21.

135   After reading Lessing, some doubts surround what can be defined as the "region of contradictions" ("Io non ardisco né affermare né negare . . .") ["I dare not confirm or deny . . ."] (G.E. Lessing, *Del Laocoonte o sia dei limiti della Pittura e della Poesia, Discorso di . . .*, recato dal tedesco in italiano dal cavaliere C.G. Londonio [translated from the German to Italian by Sir C.G. Londonio], Milano, 1833, p. 39). In conversation with Goethe, Eckermann also highlights this principle: "In Lessing . . . questo è notevole: che nei suoi scritti teoretici . . . egli non esprime mai direttamente la conclusione, ma ci porta sempre attraverso la via filosofica della opinione, della opposizione, e del dubbio, prima di lasciarci pervenire ad una materia di certezza . . . Lessing medesimo deve aver detto una volta ache, se Dio gli avesse volute dare la verità, egli avrebbe rifiutato questo dono, e preferita assai più la fatica di cercarla de se stesso" ["In Lessing . . . this is remarkable: that in his theoretical writings . . . he never directly expresses the conclusion, but always leads the way through the philosophical views of opposition and doubt, before arriving at a matter with certainty . . . Lessing must have once said that if God had wanted to give him the truth, he would refuse this gift, and much preferred the trouble of looking for it himself"]. (G.P. Eckermann, *Colloqui col Goethe*, translated by E. Donadoni, Bari, 1912, vol. I, p. 247).

136   Crowe e Cavalcaselle, *Raffaello*, Firenze, 1890, vol. II, pp. 229 and following.

137   The clear sentience of this distinction is one of the essential characteristics of Goethe's rich and prolific personality, something made obvious by his

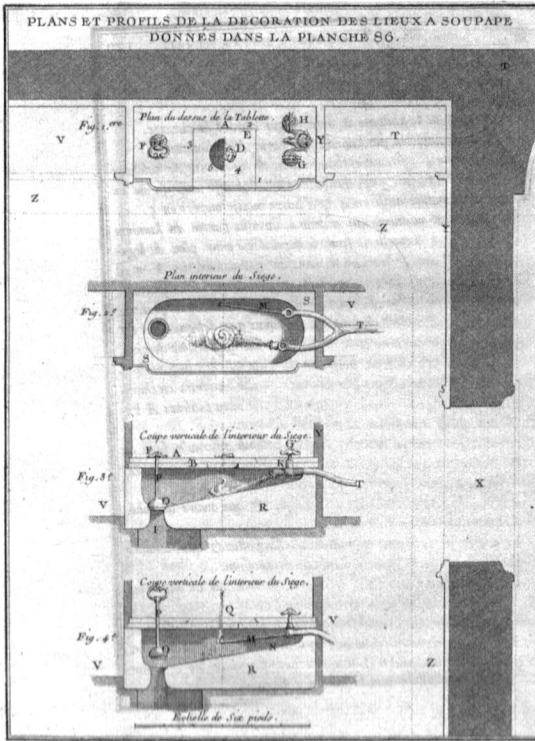

PLANS ET PROFILS DE LA DECORATION DES LIEUX A SOUPAPE DONNES DANS LA PLANCHE 86.

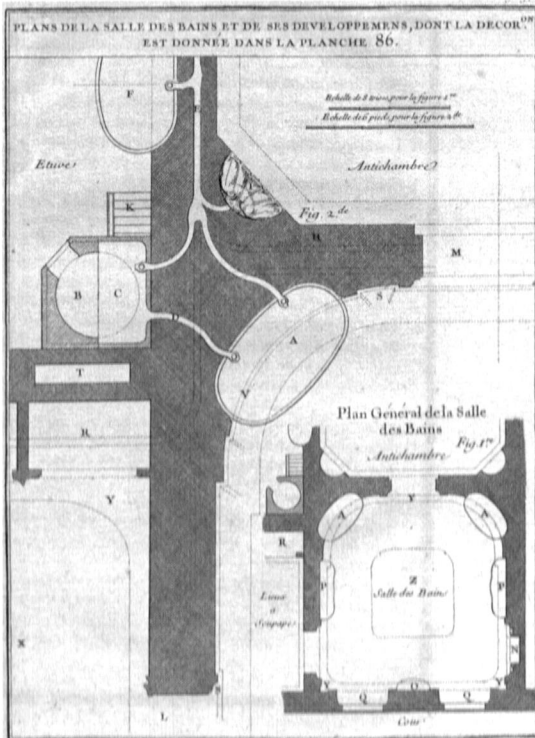

PLANS DE LA SALLE DES BAINS ET DE SES DEVELOPPEMENS, DONT LA DECOR.ON EST DONNEE DANS LA PLANCHE 86.

Construction detail, almost never taken into account until the seventeenth century (given the level achieved by the artisan, the most able assistant of the architect) begins to be considered in the eighteenth century, with the dawn of industrialization, and develops through the nineteenth century, until we reach modern "Industrial Design," an exclusive sphere of the architect and of experts in industrial design.

218 System for a "WC" proposed by Jacques François Blondel (Jacques François Blondel, *De la distribution des maisons de plaisance, et de la decoration des edifices en general*, Paris: Charles-Antoine Jombert, 1737–38, after p. 134, plate 86 n.3).

219 bathroom (*ibid.*, plate 86 n.2).

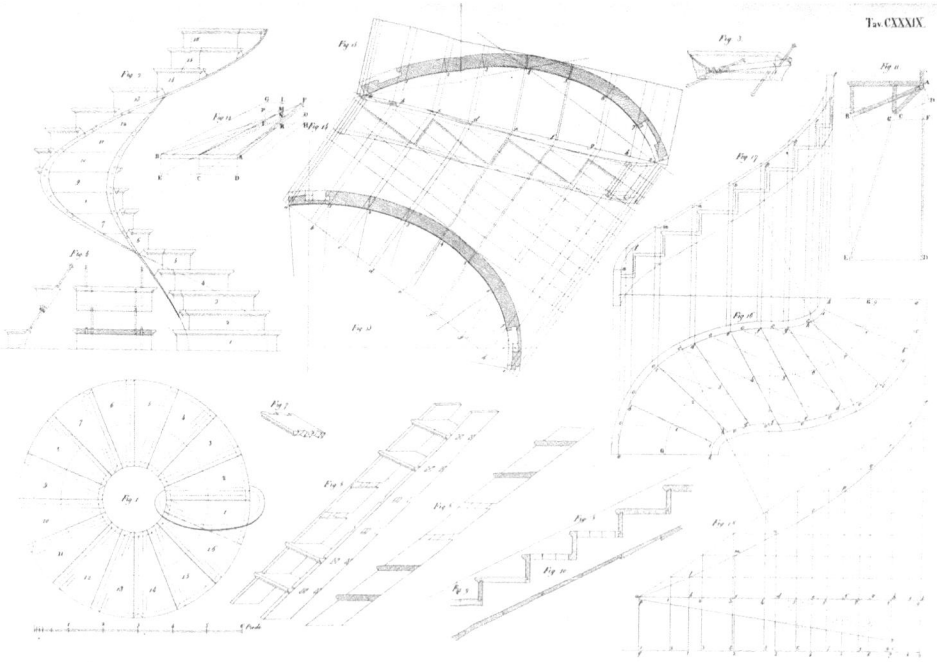

220 Stairs in the Treatise of Rondelet (*Trattato teorico pratico dell'arte di edificare di Giovanni Rondelet*, trans. Basilio Soresina, Mantua, MDCCCXXXIV (1834), vol. VII, plate CXXXIX, fig. 2). [Courtesy of Environmental Design Library Rare Books Collection, University of California, Berkeley.

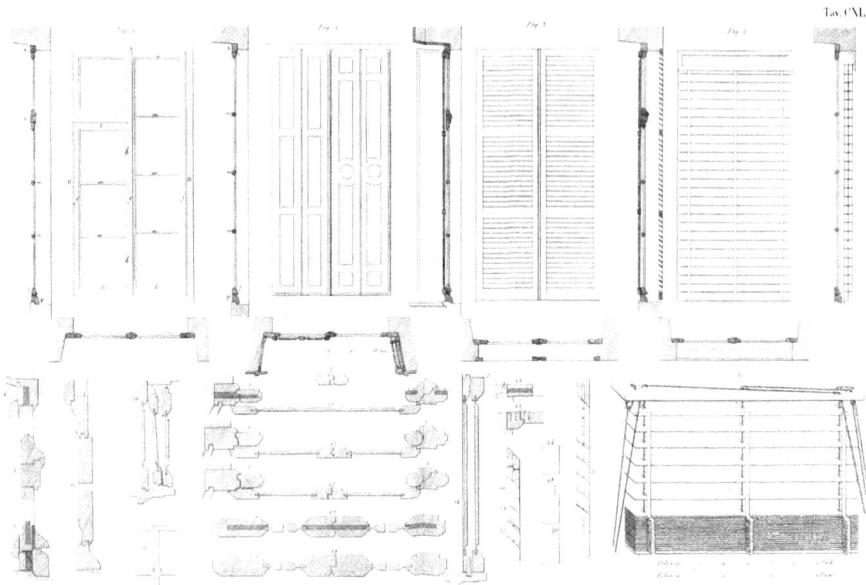

221 Persianas (*ibid.*, plate CXL). [Courtesy of Environmental Design Library Rare Books Collection, University of California, Berkeley.]

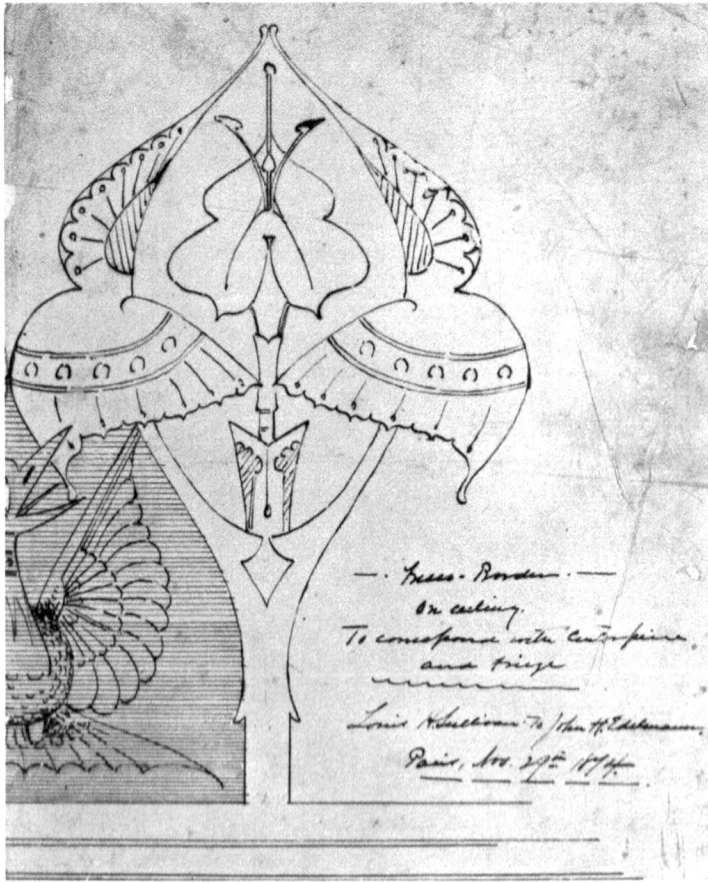

222 Louis H. Sullivan, drawing, Paris, 1871 [*sic*] [Wright, Frank Lloyd. *Genius and the Mobocracy.* New York: Duell, Sloan and Pearce, 1949, plate 1.]

223 L.H. Sullivan, detail of a door (Luigi Pellegrini, "Storicita di L. H. S.", *L'Architettura*, 1956, no. 6).

concept of "Weltliteratur." This concept is concerned with the manner in which the comprehension of national peculiarities may establish, with reciprocal understanding, a concrete unit, something that would disappear if there was a vague and indistinct leveling. Cf. concerning this: Fritz Strich, *Goethe und die Weltliteratur*, Berne, [Switzerland] 1946.

138   "Leslie Martin, who was one of the speakers at the Gold Company medal Ceremony in London last April, made one remark which pleased me very much. He said, 'I do not believe it is important to Walter Gropius that he should have established a style. It is the method on which he lays the stress and that method is being continued by his students—who are now teachers, architects, furniture designers, weavers and typographers all over the world. It is, therefore, very difficult to pin down the influence of Walter Gropius by looking at a few buildings and pointing out derivative examples. His influence is far more subtle. It is an influence of an infiltrating and multiplying kind and it is not surprising to me that that influence has spread throughout the world.' This is exactly what I meant to do, and I would find it tragic if the younger generation, in their impatience for recipes, tried to hamstring the tremendous potential of the modern medium by prematurely forcing it into fixed channels. I regret to say that not all of the "four masters" have always refrained from helping to dig such channels. In the Preface to my book, 'Scope of Total Architecture,' you find this sentence, 'In the course of my life I became more and more convinced that the usual practice of architects to relieve the dominating, disjointed pattern here and there by a beautiful building is most inadequate and that we must find, instead, a new set of values, based on such constituent factors as would produce an integrated expression of the thought and feeling of our time.' I have spent a lifetime in this search." (Letter from Gropius to E.N. Rogers in *Casabella* magazine, Milan, n. 213, in reference to p. 1) [1954].

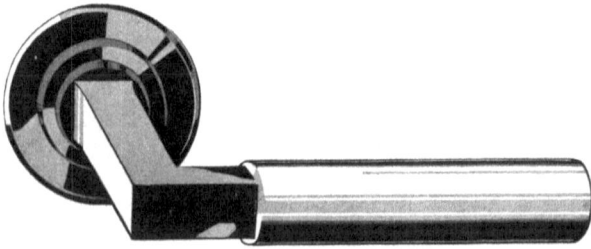

224 Door handle, nickel, 1922 (Sigfried Giedion, *Walter Gropius, work and teamwork*, New York: Reinhold Publishing. Corp., 1954. p. 103, fig. 41).

225 Heater, 1931 (*ibid.*, p.106, fig. 49).

By Walter Gropius, a plan of a metropolitan center, a drawing of a door handle, and a heater designed using the same "method."

226 Plan of the center of Boston, project of "Boston Center Architects," [sic] 1953 (*ibid.*, p.230, fig. 314).

227 "Labyrinthe" of the Cathedral of Reims (twelfth century), with the architect builders; the chief is at the center, amongst the masons, who take in their hands, the attributes of Architecture; drawing by Jacques Cellier, sixteenth century, Bibliothèque National de Paris. The inscription at the bottom of the drawing says: "C'est le dedalus qui est dedans la nef et les personnages qui sont dedans représentent les architectes qui ont conduit l'oeuvre de l'Eglise" [In the nave is Dedalus, and the characters within represent the architects who have guided the work of the Church]. (M.L. Wyffels-Simoens, "Note sur le labyrinthe de la Cathédrale de Reims," *Gazette des Beaux-Arts*,
Paris, Series 6, no. 49, May–June 1957, p. 339). [Robert Branner, "The Labyrinth of Reims Cathedral," Journal of the Society of Architectural Historians, Vol. 21, No. 1 (Mar., 1962), University of California Press on behalf of the Society of Architectural Historians, p. 18.]

WORKS CITED
BY LINA BO BARDI

Preface

Alberti, Leon Battista, *Della Architettura Libri Dieci*, trad. Italiana di Cosimo Bartoli, Milan, 1833 or *De re aedificatoria* c. 1450.

Collingwood, Robin George, *Autobiographia*, trad. Italiana Giampaolo Venezia, 1955.

Ricci, G.P., *Antonio Jannuzzi, Irmão e Cia. na Exposição Nacional*, Rio de Janeiro, 1958.

Scott, Geoffrey, *Architecture of Humanism: A Study in the History of Taste*, New York, 1954.

Chapter 1 Problems of the theory of architecture

Regarding a few treatises

Guadet, Julien, *Eléments et Théorie de l'Architecture, Cours professé à l'École Nationale et Spéciale des Beaux-Arts*, 5th edn, vol. 4, Paris, 1909.

Hamlin, Talbot, *Forms and Functions of Twentieth-Century Architecture*, New York, 1952.

Lurçat, Andre, *Forms, compositions et lois d'harmonie-elements d'une science de l'esthetique architectural*, vol. 3, Paris, 1953.

Memmo, Andrea, *Elementi dell'architettura Lodoliana ossia L'arte del Fabbricare con solidità scientifica e con eleganza non capricciosa, Libre Due, etc. . . . dall'autore Andrea Memmo*, etc., vol. 2, Zara, 1834.

Osservazioni di Antonio Viscentini architetto Veneto che servono di continuazione al Trattato di T.G. etc., Venezia, 1771.

Serlio, Sebastiano, 7 *Libri dell'architettura*, Venezia, 1537.

Trattato di Teofilo Gallaccini sopra gli errori degli Architetti ora per Primia volta, Venice, 1762. The treatise is from 1641

Viollet-le Duc, *Entretiens sur l'architecture*, Paris, 1872.

Viollet-le-Duc, *Dictionnaire raisonné de l'architecture française du XIe au XVIe siècle*. Paris, MDCCCLXVI (1866) [(10 vols), Paris, 1854–72].

Concepts and meanings

Algarotti, Francesco, *Saggio sull'Architettura e sulla Pittura*, Milano, 1756.

Blondel, M. François, *Cours d'architecture enseigné dans l'Académie Royale d'Architecture. Première partie ou sont expliquez les termes, l'origine & les Principes d'Architecture & les pratiques des cinq Ordres suivant la doctrine de Vitruve & de ses principaux Sécateurs & suivant celle des trois plus habiles Architectes qui ayent écrit entre les Modernes, qui sont Vignole, Palladio & Scamozzi. Seconde Edition, augmentée & corrigée. A Paris, chez L'AUTEUR MDCXCVIII, Et se Vend À Amsterdam, Chez Pierre Mortier, Libraire sur le Vygendam* 1698.

Dell'arte di vedere nelle belle arti del Disegno segundo i principe di Sulzer e di Mengs,
    Genoa, 1786.

Kaufman, Emil, *Three Revolutionary Architects: Boullée, Ledoux and Lequeu*,
    Philadelphia, 1952.

Lodoli, Carlo, *Elementi, etc.*, Roma, MDCCLXXXVI (1786), vol. I.

Milizia, Francesco, *Principe di Architettura civile, opera illustrata dal professore
    architetto Giovanni Antolini*, Milano, 1847.

Pellati, Francesco, *Vitruvio*, Roma, 1938.

Ragghianti, Carlo L., *Il pungollo dell'Arte*, Venezia, 1956.

Sulle Forme e caratteri dell'Architettura civile e sulle cause delle loro variazione.
    Memoria di Romolo Burri, architect-engineer, Rome, 1873.

Thomas Jefferson, architect—original designs in the collection of T.J., Boston,
    1916.

Vitruvius Britannicus; Hegemann and Peets, *The United States Vitruvius*.

Vitruvio, *De Architectura Libri*, trad. di Ugo Fleres, Villasanta, Milano, 1933;
    Vitruvio, *De Architectura*, trad. Italiana, Daniel Barbaro, Venezia, 1556;
    introd.

Architecture and nature

Bardi, P.M., "Is Man Anti-Nature?" *Habitat magazine*, no. 15, São Paulo,
    March–April 1954, p. 56.

Ruskin, John, *The Stones of Venice*, London, 1895, vol. III.

Valery, Paul, *Eupalinos ou l'architecte précédé de l'ame et de la danse*, Paris,
    1924.

White, William, *The Principles of Art as illustrated by examples in the Ruskin
    Museum*, London, 1895.

Woodbridge, Frederick J.E., *Saggio sulla Natura*, trans. Italian by Francesco
    Tató, Milano, 1956.

Zielinsky, Thaddeus, *L'antico e Noi*, trans. several authors, ed. P.E. Pavolini,
    Firenze, 1915; p. 89. The work is originally from 1903.

The measure of man

Il Quattro Libri dell'Architettura di Andrea Palladio, Venezia, 1570; Book IV,
    Proemio a I Lettori.

Le Corbusier, *Modulor 2*, Paris, 1954.

Lettere di XIII Huomini illustri, Venezia, 1560, p. 280. (One of the editions of
    Cartas de Dionigi Atanagi.)

Lomazzo, Paolo, *Trattato dell'arte della pittura sculptura e architettura*, Roma,
    1844 [original, 1585].

Pacioli, Luca, *De Divina Proportione*, Venice, 1509, cited in Julius Schlosser-
    Magnino, *La letturatura artistica—Manuale delle fonti della storia dell'arte
    moderna*, trans. Fillipo Rossi, Firenze, n.d., but 1922.

Viollet-le-Duc, *Dictionnaire raisonné*, *Op. cit.*

Weyl, Hermann, *Symmetry* Princeton, NJ, 1952.

Architecture and science

Fiedler, Conrad, *On Judging Works of Visual Art*, trans. H. Schaefer-Simmern and Fulmer Mood, Berkeley, 1949.

Nervi, Pier Luigi, *Costruire Corretamente, Caratteristiche e possibilità delle strutture cementizie armate.* Milano, 1955.

Wölfflin, Enrico, *L'arte Classica nel Rinascimento*, Rodolfo Paoli, Firenze, 1941, p. 251. [Heinrich Wölfflin, *Classical Art in the Renaissance.*]

Materials and architecture

da Vignola, Jacopo, *Gli ordinid'architettura civile corredati delle aggiunte fattevi dagli architetti G.B. Spampani e Carlo Antononi ed ombreggiati secondo il recente metodo delle R. Academie di Belle Arti del Regno etc.* Milano, MDCCCXXXII (1832).

Hessling, Bruno, *Dekorative Malerei und Flachenverzierung*, G.M.B.H. Buchandlung für Architektur und Kunstgewerbe, Berlin-New York, Architecture Catalog, 1900.

Santayana, George, *The Life of Reason*, New York, 1954.

Selvatico, Pietro Estense, *Prelezione al Corso di Storia architettonica per gli ingegneri laureati che assolvono gli studi architettonici nell'(Imperiale) R(egia) Accademia di Belle Arti in Venezia*, dated 15 gennaio 1856, in *Scritti d'Arte di Pietro Estense Selvatico*, Firenze, 1859.

Architecture and society

A Carta de Atenas—Ciam (Congrès international d'architecture moderne). Centro de Estudos Folcoloricos do Grêmio da Faculdade de Arquitetura e Urbanismo, São Paulo, 1950, no. 5.

Cicero, *De Oratore*, trans. H. Bornecque E. Courband, Paris, 1956.

Everett Gilbert, K. and Kuhn, H., *A History of Esthetics*, New York, 1939.

McMahon, Philip, *Preface to an American Philosophy of Art*, Chicago, 1945.

Meyers, I.E., *Mexico's Modern Architecture*, New York, 1952.

Moholy-Nagy, L.M.N., *Vision in Motion*, Chicago, 1947.

Mort de la Rue par Le Corbusier, Revista plans, Paris, 1931.

Vitry, Urbano, *Il proprietario architetto*, etc. Venezia, 1832.

The architect and the client

Merzario, Giuseppe, *Il Maestri Comacini-Storia artistica di Mille duecento anni (600–1800)*, vol. I, Milan, 1893.

Romanticism and architecture

Benz, Richard, *Die Deutsche Romantik*, Stuttgart, 5th edn, 1956, p. 8). [Originally, *Die Deutsche Romantik. Geschichte einer geistigen Bewegung*, Leipzig, 1937.]

Cousin, Victor, *Œuvres complètes*, Paris, 1840.

Garbett, Edward, *Rudimentary Treatise on the Principles of Design in Architecture.*

Gerbi, Antonello, *La politica del romanticismo*, Bari, 1932.

Hopkins, Vivian C., *Spires of Form, a Study of Emerson's Aesthetic Theory*, Cambridge, 1951.

Chapter 2 Problems of method

The example of the masters

Aristotle, *Etica a Nicómaco* [Nicomachean Ethics], 350 BC.

Tari, Antonio, *Del Sistema delle Arti*, Naples, 1864; reprinted in *Saggi di Estetica e Metafisica*, ed. Benedetto Croce, Bari, 1911.

On the theory of internal space

Borissavliévitch, Miloutine, *Les Théories de l'Architecture*, Paris, 1951.

Bottari, Stefano, *La critica figurativa e l'estetica moderna*, Bari, 1935.

Focillon, Henri, *Vie des Formes, suivi de L'éloge de la main*, Paris, 1955. The lesson is from 1934.

Investigazioni preliminari per la scienza dell'architettura civile di Nicola d'Apuzzo architetto, Naples, 1844.

Lehmann-Hartleben, K., *Lettere Scelte di Plinio il Giovane*, Firenze, 1936.

Milizia, Francesco, *Memorie degli Architetti antichi e moderni*, Bassano, 1795.

Morelli, Giovanni, *Della Pittura Italiana*, Milano, 1897.

Ostendorf, Friedrich, *Sechs Buecher von Bauen*, Berlin, W. Ernst u. Sohn, 1914.

Schmarsow, August, *Grundbegriffe der Kunstwissenschaften*, Leipzig and Berlin, 1905.

Schmarsow, August, *Traité d'Esthétique Scientifique de l'Architecture*, Paris, 1954.

Treves, Vittorio, *L'Architettura d'oggi—Gli architetti e le Scuole d'A. in Italia*, Torino, 1890.

Valente, Pietro, *Dell'Essenza e Dignita dell'architeturra, e de Doveri dell'Architetto, Discorso pronunziato nella cattedra di architettura civile della Regia Universita degli Studii di Napoli il di' 28 novembre 1835*, Napoli, 1836.

Venturi, Adolfo, *Storia dell'Arte Italiana*, Milano, 1901–40.

Venturi, Lionello, *History of Art Criticism*, New York, E.P. Dutton & Co., 1936.

von Hartmann, Eduard, *Philosophie des Schoenen*, Berlin, 1887.

Wotton, Henry, *The Elements of Architecture collected by Henry Wotton from the Best Authors and Examples,* London, MDCCCIII (1803), reproduced from the book published in London in 1624.

Wright, F.L., *The future of Architecture*, London, 1955.

Zevi, Bruno, *Saper Vedere l'Architettura*, Torino, 1948.

Theory and "caractères" of buildings

Giovannoni, Gustavo, *Corso di architettura*, vol. 2, Roma, 1932.

Hamlin, Talbot, *Architecture: An Art for All Men*, New York, 1947.

Hautecoeur, Louis, *L'architecture française*, Paris, 1950.

Manuale dell'architetto compilato a cura del consiglio nazionale delle Richerche, pubblicato dall'ufficio informazioni Stati Uniti in Roma, 1946.

Melis, Armando, *Caratteri degli edifice-Distribuzione proporzionamento organizzazione degli edifici tipici-Schemi funzionali*, Torino, 1947.

Morasso, Mario, *L'imperialismo artistico*, Torino, 1903.

Neufert, Ernst, *Enciclopedia practica per progettare e costruire etc.*, 1ª edizione italiana a cura di Luigi Lenzi. Milano, 1949.

Universite degli Studi di Roma, Facolta di Architettura, *Ordine degli Studi, 1956–57*, 1956.

Methodological update

Bettini, Sergio, *L'architettura di San Marco. Origini e significato*, Padova, 1946.

Calandra, Enrico, *Breve storia della Architettura in Sicilia*, Bari, 1938.

Condit, Carl W., *The Rise of the Skyscraper*, Chicago, 1952.

Crowe e Cavalcaselle, *Raffaello*, Firenze, 1890.

Eckermann, G.P., *Colloqui col Goethe*, vol I, trans. E. Donadoni, Bari, 1912.

Fasola, Giusta Nicco, *Ragionamenti sull'architettura, Città*, Marci di Castello, 1949.

Gernskeim, Helmut, *Focus on Architecture and Sculpture, etc.*, London, 1949. Introduction by Nicholas Pevsner.

Grita, Salvatore, *Polemiche Artistiche*, Roma, 1884.

Gropius, Walter and E.N. Rogers, *Casabella* magazine, Milano, no. 213, p. 1.

Gropius, Walter, *Scope of Total Architecture*, New York, 1943.

Gropius, Walter, *O arquiteto na sociedad industrial*, conferencia proferida em São Paulo, in *Habitat*, no. 14, São Paulo, January–February 1954.

Gropius, Walter, *In Search of a Common Denominator in Building for Modern Man*. A symposium edited by Thomas H. Creighton, Princeton, 1949.

Le Corbusier, *Quand les Cathédrales étaient blanches*, Paris, 1937.

Lessing, G.E., *Del Laocoonte o sia dei limiti della pittura e della Poesia, Discorso di G.E. Lessing recato dal tedesco in italiano dal cav. C.G. Londonio, Milano, per A. Fontana*, 1833.

Matlack Price, C., *The Practical Book of Architecture*, Philadelphia and London, 1916.

Nervi, Pier Luigi, *Scienza o Arte del costruire?* Roma, 1945.

Nicco Fasola, Giusta, *De prospectiva pindendi*, in *Raccolta di fonti per la storia dell'arte*. Firenze, 1942.

Strich, Fritz, *Goethe und die Weltliteratur*, Bern, 1946.

Viollet-le-Duc, *Dictionnaire raisonné, Op. cit.*

Wright, F.L., *Genius and the Mobocracy*, New York, 1949.

Wright, F.L. *The Future of Architecture*, London, 1955.

SELECTED BIBLIOGRAPHY

Archives

Avery Classics Collection, Columbia University Libraries, Columbia University, New York, NY.

Drawing Collection of the Faculdade de Arquitetura e Urbanismo da Universidade de São Paulo (FAUUSP), São Paulo, Brazil.

Instituto Lina Bo e P.M. Bardi, São Paulo, Brazil.

Lina Bo e P. M. Bardi Collection, São Paulo, Brazil: Museu de Arte de São Paulo, São Paulo, Brazil.

Rare Books Collection of the Library and Documentation Center of the Museum of Art of São Paulo (MASP), São Paulo, Brazil.

Primary sources

Alberti, Leon Batista, *On the Art of Building in Ten Books*, trans. Joseph Rykwert, Neil Leach, and Robert Tavernor, Cambridge, MA: MIT Press, 1988.

Architecture d'Aujourd'hui 24, no. 49 (October 1953). Entire issue devoted to twentieth-century domestic architecture.

Argan, Giulio Carlo, "A proposito di spazio interno," *Metron* 28 (October 1948): 20–21.

Bardi, Lina Bo, "Serre," *Lo Stile*, Milan, no. 5–6 (May 1941): 113.

Bardi, Lina Bo, "Un interessante libro sulle piante d'architettura," *Lo Stile*, Milan, no. 10 (October 1941): 34.

Bardi, Lina Bo, "Finestre," *Lo Stile*, Milan, no. 16 (April 1942): 18–19.

Bardi, Lina Bo, "Quel che c'insegna un confronto numerico fra scuole tedesche e italiane," *Lo Stile*, Milan, no. 26 (February 1943): 24–25.

Bardi, Lina Bo, "Un esperimento riuscito: La Casa a nuclei habitativi in Roma," *Lo Stile*, Milan, no. 31 (July 1943): 15–23.

Bardi, Lina Bo, "Architettura e natura: la casa nel paesaggio," *Domus*, Milan, no. 191 (November 1943): 464–471.

Bardi, Lina Bo, "Sistemazione degli interni," *Domus*, Milan, no. 198 (June, 1944): 74–84.

Bardi, Lina Bo, "La Propaganda Per La Ricostruzione," contribution to the 1st Italian Reconstruction Congress, Milan, December 14–15, 1945, reprinted in F. Brunetti, *L'Architettura in Italia Negli Anni della Ricostruzione; Le vicende e le immagini*, Maria Coli Brunetti, ed., Appendice: Interventi dal Primo convegno nazionale per la ricostruzione edilizia, Paola Signori, ed., Firenze: Alinea (1986): 239–241.

Bardi, Lina Bo, "Na Europa a casa do Homem ruiu," *Rio*, Rio de Janeiro, no. 92 (February 1947): 53–55, 95; translated into English in *Lina Bo Bardi, 1914–1992*, Marcelo Carvalho Ferraz, ed. Milan: Charta, 2nd edn, 1996, pp. 10–11.

Bardi, Lina Bo (ed.), *Habitat*, São Paulo, nos 1–9 (1950–52).

Bardi, Lina Bo, "Prefácio," *Habitat*, São Paulo, no. 1 (October–December 1950): 1; "Preface" in *Habitat 1: English Translation* (insert, not paginated.)

Bardi, Lina Bo, "Casas de Artigas," *Habitat*, São Paulo, no. 1 (October–December 1950): 2–16; "Houses by Artigas" in *Habitat 1: English Translation* (insert, not paginated).

Bardi, Lina Bo (attributed), "Vitrinas das formas," *Habitat*, São Paulo, no. 1 (Oct.–Dec. 1950): 35.

Bardi, Lina Bo, "O Museu de Arte de São Paulo, Funçao social dos Museus," *Habitat*, São Paulo, no. 1 (October–December 1950):17; "The social function of art museums," in *Habitat 1: English Translation* (insert, not paginated).

Bardi, Lina Bo (attributed), "Novo mundo do espaço de Le Corbusier," *Habitat*, São Paulo, no. 1 (October–December 1950): 37; "New world of space," in *Habitat 1: English Translation* (insert, not paginated.)

Bardi, Lina Bo (attributed), "Frei Lodoli e a cadeira," *Habitat*, São Paulo, no. 1 (October–December 1950): 52; "Carlo Lodoli and the chair," in *Habitat 1: English Translation* (insert, not paginated).

Bardi, Lina Bo, "Bela Criança," *Habitat*, São Paulo, no. 2 (January–March 1951): 3; "A new-born child," in English Summary insert, not paginated.

Bardi, Lina Bo, "Primeiro: escolas," in English Summary, *Habitat*, São Paulo, no. 4 (July–September 1951): 1; "First of all schools," in English Summary (insert, not paginated).

Bardi, Lina Bo, "Vitrinas," *Habitat*, São Paulo, no. 5 (October–December 1951): 60.

Bardi, Lina Bo, "Desenho industrial," *Habitat*, São Paulo, no. 5 (October–December 1951): 62–63.

Bardi, Lina Bo (attributed), "Morumbi," *Habitat*, São Paulo, no. 5 (October–December 1951): 66.

Bardi, Lina Bo (attributed), "Necessidade da crítica na Arquitetura," *Habitat*, São Paulo, no. 7 (April–June 1952): 53.

Bardi, Lina Bo (attributed), "Construir com simplicidade," *Habitat*, São Paulo, no. 9 (October–December 1952): 15.

Bardi, Lina Bo (attributed), "Max Bill: Iconoclasta," *Habitat*, São Paulo, no. 12 (July–September 1953): 34; "The iconoclast," in English Summary (insert, not paginated).

Bardi, Lina Bo, "Lettera dal Brasile," *Architettura: cronache e Storia 2*, no. 9 (July 1956): 182–187.

Bardi, Lina Bo, *Contribuição propedêutica ao ensino da teoria da arquitetura*, São Paulo: Habitat Ltd. 1957; facsimile reprinted in *Contribuição propedêutica*

ao ensino da teoria da arquitetura: *Um Inédito de Lina Bo Bardi*, Instituto
Lina Bo e. P.M. Bardi, 2002.

Bardi, Lina Bo (ed.), *Diario de Noticias de Salvador*, Salvador de Bahia, no. 1–9
(September–November 1958).

Bardi, Lina Bo, "Lina Bo Bardi, Brazil: SESC—Pompéia Leisure Center,"
Zodiac, no. 8 (September 1992–February 1993): 224–229.

Bardi, Lina Bo, *Tempos de grossura: o design no impasse*, São Paulo: Instituto Lina
Bo e P.M. Bardi, 1994.

Bardi, Lina Bo, Interview, "Uma aula de Arquitetura," *Revista Projeto* 133
(1990): 103–108; reprinted in *Projeto* no. 149, Special edition, January–
February 1992: 59–64; edited and abridged as "Lina Bo Bardi, l'ultima
lezione," *Domus*, no. 753 (October 1993): [17]–24.

Bardi, Lina Bo, *Lina Bo Bardi, 1914–1992*, Marcelo Carvalho Ferraz, ed.
Milan: Charta, 1994; reprinted, 2nd edn, São Paulo: Instituto Lina Bo e
P.M. Bardi, 1996; 3rd edn, São Paulo: Instituto Lina Bo e P.M. Bardi:
Impr. Oficial, 2008.

Bardi, Lina Bo and P.M. Bardi (eds), *Habitat*, São Paulo, nos 14–15 (1954).

Bardi, Lina Bo and Carlo Pagani, "3 arredamenti," *Lo Stile*, Milan, no. 1
(January 1941): 88–104

Bardi, Lina Bo and Carlo Pagani, "Terrazze in città," *Lo Stile*, Milan, no. 4
(April 1941): 70–71.

Bardi, Lina Bo and Carlo Pagani, "L'acquario in casa," *Lo Stile*, Milan, no. 10
(October 1941): 24–25.

Bardi, Lina Bo and Carlo Pagani, "Lúmen," *Lo Stile*, Milan, no. 10 (October
1941): 26–27.

Bardi, Lina Bo and Carlo Pagani, with Bruno Zevi (eds), "A—Un settimanale
di architettura scaturito della Resistenza," *Architettura* 37, nos 7–8
(441–442) (July–August 1992): 541–[560].

Bardi, P.M., *Rapperto Sull' Architettura (per Mussolini)*, Roma: Tip. Arte della
stampa, 1931.

Bardi, P.M., *Un Fascista Al Paese Dei Soviet*, Rome: Edizioni d'Italia, 1933.

Bardi, P.M., "Belvedere Dell'Architettura Italiana d'oggi," Milano: Edizione
Quadrante, 1933.

Bardi, P.M., "Architettura Di Una 'Civilta Giornalistica,'" *Lo Stile*, no. 10
(October 1941): 2–5.

Bardi, P.M., "Stile Di Pier Luigi Nervi," *Lo Stile*, nos 19–20 (July–August
1942): 9.

Bardi, P.M., "Stato e Architettura," *Lo Stile*, no. 21 (September 1942): 3.

Bardi, P.M., "Il Socrate Dell'Architettura," *Lo Stile*, no. 30 (June 1943):
5–11.

Bardi, P.M., *Neutra: residências/residences*, 2nd edn [1st edn, October 1950 for
exhibition at Diários Associados Building, MASP].

Bardi, P.M., *A Critical Review of Le Corbusier: Leitura critica de Le Corbusier*, São
Paulo, Brazil: Habitat Editora Museu de Arte de São Paulo, 1951.

Bardi, P.M. *Chefs-d'oeuvre Du Musée D'art De Sao-Paulo*. Paris: Edns des Musées Nationaux, 1953.

Bardi, P.M. *Masterpieces from the São Paulo Museum of Art at the Tate Gallery, June 19 to August 15, 1954*. London: s.n., 1954.

Bardi, P.M., *Paintings from the São Paulo Museum {Catalog of the Exhibition} at the Metropolitan Museum of Art, March 21–May 5, 1957*, New York: Metropolitan Museum of Art, 1957.

Bardi, P.M., *Art Treasures of the São Paulo Museum and the Development of Art in Brazil*, trans. John Drummond, New York: Harry N. Abrams, Inc., 1956.

Bardi, P.M., *The tropical gardens of Burle Marx*, photos by M. Gautherot, New York: Reinhold, 1964.

Bardi, P.M., *Architecture: The World We Build*, London: Collins, 1972.

Bardi, P.M., *História do MASP*, São Paulo: Instituto Quadrante, 1992.

Bardi, P.M., *Lembrança de Le Corbusier: Atenas, Itália, Brasil*, prefácio de Alexandre Eulálio; tradução das conferências, Ana Carboncini e Leda Maria Figueiredo Ferraz, São Paulo: Nobel, 1984.

Bardi, P.M., and Hélène AdhéMarch, *L'Art Français Au Musée D'art De São Paulo: Un Musée Au Tropique*, Paris: Imprimeries Desfossés et Sapho, 1954.

Bardi, P.M., and Hans Conried, *A Colorslide Tour of the Museum of São Paulo, Brazil: 32 Masterpieces of Painting Visited with P.M. Bardi, Director*, New York: Columbia Record Club, 1961.

Bettini, Sergio, *L'architettura di San Marco; origini e significato*, Venice, San Marco (Cathedral): [Padova] Tre Venezie, 1946.

Bill, Max, "Beleza Provida da Funcao e como Funcao," *Habitat*, São Paulo, no. 2 (January–March 1951): 61–65; "Beauty generated by function and as function," in English Summary insert, not paginated.

Bill, Max, "De la surface à l'Espace", Paris, *XXeme siècle*, no. 2 (January 1952): 65.

Bill, Max, *Eine Bilanz über die Formentwicklung um die Mitte des XX Jahrhunderts*, Basel: Verlag Karl Werner A.G., 1952.

Bill, Max, "O Arquiteto, a Arquitetura e a Sociedade," *Habitat*, São Paulo, no. 14 (January–February 1954): insert, "Polemica" A–B.

Bill, Max, "Report on Brazil," *Architecture Review* 116, no. 694 (October 1954): 234–250.

Borissaviliévitch, Miloutine, *Les theories de l'architecture*, Paris: Payot, 1926.

Borissaviliévitch, Miloutine, *Les theories de l'architecture*, introduction by Louis Hautecoeur, Paris: 1951.

Boyd, Robin, "These Critical Times," *Journal of Architectural Education* 12, no. 2 (summer 1957): 33–36.

"Brazilian modern re-orients an old tradition," *House & Garden* (March 1943): p. 30–31.

"Brazilian preview," *Architectural Review* 114 (July 1953):10–15.

Collingwood, R.G., *Autobiographia*, Italian trans. by Giampaolo Gandolfi, Venice, 1955, p. 88. Original title: *An Autobiography*, London, 1938.

de Souza, Abelardo, "Ensino da arquitetura," *Habitat*, São Paulo, no. 18 (September–October 1954):1.

Debenedetti, Emma and Anita Salmoni, *Architettura italiana a San Paolo*, São Paulo: Instituto Cultural Italo-Brasileiro, 1953.

Duarte, Helio, "O problema das escolas e Arquitetura," *Habitat*, São Paulo, no. 4 (July–September 1951): 4; "The problem of schools and architecture," in English Summary (insert, not paginated).

Ferraz, Geraldo, "Habitat initiates a survey on the conditions of university education in statements made by leaders of different chairs FAU," *Habitat*, São Paulo, no. 26 (1956): 5.

Giedion, Sigfried, "History and the architect," *Journal of Architectural Education* 12, no. 2 (summer 1957): 14–16.

Giovannoni, Giovanni, *Vecchi città ed edilizia nuova*, Torino: Unione Tipografico-Editrice Torinese, 1931.

Gordon, D.J., "Poet and architect: the intellectual setting of the quarrel between Ben Johnson and Inigo Jones," *Journal of the Warburg & Courtauld Institutes* 12 (1949): 152–178.

Gropius, Walter, "In search of a better architectural education," transcribed in *A Decade of New Architecture*, ed. Sigfried Giedion, Zurich, 1951, pp. 41–46.

Gropius, Walter, "History and the student," *Journal of Architectural Education* 12, no. 2 (summer 1957): 8.

Gropius, Walter, *Scope of Total Architecture*, New York: Harper, 1955; reprinted Collier Books, 1962, 1966.

Guadet, Julien, *Éléments et Théorie de l'Architecture, Cours professé à l'École Nationale et Spéciale des Beaux-Arts*, 5th edn, vol. 4, Paris, 1909.

Hudnut, Joseph, "On teaching the history of architecture," *Journal of Architectural Education* 12, no. 2 (summer 1957): 6–8.

Marangoni, Matteo. *Saper vedere: come si guarda un'opera d'arte*. [Milano]: Garzanti, 1945.

Marangoni, Matteo. *The Art of Seeing Art*, London: Shelley Castle, 1951.

Mazzocchi, Mauricio, "The house, its construction and industrialization," *Habitat*, São Paulo no. 29 (April 1956): 33–36.

McMahon, A. Philip, *Preface to an American Philosophy of Art*, Chicago, University of Chicago Press, 1945.

Memmo, Andrea, *Elementi dell'Architettra Lodoliana*, Roma, 1786, 1834.

Mindlin, Henrique E., *Modern Architecture in Brazil*, London: Architectural Press, 1956.

Moholy-Nagy, László, *A New Vision*, New York: Wittenborn, Schultz, 1947.

Moretti, Luigi, "Strutture e sequenze di spazi," *Spazio* 7 (December 1952–April 1953): 9–20, 107–108; "Structures and sequences of spaces," English translation (insert, not paginated).

Motta, Flavio, "Problemas Educacional," *Habitat*, São Paulo, no. 10 Editorial, (January–March 1953) p. 1; "Educational problems," in English translation (insert, not paginated).

Nicco Fasola, Giusta, "Fattori sociali nell'architettura" ["Social Factors in Architecture"], trans. Gilbert Creighton, *The Journal of Aesthetics and Art Criticism* (June 1950).

Nicco Fasola, Giusta, (ed.), *De Prospectiva Pingendi*, edizione critical, Raccolta di Fonti per la Storia dell'Arte, no. 5, Firenze, Sansoni, 1942.

Pagano, Giuseppe, *Architetture e scritti/Giuseppe Pagano Pogatschnig (1896–1945)*, Milano: Domus, 1947.

Pagano, Giuseppe and G. Daniel, *Architettura rurale Italiana*, Milano: Ulrico Hoepli Editore, 1936.

Perret, Auguste, *Une Contribution à une théorie de l'architecture*, Paris: A. Wahl, 1952.

Piacentini, Marcello, *Architettura d'oggi*, Roma: Cremonese, 1930.

Ponti, Gio, "Arredamenti degli architetti Lina Bo e Carlo Pagani," *Stile*, Milan, no. 1 (January 1941): 88–104.

Ponti, Gio, "Un arredamento a Milano," *Lo Stile*, Milan, no. 21 (September 1942):15–22.

Ponti, Gio, "Taglianetti House," *Domus*, no. 283, 1953.

Ponti, Gio, "Project for a Faculty of Theoretical Nuclear Physics at the University of São Paulo," *Domus*, no. 284, 1953.

Ponti, Gio, "Predio Italia," *Domus*, no. 379, 1961.

"Renovation in Architectural Education," *Habitat*, São Paulo, no. 37 (December 1956): 1.

Rogers, Ernesto N., Editorial: "Our responsibilities towards tradition," *Casabella Continuita*, Milan, no. 199 (1954): 1.

Rogers, Ernesto N., "Continuity," *Casabella Continuita*, Milan, no. 199 (1954): 2.

Rogers, Ernesto N., Editorial: "Towards a non-formalist criticism," *Casabella Continuita*, Milan, no. 200 (1954): 1.

Santos, Paulo F., "A arquitetura da sociedade industrial: I. Posição dos artistas," *Habitat*, São Paulo, no. 20 (January–February 1955):10.

Santos, Paulo F., "A arquitetura da sociedade industrial: II. Artesanato e produção fabril," *Habitat*, São Paulo, no. 23 (July–August 1955):10.

Santos, Paulo F., "A arquitetura da sociedade industrial: III. O fator estrutural. Morris, Ruskin, Labrouste and Viollet-le-Duc," *Habitat*, São Paulo, no. 27 (February 1956):16–19.

Santos, Paulo F., "A arquitetura da sociedade industrial: IV. O fator estrutural, Concreto armado," *Habitat*, São Paulo, no. 28 (March 1956): 56–60.

Santos, Paulo F., "A arquitetura da sociedade industrial: V. O fator estrutural, Estrutura independente," *Habitat*, São Paulo, no. 30 (May 1956): 50–54.

Santos, Paulo, F., "A arquitetura da sociedade industrial: VI. O fator estrutural, Fatores socioeconômicos," *Habitat*, São Paulo, no. 31 (June 1956): 38–42.

Schlosser-Magnino, Julius, *De Kunstliteratur*, Vienna: Schroll & Col, 1924.

Scott, Geoffrey, *The Architecture of Humanism—A Study in the History of Taste*, Garden City, New York, 1954 (1st edn, 1914).

Sekler, Eduard, "Research and criticism in architecture," *Journal of Architectural Education* 12, no. 2 (summer 1957): 31–32.

Shellman, William, "An introduction to the study of architecture," *Journal of Architectural Education* 12, no. 2 (summer 1957): 20–23.

Summerson, John, "The case for a theory of modern architecture," *Royal Institute of British Architects Journal* (June 1957): 307–313.

Teixeira, Anisio, S. "Considerações sobre o Contrato Educacional," *Habitat*, São Paulo, no. 4 (July–September 1951) p. 3; "Considerations about the educational agreement," in English Summary insert, not paginated.

Trapp, Frank Anderson, "Fundamentals of Design: outline for a full-year college course," *College Art Journal* 14, no. 4 (summer, 1955): 347–357.

Ordine Degli Studi : Approvato dal Consiglio du Facoltà nella seduta del 26 settembre 1956, Programmi e Orari dei Corsi, Università Degli Studi Di Roma, Facoltà di Architettura, Stab.Tipo-Lit. V. Ferri, Roma, 1956–1957.

Viollet-le-Duc, Eugène-Emmanuel, *Dictionnaire raisonné de l'Architecture française du XI au XVI siècle*, vol. I, Paris: B. Bance, MDCCCLXVI.

Wyffels-Simoens, M.L., "Note sur le labyrinth de la Cathédral de Reims," *Gazette des Beaux-Arts*, Paris, series 6, no. 49 (May–June, 1957): 337–340.

Wright, Frank Lloyd, *The Story of the Tower; The Tree That Escaped the Crowded Forest*. New York: Horizon Press, 1956.

Wright, Marie Robinson, *The Brazilian National Exposition of 1908 in celebration of the centenary of the opening of Brazilian ports to the commerce of the world by the Prince Regent Dom João of Portugal in 1808, Philadelphia*, G. Barrie & Sons, 1908.

Zevi, Bruno, *Verso un'architettura organica*, Milano: 1945.

Zevi, Bruno, *Architecture as Space*, trans. Milton Gendel, New York: Horizon Press, 1957. (Original Italian publication, 1948).

Zevi, Bruno, *Architettura e Storiografia*, Milano: Politecnica Tamburini, 1951.

Zevi, Bruno, "John Summerson: una teoria per l'architettura moderna," *Architettura: cronache e storia* 3, no. 25 (November 1957): 436–437.

Zevi, Bruno, "For Architects: A Productive University," *Architettura: cronache e storia* 5, no. 53 (March 1960): 726–727.

Secondary sources

Allen, Stan and Diana Agrest, *Practice: Architecture, Technique and Representation*, OPA, G+B Arts International, 2000.

Alpers, Svetlana, *The Art of Describing: Dutch Art in the Seventeenth Century*, Chicago, University of Chicago Press, 1983.

Amado, Jorge, "Lina Bo Bardi," *Projeto*, no. 149 (January–February 1992): 23–58, cover.

Anderman, Jens and William Rowe, *Images of Power: Iconography, Culture and the State in Latin America*, New York, Oxford: Berghahn Books, 2005.

Anelli, Renato, *Rino Levi: arquitetura e cidade*, São Paulo: R. Guerra, 2001.

Aubert, Marcel, "L'ordre des architectes de la cathe_dral de Reims," *Bulletin société nationale des antiquares de France* (1955): 165–166.

Aubert, Marcel, "Les architectes de la cathédrale de Reims," *Bulletin monumental* 114 (1956): 123–125.

Barthes, Roland, "The third meaning," *Image Music Text*, trans. Richard Howard, New York: Hill and Wang, 1982.

Blanc, Philippe, "Lectura de Lina Bo: Pompéia [São Paulo]," *ARQ*, no. 55 (December 2003): 60–65.

Bouisset, Maïten, *Arte povera*, Paris: Editions du regard, 1994.

Branzi, Andrea, "Exhibition design and the metaphor of the new modernity," *Lotus International* 115 (December 2002): 96–99.

Bryson, Norman, *In Vision and Painting*, New Haven, CT: Yale University Press, 1986.

Campeio, Maria de Fátima de Mello Barreto, "Lina Bo Bardi: as moradas da alma," unpublished disssertation, FAU/USP, São Paulo, 1997.

Casciato, Maristella and Claudia Mattogno, "Les femmes et l'architecture, une histoire à écrire," *Architecture intérieure – Créé*, no. 291 (1999): 36–41.

Ciucci, Giorgio, "Italian architecture during the Fascist Period: classicism between neoclassicism and rationalism: the many souls of the classical," *The Harvard Architecture Review* 6 (1987): 76–87.

Collins, Peter, "The doctrine of Auguste Perret," *The Architectural Review*, London, 114 (August, 1953): 90–98.

Colomina, Beatriz, *Clip, Stamp, Fold: The Radical Architecture of Little Magazines 196X–197X*, Actar-D, 2009.

Colomina, Beatriz, "Introduction: on architecture, production and reproduction," in *Architectureproduction*, Princeton, NJ: Princeton Architectural Press, 1988.

Colomina, Beatriz, *Privacy and Publicity: Modern Architecture as Mass Media*, Cambridge, MA: MIT Press, 1994.

Crary, Jonathan, *Techniques of the Observer: On Vision and Modernity in the Nineteenth Century*, Cambridge, MA: MIT Press, 1990.

de Oliveira, Olivia Fernandes and Marcelo Carvalho Ferraz, "Lina Bo Bardi: architetture senza éta e senza tempo," *Casabella* 64, no. 681 (September 2000): 36–55.

de Oliveira, Olivia Fernandes "Lina Bo Bardi: obra construida: Built Work," *2G: Revista Internacional de Arquitectura*, Barcelona: Gustavo Gili, nos 23–24 (2002): double issue.

de Oliveira, Olivia Fernandes, "Lina Bo Bardi: frontieres—passages," *Faces*, no. 51 (autumn 2002): 14–21.

de Oliveira, Olivia Fernandes, *Subtle Substances: The Architecture of Lina Bo Bardi*, Barcelona: Gustavo Gili, 2006.

de Oliveira, Olivia Fernandes, "Lina Bo Bardi, des dessins comme des récits," *Architecture d'Aujourd'hui*, Paris, no. 371 (July–August, 2007): 70–77.

De Seta, Cesare, *Pagano: architettura e città durante il fascismo*, Bari: Laterza, 1990.

Deplazes, Andrea, *Constructing Architecture: Materials Processes Structures—A Handbook*, Basel: Birkhauser, 2006.

Dunn, Christopher, *Brutality Garden:* Tropicalia *and the Emergence of a Brazilian Counterculture*, Chapel Hill: University of North Carolina Press, 2000.

Evans, Robin, "Translations from drawing to building" (1986), in *Translations from Drawing to Building and Other Essays*, London: Architectural Association Publications, and Janet Evans, 1997, pp. 153–193.

Evans, Robin, *The Projective Cast: Architecture and its Three Geometries*, Cambridge, MA: MIT Press, 1995.

Ferraz, Marcelo Carvalho, "Lina, architecture and Brazil," *A + U: Architecture and Urbanism*, no. 2 (341) (February 1999): 92–102.

Ferraz, Marcelo Carvalho, "Minha Experiência com Lina," (November 1991) *urbanismo* 40 (January/February 1992): 39.

Ficher, Silvia, *Os Arquitetos da Poli: ensino e profissão em São Paulo*, São Paulo, Brazil: Edusp., 2005.

Foster, Hal (ed.), *Discussions in Contemporary Culture: Vision and Visuality*, Seattle: Bay Press, 1988.

Frampton, Kenneth, *The Evolution of 20th Century Architecture: A Synoptic Account*, Springer, 2007.

Frampton, Kenneth, *Modern Architecture, A Critical History*, New York: Oxford University Press, 1980.

Gabetti, Roberto, "La didattica tra Academia Politecnico," *Casabella* 50, nos 520–521 (January– February 1986): 90–94.

Gallo, Antonella, *Lina Bo Bardi architetto*, Exhibition catalog, Biennale di Venezia. Mostra Internazionale di Architettura, Venezia: Marsilio, 2004.

Guedes Sobrinho, Manoel Joaquim, *Lembrancas de Lina Bo Bardi*, Venezia: Marsilio, 2004.

Hertzberger, Herman, *Space and the Architect: Lessons in Architecture*, The Netherlands: 010 Publishers, 2000.

Hertzberger, Herman, *Space and Learning: Lessons in Architecture 3*, The Netherlands: 010 Publishers, 2008.

Jay, Martin, *Downcast Eyes: The Denigration of Vision in Twentieth Century French Thought*, Berkeley: University of California Press, 1993.

Lima, Zeuler, R.M.A., "Preservation as confrontation: the work of Lina Bo Bardi," *Future anterior: journal of historic preservation history, theory & criticism*, 2005 Winter, v.2, n.2, p. 24–33.

Lima, Zeuler, R.M.A., "The faces of Janus: modernism and hybridisation in the architecture of Lina Bo Bardi," *Journal of Architecture* 11, no. 2 (April 2006): 257–267.

Lima, Zeuler, R.M.A., "Nelson A. Rockefeller and the Art Patronage in Brazil after World War II: Assis Chateaubriand, the Museu de Arte de São Paulo (MASP) and the Musee de Arte Moderna (MAM)", unpublished research report, The Rockefeller Archive Center, 2010.

"Lina Bo Bardi, mestre de obra e de vida," *Projeto*, no. 151 (April 1992): 85–86.

Lotz, Wolfgang, "The rendering of the interiór in architectural drawings of the Renaissance," in *Studies in Italian Renaissance Architecture*, 1977 (1956): 1–65.

MacLaren, Brian, "Under the sign of the reproduction," *Journal of Architectural Education* 45, no. 2 (February 1992): 98–106.

Martignoni, Massimo, *Gio Ponti: gli anni di stile: 1941–1947*, Milan: Abitare Segesta, 2002.

Millon, Henry A. "Rudolf Wittkower, *Architectural Principles in the Age of Humanism:* Its influence on the Development and Interpretation of Modern Architecture," *Journal of the Society of Architectural Historians* 31, no. 2 (May 1972): 83–91.

Miotto, Laura and Savina Nicolini, *Lina Bo Bardi: Aprirsi All' Acadimiento*, Torino: Testo & Immagine, 1999.

Mitchell, W.J.T. (ed.), *The Language of Images*, Chicago: University of Chicago Press, 1974.

Moholy-Nagy, Sibyl, "Architectural history and the student architect: a symposium," *Journal of the Society of Architectural Historians* 26, no. 3 (October, 1967): 179–199.

Moholy-Nagy, Sibyl, *Native Genius in Anonymous Architecture in North America*, New York: Schocken Books, 1976, c.1957.

Morais, Fernando, *Chatô, o rei do Brasil*, São Paulo: Companhia das Letras, 1994.

Mulvey, Laura, *Visual and Other Pleasures*, London: The Macmillan Press, 1989.

Neveu, Marc, J., *Architectural Lessons of Carlo Lodoli (1690–1761): Indole of Material and of Self* (unpublished dissertation, McGill University, 2005).

Owens, Craig, "Photography *en abyme*," in *Beyond Recognition: Representation, Power and Culture*, Berkeley: University of California Press, 1992, pp. 16–29.

Payne, Alina, *The Architectural Treatise in the Italian Renaissance: Architectural Invention, Ornament, and Literary Culture*, Cambridge: Cambridge University Press, 1999.

Perez-Gomez, Alberto, "Architecture as drawing," *Journal of Architectural Education* 6, no. 2 (winter 1982): 2–7.

Rifkind, David, "*Quadrante* and the politicization of architectural discourse in Fascist Italy" (PhD dissertation, Columbia University, 2007).

Rifkind, David. *The Battle for Modernism: Quadrante and the Politicization of Architectural Discourse in Fascist Italy*, Vicenza: Centro Internazionale di Studi di Architettura Andrea Palladio, 2012.

Ripa, Cesare, *Iconologia*, New York: Garland Pub., 1979; reprint of the 1779 edn, London: G. Scott, [selected by] George Richardson, introductory notes by Stephen Orgel.

Risério, Antonio, *Avant-garde na Bahia*, São Paulo: Instituto Lina Bo e P.M. Bardi, 1995.

Rubino, Sylvia and Marina Grinover (eds), *Lina Por Ecrito: Textos Escolhidos de Lina Bo Bardi, 1943–1991*, São Paulo: COSAC NAIFY, 2009.

Rykwert, Joseph, "Lodoli on function and representation," *The Architectural Review*, London, 160, no. 953 (July 1976): 21–26.

Rykwert, Joseph, "Organic and mechanical," *RES: Anthropology and Aesthetics*, no. 22 (autumn, 1992): 11–18.

Silva, Mateus Bertone, "Lina Bo Bardi. Arquitetura cênica," unpublished disssertation, FAU/USP, São Paulo, 2005.

Skidmore, Thomas, *Brazil: Five Centuries of Change*, New York and London: Oxford University Press, 1999.

Spitz, Rene, *HfG Ulm. The View Behind the Foreground, The Political History of the Ulm School of Design 1953–1968*, Stuttgart: Edition Axel Menges, 2002.

Suzuki, Marcelo, *Lina Bo Bardi: L'impasse Del Design—L'esperienza Nel Nordest Del Brasile*, Milano: Editions Charta, 1997.

Tentori, Francesco, "P.M. Bardi e Lina Bo," *Abitare*, no. 374 (June, 1998): 94–107, 230.

Tentori, Francesco, "Persico e Bardi," *Zodiac*, no. 21 (July–December, 1999): 86–95.

Tentori, Francesco, *Pietro Maria Bardi: primo attore del razionalismo*, Torino: Testo & Immagine, 2002.

Treib, Marc (ed.), *The Architecture of Landscape, 1940–1960*, Penn Studies in Landscape Architecture, University of Pennsylvania Press, 2002.

Veikos, Cathrine, "To enter the work: ambient art," *Journal of Architecture Education*, Special Issue: Installation Art, 59, no. 4 (Blackwell Publishing, 2006): 71–80.

Venturi, Lionello, *History of Art Criticism*, New York: E.F. Dutton & Co., 1924.

Vera, Paloma, "Después del sueño moderno: Lina Bo Bardi y la enseñanza de la arquitectura [Beyond the modern dream: Lina Bo Bardi on teaching architecture]," *Arquine: revista internacional de arquitectura*, Mexico, no. 52 (Summer, 2010): 95–97.

Vivanco, Sandra, "Lina Bo Bardi: the chameleon of Brazilian modern architecture," *Aula: architecture & urbanism in las Américas, California*, no. 1 (Spring 1999): 14–19.

Buildings and projects (chronological)

MASP rua 7 de Abril, São Paulo, 1947

"Architetti e Critici d'Arte Italiani in Brasile: Un Museo Dell'Architetto Lina Bo," *Metron* 30 (December 1948): 34–35.

"Museum of Art, São Paulo, Brazil," *Architectural Review* 112, no. 669 (September 1952): 160–163.

"Introduzione al Museo de Arte de San Paolo," *Domus*, no. 284 (Milan, Italy) (July 1953).

"Brazilian Preview," *Architectural Review* 114 (July 1953): 10–15.

Museum of Arte, São Vicente, 1951 (unbuilt project)

"Museo sulla sponda dell'oceano," *Domus*, no. 286 (September 1953): 15.

"Museum by the Sea," *Architectural Review* 114 (July 1953): 10–15.

Glass House, Morumbi, São Paulo, 1951

"Entre o ceu e a vegetacao pousa a casa de dois artistas," [Between the sky and vegetation lands the house of two artists], *Casa e Jardim*, no. 1 (Rio de Janeiro, Brazil) (1953): 8–13.

"La 'Casa de Vidro' Gio Ponti, Milan," *Domus*, no. 279 (February 1953): 19–26.

"Residencia no Morumbi, Arq. Lina Bo Bardi, São Paulo," *Habitat*, São Paulo, no. 10, ed. Flavio Motta (March 1953): 31–41; "Residence on the Morumbi" in English Summary, not paginated.

"Architects' own house, São Paulo, Brazil," *Architect and Building News*, London, 203 no. 17 (April 1953): 488–494.

"Built in Brazil: a light glass casa in the air," *Contract Interiors*, no. 10, vol. 112 (May 1953): 74–83.

Silveira, Helena, "Un Casa no Morumbi," *Folha da Manhã Journal* (São Paulo) (May 31, 1953): 6–7.

Aberdeen, David, "Casa de Vidro," *Architectural Design*, no 8, London (August 1953): 230–31.

"Built in Brazil: a light glass casa in the air," *Habitat*, no. 12 (September 1953): 5 (reprint of the article from *Interiors*).

"Maison pour un critique d'art aux environs de São Paulo," *Architecture d'Aujourd'hui* 24, no. 49 (Twentieth-century domestic architecture issue) (October 1953).

"Glass House," *World's Contemporary Houses*, no. 8 (Latin America) (1954), Shokoku-sha Publishing, Tokyo: 11–15.

"Habitation près de São Paulo," *La Maison*, Brussels, no. 4 (April 1954).

"Escaliers intérieurs, escaliers extérieurs," *Architecture d'Aujourd'hui* (October 1954): 84.

"House in Brazil: Extrovert Structure: Steel and Glass," *Architecture & Building* (September 1955): 351–354.

"Uma Casa para dois artistas," *Casa Claudio*, no. 164 (May 1975): 50–52.

Bardi, P.M., "Em meio ao verde a casa do Morumbi," *Casa Vogue*, no. 3 (May–June 1984): 160–163.

Acayaba, Marlene, "Residencias em São Paulo 1947–1975," *Projeto* (1986): 43–50.

"The Glass House, São Paulo, Brazil 1951," *A + U: Architecture and Urbanism*, no. 2 (341) (February 1999): 10–17.

Bardi, Lina Bo, *Casa de Vidro, The Glass House: São Paulo, Brasil, 1950–1951*, with text by Marcelo Carvalho Ferraz, trans. C. Stuart Birkinshaw, Lisbon: Editorial Blau; São Paulo: Instituto Lina Bo e P.M. Bardi, c.1999.

"Residential masterpieces: Lina Bo and P.M. Bardi: Casa de Vidro, São Paulo, Brazil 1951," *GA Houses*, no. 65 (November 2000): 10–25.

Dias Comas, Carlos Eduardo, "Casino, cobijo, capilla: tres casas de cristal modernas en Brasil," *Summa*, no. 50 (August–September 2001): 70–75.

da Costa Meyer, Esther, "After the flood: Lina Bo Bardi's Glass House," *Harvard Design Magazine*, no. 16 (Winter/Spring 2002): 4–13.

Dortignac, Geneviève, *World of Interiors*, London, 30, no. 5 (2010 May): 196–203.

Valéria P. Cirell House, Morumbi, São Paulo, 1958 ("Crystal Garden House" and La Torracia guest residence, 1964)

Ferraz, Marcelo Carvalho, "Valéria P. Cirell's home, São Paulo, Brazil 1958," *A + U: Architecture and Urbanism*, no. 2 (341) (February 1999): 34–41.

Taba Guaianases Building, São Paulo (unbuilt project)

Bardi, Lina Bo and Pier Luigi Nervi, "Il complesso Guajanazes a San Paolo," *Domus*, no. 282 (May 1953): 4–7.

Bardi, Lina Bo and Pier Luigi Nervi, "Taba Guaianases, São Paulo," *Habitat*, São Paulo, no. 14 (January–February 1954): 4–10.

MASP Avenida Paulista, São Paulo, 1957–1962; 1966–1969

"Museu de Arte di São Paolo del Brasile," *L'Architettura*, no. 210, Roma (April 1973).

"Museo de Arte de São Paulo," *A + U: Architecture and Urbanism*, no. 6 (1975): 51–66.

Bardi, Lina Bo, *Museu de Arte de São Paulo, 1957–1968*, with text by Aldo Van Eyck, Isa Grinspum Ferraz, ed. Blau Portfolio Series, São Paulo: Instituto Lina Bo e P.M. Bardi; Lisbon: Editorial Blau, 1997.

"Musée En Péril: Un Espace Trop Libre (MASP, Musée d'Art de São Paulo de Lina Bo Bardi)," *Architecture d'Aujourd'hui*, no. 320 (January 1999): 134–139.

"São Paulo Art Museum: São Paulo, Brazil 1957–1968," *A + U: Architecture and Urbanism*, no. 2 (341) (February 1999): 18–33.

Solar do Unhão, Bahia Museum of Modern Art and Folk Art, Salvador, Bahia, 1958–1963

Bardi, Lina Bo, "Popular Art Museum, Salvador de Bahia, Brazil 1959," *A+U: Architecture and Urbanism*, no. 2 (341) (February 1999): 42–47.

"Cultural Brazil—Bahia's Popular Art Museum," Washington, DC, USA (January 1964).

SESC—Pompéia Factory Leisure Center, São Paulo, 1977

Mariani, Riccardo, "Utilizzare l'architettura minore: San Paolo (Brasile), da una fabbrica," *Abitare*, no. 220 (December 1983): 64–67.

David, Theo, "Brazil: Old Brick Factory made into Recreation Center," *Architecture: The AIA Journal* 73, no. 9 (September 1984): 180–181.

"Centre Socio-Culturel Sesc Pompéia [São Paulo]: Lina Bo Bardi," *Architecture d'Aujourd'hui*, no. 251 (June 1987): 6–9.

"Gli Scabri Simboli Del passato/futuro [Sesc Pompéia, São Paulo]," *Architettura* (1988).

"Siete obras en Brazil," *ARS*, no. 11 (July 1989): 40–51.

Magnago Lampugnani, Vittorio, "Lina Bo Bardi: Centro Sociale e Sportivo 'Fábrica Pompéia,' San Paolo," *Domus*, no. 717 (June 1990): 56–57.

Magnavita, Paqualino, "Lina Bo Bardi: Salvador, uma paixão," *Projeto*, no. 155 (August 1992): 75–78.

Comas, Carlos Eduardo, "Centro De Recreación SESC–Pompeya, São Paulo, Brazil," *Escala* 30, no. 173 (1996): 50–52.

Bardi, Lina Bo, *Centro de Lazer, SESC, Fábrica Pompéia: São Paulo, Brasil, 1977–1986*, with texts by Cecília Rodrigues dos Santos, André Vainer, and Marcelo Carvalho Ferraz, São Paulo: Instituto Lina Bo e P.M. Bardi; Lisbon: Editorial Blau, 1998.

"SESC—Pompéia Factory Leisure Center, São Paulo, Brazil 1977," *A + U: Architecture and Urbanism* (February 1999): 54–71.

"Cidadela da Liberdade" (exhibition), November 19–December 30, 1999, SESC–Pompéia: Instituto Lina Bo e P.M. Bardi, 2002.

Corbioli, Nanci, "Revitalização Em Unidade do Sesc Preserva Projeto Original De Lina Bo Bardi," *Projeto*, no. 276 (February 2003): 78–80.

Espírito Santo do Cerrado Church, Uberlândia, Minas Gerais, 1976–1982

"Espírito Santo do Cerrado Church, Minas Gerais, Brazil 1976–1982," *A+U: Architecture and Urbanism*, no. 2 (341) (February 1999): 48–53.

Bardi, Lina Bo, *Igreja Espírito Santo do Cerrado: Uberlândia, Brasil, 1976–1982*, texts by Lina Bo Bardi and Edmar de Almeida, trans. C. Stuart Birkinshaw, Lisbon: Editorial Blau; São Paulo: Instituto Lina Bo e P.M. Bardi, c. 1999.

Salvador de Bahia, Interventions in the historic center, Salvador, Bahia, with João Filgueirias Lima, Marcelo Carvalho Ferraz and Marcelo Suzuki, 1986–1990

"Ladeira de misericórdia: plano piloto," *Projeto*, no. 133 (July 1990): 49–55.

Brazilian Pavilion, Universal Exposition of Seville, Spain, 1991 (unbuilt project by Lina Bo Bardi, Marcelo Carvalho Ferraz and Marcelo Suzuki, Francisco de Paiva Fanucchi)

"A grande caixa: un memorial para o homen do novo mundo," *Projeto*, no. 141 (May 1991): 78–80.

Film

Lina Bo Bardi directed by Aurélio Michiles; writing and editing by Isa Grinspum Ferraz, São Paulo: Instituto Lina Bo e P.M. Bardi, 1993.

Appendix 1

Senhor Professor,

By order of the office of Senhor Vice-Director, Prof. Pedro Bento José Gravina, I hereby direct to your excellency a copy of the Notice of Contest to fill the post of Professor of the Chair n.14 "Architecture Theory" of the 2nd-year of the course of Architecture in the Faculty.

I take the occasion to renew to your Excellency the assurance of my highest consideration and appreciation.

Paulo Quadri Prestes
Secretary

In accordance with the law—Federal n. 2.938, of 2 November, 1956— the following competition was organized by the "Egrégio Conselho Universitário," [Distinguished University Council] acting as a Congress for this Faculty:

A Elements of Architecture

1 Structural Elements. Continuous loads and Point loads. Wall and Column. Evolution of the periods, Classical, Byzantine, Romanesque, Gothic, Renaissance, Baroque, Neo-Classical, eclectic and contemporary. The trilithon and the arch. The truss and the morphology of modern structures of wood, steel and reinforced concrete. Economic structure, function and form.
2 Protective Elements. Membranes. Roofs. Terraces. Domes and vaults. Balustrades. Ceilings and floors.
3 Elements of Circulation. Openings. Doors and Windows and their evolution. Walkways, ramps, stairs and elevators and escalators.
4 Elements of Decoration. "Mother Nature": the touchstone of the architect. The law of Ornament. Color. Light. Texture. Living plants and flowers. Water.
5 Painting, Sculpture and their mutual relation. The problem of integrating the arts. Historical process.

B Elements of Aesthetics

1 Propaedeutic Philosophy.
2 Aesthetics: definition, objective and methods.
3 Art. Beauty. Taste. Style. Rhythm.
4 Impressionism and Dogmatism.

5 Principal Aesthetic Theories.

6 Psychological Aesthetics. Technique.

7 Sociological Aesthetics. Art and Society.

8 The Fine Arts.

9 Art, Industry and Machines.

C Concepts of Architecture

1 Definition of Architecture and Urbanism. Expression, correlation, integration and organic order. Exterior space and interior space.

2 Complexity of Architecture. Function, structure, economy. Fulfilling the emotional force of aesthetic synthesis, form and function. The "isms."

3 The setting and its atmospheric elements, thermal, lighting, acoustics, space and motion. Comfort. Metabolic equations.

4 Salubrity. The physically and spiritually healthy building. Aspects of health. Principles of the healthy home.

5 Elementary construction systems. The great constructions of culture. The battle against gravity and [horizontal] thrust. Vertebrae of the crustacean. Structure and equipment. Skeleton and selective membranes.

6 Steel, concrete, wood, glass and plastics. History and evolution.

7 Resistance and lifespan. Industrialization. Pre-fabrication. Standardization. Engineering and the link to the machine. Nature and its resistant forms.

8 Economy. Metaphysical sense. Purity of form and truth in construction. Monumentality and its problems today. Criteria for efficiencies.

9 Planning (programming) and manipulation of space. The plan as the generator. Biological concepts. Plans as determinates of social processes. Functional plans. Human scale.

10 Democracy and Habitation. Economic studies, civic debt, social problems.

D Aesthetics of Architecture

1 Architecture—Material expression of the soul of the people. The architect and his social function.

2 The impact of science and technology on architecture.

3 "Morphogenetic" factors of architecture.

4 Factors of the material order: climate, soil and materials.

5 Factors of the social and economic order: client, program and resources. Pricing. Regulations for construction and zoning. Standardization in construction and pre-fabrication. Urbanistic correlation between buildings.

6   Factors of the psychological order. "Parti," composition, proportions, scale, optical corrections.

7   Form and forms. The research of form. The creative instinct. Art and Nature. Expression, correlation, organic order. The aura of Form.

8   Form and time. Tradition. Style and styles.

9   Form and theory. Artistic education and its objectives.

10 Form and Theory. Artistic education and its objectives.
    [Items 9. and 10. repeated thus in the original.]

11 The evolution of Form. The life of Forms; architectural vocabulary. The spirit of Forms. Historic styles, structures and decorations. The "neos" and the "revivals." Eclectism. Contemporary Architecture.

12 Space—protagonist of Architecture. Space and its manipulation. The diverse conceptions of Space through History:

    a)   Ignorance of internal space and the human scale of the Greeks
    b)   The static and monumental space of the Romans
    c)   The human direction of Christian Space
    d)   The dilation and magical fluctuation of Byzantine Space
    e)   The rhythmic caesura of the pre-Romanesque epoch
    f)   The spatial metrics and structure of the Romanesque
    g)   The spatial continuity of the Gothic
    h)   Laws and measures of the rhythmic space of the Renaissance
    i)   Movement and interpenetration of the Baroque
    j)   Neo-Classical urban space
    k)   The free plan and organic space—contemporary period.

E Caractère of Buildings

1   Caractère: transformation of the program into a work of art; subjective qualities of architecture as expressions of the collective soul. Methods and bibliographical sources. Functional schemes.

2   Habitation. Elements of design. Elements of order in the environment, atmospheric, thermal, lighting, acoustics, space and motion. Structure and selected membranes. Mechanization and flexibility. The notion of comfort. Integration into the environment. The garden and green space.

3   Classification of Buildings. The social process as a determining factor of the plan. Development and integration of the various units, horizontally and vertically. Scheme for general classification. The social process. The corresponding type of plan. 1. Production. Factories. Slaughterhouses. 2. Energy, Dams, Powerplants. 3. Transport and Communications. Hydro system, road, railroad and air and their terminals, postal systems, telegraph, telephone, television and radio transmission. 4. Guard (Storage) Depots, warehouses, refrigerators, silos, tanks and reservoirs. 5. Exchanges. Shops, offices, markets,

banks and stock exchanges. 6. Directors, executive offices of the legislative and judicial powers. Municipalities and offices. 7. Protective. Detention facilities, services against fires. 8. Residences. Houses, apartments, hotels, tourism. 9. Education and Research. Schools, universities, laboratories, libraries, museums, botanical and zoological gardens. 10. Recreation. Parks, "playgrounds," stadiums, gymnasiums, spas, swimming pools. 11. Prevention and cure. Clinics, health centers, hospitals, asylums, reformatories, penitentiaries. 12. Worship. Chapels and churches. 13. Conservation or elimination of waste. Cemeteries, crematoria, sewage systems, incinerators, furnaces. 14. War. Military installations. Expression, correlation, and integration of these elements in the local region.

The deadline for applications is 21 September, 1957, at 10:00.

Secretary of the Faculty of Architecture and Urbanism of the University of São Paulo, 25 May, 1957.

Paulo Quadri Prestes
Secretary

A1.1 Cover Letter for the Notice of Contest for Chaired Professor n.14 in Architecture Theory, with handwritten note by Lina Bo Bardi © Institute Lina Bo and P.M.Bardi

UNIVERSIDADE DE SÃO PAULO FACULDADE DE ARQUITETURA E URBANISMO

Senhor Professor,

De ordem do Senhor Vice-Diretor em exercicio Prof. Pedro Bento José Gravina, tenho a honra de encaminhar a V.Excia., cópia do Edital de concurso para provimento do cargo de Professor Catedrático da cadeira nº14 "Teoria da Arquitetura". do 2º ano do curso de Arquitetura desta Faculdade.

Valho-me do ensejo para renovar a V.Excia. os meus protestos de elevada consideração e apreço.

Paulo Quadri Prestes
-Secretario-

A1.2 Competition Program, page 1. © Institute Lina Bo and P.M.Bardi

De acôrdo com que dispõe a Lei-Federal nº2.938, de 2 de novembro de 1956, foi organizado pelo Egrégio Conselho Universitário ,funcionando como Congregação desta Faculdade, o seguinte programa de concurso:

A) -Elementos de Arquitetura

1. -Elementos estruturais.

Apoio contínuo e isolado. O muro e a coluna. Evolução nos períodos clássico,bizantino,românico, gótico, do renascimento,barrôco,neo-clássico, eclético e contemporâneo. O trilito e o arco. A tesoura e o consolo.Morfologia das estruturas modernas de madeiras, aço e concreto armado. Função,estrutura,economia e forma.

2. - Elementos de proteção .

Membranas. Telhados. Terraços. Abóbodas e Cúpolas.Pendentes e Trompas. Balaustradas. Tetos e Pavimentos.

3.- Elementos de circulação .

Aberturas. Portas e Janelas e sua evolução.Passajens, Rampas, Escadas, Elevadores e Escaladores.

4.- Elementos de Decoração.

Modernatura: a pedra de toque do arquiteto. O ornato e suas leis. Côr, Luz.Texturas. A planta viva e a flor. A agua.

5).- Pintura,escultura e relações mutuas.

O problema da integração das artes.Processo Historico.

B) Elementos de Estetica .

1.- Propedêutica filosófica

2.- Estetica: definição, objeto e métodos.

3.- Arte.Belo.Gôsto.Estilo.Ritmo.

4.- Impressionismo e Dogmatismo.

5. As principais teorias estéticas.

6.- A estética psicologica . A técnica.

7.- A estética sociologica.Arte e sociedade.

8.- As Belas Artes.

9.- Arte, Industria e máquinas

A1.3 Competition Program, page 2. © Institute Lina Bo and P.M.Bardi

C).- Conceito de Arquitetura.

1).- Definição de Arquitetura e Urbanismo.Expressao, correlaçao, integração e ordem orgânica . Espaço interior e exterior.

2.- Complexidade do fato arquitetônico.Função, estrutura, economia. A
força emotiva realizadora da sintese estética.A forma e a função.
Os"ismos."

3.- O ambiente e seus elementos de ordem atmosférica,termal, luminosa,
sônica, espacial e animada.O conforto. Equação do metabolismo.

4.- A salubridade. O edificio e a saúde fisica e espiritual. A Saúde e
seus aspetos. Princípio da casa salubre.

5.- Os sistemas costrutivos elementares. As grandes culturas construti-
vas.A luta contra a gravidade e o impuxo.De crustaceo a vertebrado.
Estrutura e equipamento. Esqueleto e membranas selettivas.

6.- O aço, o concreto, a madeira, o vidro e os plasticos.Historico e
evolução.

7.- Resistencia e longevidade. Industrialização. Pre-fabricação.Tipisa-
ção.Normalização. A engenharia e a lição da maquina.A natureza e sua
formas resistentes.

8.- A economia.Sentido metafisico.Pureza de forma e sinceridade constru-
tiva.Monumentalidade e seus problemas hodiernos. Criterios de efici
eficiencias.

9.- Planejamento e manipulaçao do espaço.O plano como gerador. Conceito
biologico.Processos sociais como determinantes dos planos. Esquemas
funcionais. Escala humana.

10.- Democracia e Habitação.Estudo economico, dever civico, problema soci
social.

D).- Estetica da Arquitetura.

1.- Arquitetura-expressao material da alma dos povos.O arquiteto e sua
funçao social.

2.- Impacto da ciencia e da tecnologia.sobre a arquitetura.

3.- Os fatores morfogeneticos da arquitetura.

4.- Fatores de ordem material:clima, solo e materiais.

A1.4 Competition Program, page 3. © Institute Lina Bo and P.M.Bardi

5.) Fatores de ordem social e economica:cliente, programa e recursos.
Preços.Regulamento de construção e zoneamento.Normalização industria
e prefabricação.Correlação urbanistica entre edificios.

6.- Fatores de ordem psicológica. Partido, composição, proporções, escala, correções oticas.

7.- A Forma e as Formas. A pesquiza da forma.Instinto criador. Arte e
natureza. Expressão, correlação, ordem organica. A aura da Forma.

8.- A Forma e o tempo. A tradição. Os Estilo e os Estilos.

9.- A Forma e a teoria. Educação artistica e seus objetivos.

10.- A Forma e a Teoria. Educação artistica e seus objectivos.

11.- A evolução das Formas. A vida das Formas: vocabularió do arquiteto.
O espirito e as Formas. Os estilos historicos, estruturais e decora
tivos.Os "neos" ou "revivals". Ecletismo. Arquitetura contemporanea

12.- O Espaço protagonista da Arquitetura. Oespaço e sua manipulação.
As diversas concepções espaciais, atraves da Historia:

a) a ignorancia do espacio interno e a escala humana dos gregos;

b) o espaço estatico e monumental dos romanos;

c) a diretriz humana do espaço cristão;

d) a dilatação e flutuação magica do espaços bizantino;

e) a cezura ritmica da epoca pre-romanica;

f) a metrica espacial e a estrutura romanica;

g) a continuidade espacial da epoca gotica;

h) leise medida do espaço ritmico renascentista;

i) movimen to e'interpenetração do espaço barroco;

j) o espaço urbanistico neo-classico;

k) o plano livre e o espaço organico da epoca atual.

E) Caraterol os Edificios
Caraterologia

1.- Carater: trasformação do programa em obra de arte; qualidade subjeti
va do arquiteto nas expressões das alma coletiva. Metodos e fontes
bibliograficas.Esquemas funcionais.

2.- A habitação. Elementos da composição. Elementos do ambiente de ordem
atmosferica, termal, luminosa, sonica;espacial e animada.
Estrutura e membrana seletiva.Mecanização eflexibilidade. O conceito

A1.5 Competition Program, page 4. © Institute Lina Bo and P.M.Bardi

O conceito de conforto.A integração dos ambiente. O Jardim e o verde.

3.- Classificação dos edificios. O processo social como determinante do
plano.Desenvolvimento e integração das diversas unidades, horizontal
e verticalmente.

Esquema de classificação geral. Processo social Tipo de plano corre-
spondente. 1.Produção.Fabricas, Matadouros.2.Energia, Barragens,usina
3.Transportes e comunicações.Sistema de hidro, rodo, ferro e areovias
e suas terminais;sistemas postais, telegraficas, telefonicos, radio
emissão e televisão.4 Guarda(Storage) Depositos, armazens, frigorifi
cos, silos, tanques e reservatorios.5 Trocas.Lojas, escritórios, mer-
cados, bancos e bolsas. 6. Administração, sedes dos poderes executivo
legislativos e judiciarios.Autarquias e escritorios.7. Proteção. Casa
de detenção,servicio contra incendios.8.Residencias.Casas,apartamento
hoteis, campos de turismo.9. Educação e pesquiza.Escolas, Universidade
laboratorios, bibliotecas,museus, jardins botanicos e zoologicos,10. R
creio. Parque, "playgrounds", estadios, ginasios, balnearios,piscinas.
11. Prevenção e cura.Clinicas, centros de saude, hospitais, azilos, re-
formatorios,penitenciarias.12.Adoração. Capelas, igrejas.13. Conserva-
ção ou eliminação de residuos. Cemiterios, crematorios, sistemas de
esgotos, fornos incineradores.14.Guerra.Instalações militares.
Expressão, Correlação, e Integração desses elementos nos planos regi
local e regional.

O encerramento das inscriçoes termina no dia 21 de Setembro de 1957, as
10 horas.
Secretaria daFaculdade de Arquitetura e Urbanismo daUniversidade de Sao
Paulo, em 25 de Maio de 1957.

                                    Paulo Quadri Prestes
                                       -Secretario-

SYLLABUS OF THE COURSE OF DECORATIVE COMPOSITION (INTERIOR DESIGN; INDUSTRIAL DESIGN)

Introduction

The environment of Man. (Habitation, collective buildings, stores, etc.) in relation with the proportions of human body. General Composition.

The main element of composition: "Furniture".

The study of "measures" and various constructive techniques; properties of materials (steel, wood, fabrics, etc.)

Relations between furniture and the environment: colors, fabrics, coating materials, stained glass, plants, curtains, rugs etc.

Historical summaries of the Epochs and Decorative Styles

The three weekly hours will be divided as follows:

1st 50 minutes of class: projections or drawings on the blackboard, referring to past styles or elements of contemporary composition. Little exhibitions dedicated to the history of the chair, of ceramics, glass, etc. will be organized by the students in a location of the University under the direction of the Professor. The material will be borrowed from the architect Lina Bardi. (Collection of vintage fabrics etc.)

2nd The rest of the time in class will be dedicated to drawing, studies, projects and the execution of models.

A catalog of materials will be organized during the course.

Visits will be organized to studios and furniture factories, for the students to acquire direct knowledge of different methods of production and work with materials.

At the end of the year, each student will have executed a model of a piece of furniture of their own design selected by the Professor.

A2.1 Course Syllabus: Decorative Composition (Interior Design, Industrial Design) signed "Lina Bo" © Institute Lina Bo and P.M.Bardi

lina bo

Programa curso Composição Decorativa (Arquitetura de Interiores
Desenho Industrial)

Introdução

O Ambiente do Homem.(habitação, edificios coletivos, lojas,etc.)Seu raporto
com as proporcoõs do corpo humano.Generalidades compositivas.
O elemento principal da composição" O Movel".
Estudo das "medidas" e das diversas tecnicas construtivas;propriedades dos
materiaes (ferro, madeira, tecidos etc.)
Raporto dos moveis com o ambiente: cõres, fazendas, materiaes de revestimento,
vitraes,plantas vivas, cortinas, tapetes etc.
Resumo historico das Epocas e dos Estilos decorativos.

As tres horas semanais serão assim divididas:

                                        1º 50 minutos de aula com
                                           projeções ou desenhos
                                           ao quadro negro, referente
                                           seja aos Estilos do passado
                                           seja aos elementos da com-
                                           posição contemporanea.
Serão organizadas pelos estudantes mesmo num local da Universidade sob a orienta
ção do Professor, pequenas exposições dedicadas a historia da cadeira,das
ceramicas, vidros etc. O material será emprestado pelo arquiteto Lina Bardi.
Coleção de tecidos antigos etc.

                                        2º Orestante tempo, até a fim da
                                           aula será dedicado ao desenho
                                           estudos, projetos e execução de
                                           maquete.

Será organizado durante o curso um mostruario de materiaes.
Serão organiz das visitas a oficinas e fabricas de moveis, fazendasxtapetes
xxterinsxxdxx para os alunos ter conhecimentos direto com os diferentes metodos
de produção e trabalho dos materiais.

Cada estudante no fim do ano academico terá que ter executado uma maquete dum
movel por ele projetado e escolhido pelo professor.

CHAIR: DECORATIVE COMPOSITION (5TH YEAR)

Number of theory and practice classes advisable for the efficient development of the chair in my office.

A   1st A Theory class every week, (of a minimum of one hour) for the development of the didactics program referring to the subject, that is:

  – Professional Techniques of planning for "decoration" (Interior Design and Decorative Compositions in gardens, exhibitions etc. . . .) Establishment of the project and practical details for its execution.
  – Detailed analysis of the diverse organisms (residences, collective buildings, studies, meetings etc.), all studied from the point of view of "decoration" (Interior Design).
  – Presentation of the problems of the "industrial design," basic measures for furniture design etc.
  – Short history of diverse decorative styles and the "applied arts."

B   2nd The weekly class will be illustrated with projections (of books, magazines, original prints etc.) and drawings made by the professor on the blackboard.

C   Practice class (minimum, three hours) for "application," the execution of a complete project of decoration (year-long project), with technical and decorative details, samples of materials etc.

   Every month an "extemporaneous" test will be given; the subject will be taken from one of the theory classes of the month (historical, technical or decorative).

D   Visits to factories and workshops will be planned for practical demonstration of work and execution.

E   During the three weekly hours, students will make models of the furniture projects they have designed that have been chosen by the professor.

F   It is absolutely necessary, in order to make good use of the practice classes, to present material catalogs (fabrics, coatings, woods, metals, ceramics, colors etc.).

A year's teaching experience in the chair of "Decorative Composition" demonstrated to the professor the potential of the students, which is great from any point of view, but is undermined because of the lack of space and

A2.2 Self-assessment of 5th year course in Decorative Composition © Institute Lina Bo and P.M.Bardi

Cadeira : Composição Decorativa (v- ano)

Número de aulas teoricas e práticas recomendavel para um eficiente
desenvolvimento da cadeira a meu cargo.

A   1º Uma aula teórica por semana,(de uma hora no minimo) para o desenvolvimento do programa didatico referente a materia, seja:
           Tecnica profissional de planejamento para "decorações" (archi-
tetura de interiores e composições decorativas em jardims, exposições etc)
impostação do projeto e detalhes praticos para execução.
           Analise em detalhe dos diversos organismos ,(residencias, edifi-
cios coletivos, de estudos,de reunião etc. todos estudados do ponto de vista
da "decoração" (arquitetura de Interiores).
           Apresentação dos problemas do "desenho industrial", medidas ba-
sicas para projeto de moveis etc.
           Pequena historia dos diversos estilos decorativos e das "artes
aplicatas".

B   2º A aula semanal teorica será ilustrada com projeções (de livros, revistas
gravuras originaes etc.) e desenhos feitos pelo professor mesmos no quadro
negro.
C   Aula pratica (de tres horas no minimo) para a "aplicação",seja a execução
de um projeto completo de decoração (trabalho do ano), comdetalhes tecnicos e
decorativos,amostras de materiais etc.
    Cada mez será feita uma prova "ex-tempore" para aproveitamato; o assunto será
tirado duma das aulas teoricas do mez (historica, tecnica o decorativa).
D   Serõ programada visitas em fabricas e oficinas para a demonstração pratica de
trabalho e execução.
E   Nas tres horas semanais serão feitas pelos alunos as maquetes de alguns dos
moveis por eles projetados e escolhidos pelo professor.
F   é absolutamente necessaria pelo bom aproveitamento das aulas praticas a ajuda
de um assistente.
G   É necessario escolher um local o uma parede para apresentação de um mostruario
de mate riais (fazendas, revestimentos, madeiras, metais,ceramicas cores etc.).

O balanço de um ano de ensino na cadeira de "Composição Decorativa" deu ao
professor a demonstração das possibilidades dos alunos, otimas sb qualquer
pontos de vista,mas obstaculadas pela falta de espaço e de organização do
trabalhos e pelaexiguidade do tempo a disposiçã (uma hora a mais ar uma
aula teorica resolveria a situação, deixando livres para a parte pratica as tres
horas atuais.) A presença de um assistente ajudaria o professor na tarefa das
explicações e esclarescimentos necessarios aos alunos nas tres horas de trabalhos praticos.

organization of the work and the shortness of the time at our disposal (one hour more for theory would solve the issue, leaving free, for practice, the actual three hours). The presence of an assistant would help the professor with the tasks of providing explanations and necessary clarifications to the students during the three hours of practice.

SYLLABUS FOR THE COURSE OF INDUSTRIAL DESIGN

1st part of the course

The function of "furniture" in human habitation. Study of the functional characteristics of each type of furniture. (The study will have a practical character, with drawings and general diagrammatic studies. In parallel, there will be a series of lectures with slides, drawings, illustrating the main characteristics of furniture and of habitation in our time.

2nd part of the course

Furniture in its organism

Study of the materials' behavior, the plastic composition of furniture in relation to function. Practice exercises of composition, design, detail. (There will be a series of visits to workshops for carpentry, upholstery, mechanical systems, to see real work being executed.)

Design of furniture in relation to its details: curtains, rugs, paintings, plants etc.

At the end of the course, each student will have executed one model of a piece of furniture designed by the student and selected by the professor. (The model should be made in the studio of the school, if possible, or in a laboratory outside the school rented for a few hours per week).

During the course, a permanent catalog of the materials related to decoration and furnishing will be constituted: fabrics, rugs, wood, glass, etc.

A2.3 Course Syllabus: Industrial Design © Institute Lina Bo and P.M.Bardi

Pro.ram.   para um curso de Desenho Industrial

1ª turno o curso

A função do "movel" na abitaçaõ humana.Estudo dos carateres funcionais de cada
tipo de movel.(O estudo terá caratere pratico com desenhos e estudos distributivos
generais). Paralelmente será feita uma serie de conferencias com projeções desenhos
ilustrando os carateres principais dos moveis e da habitaçaõ no tempo.

2º turno do curso

O Movel no seu Organismo.
Estudo do comportamento dos materiaes, composiçaõ plastica dos moveis em raporto da
funçaõ. Exercitações praticas de composiçaõ, desenho, detalhe.(Será feita uma serie
de visitas em olicinas de Madeiras, Estofamento, Mecanicas, para ver na realidade
o trabalho executivo).
Composiçaõ do movel em raporto nos detalhes:cortinas , tapetes,quadros, plantas vivas etc.

Ao terminar o curso onde estudante deverá ter executado uma maquete dum movel projetado por ele e escolhido pelo professor.(O trabalho da maquete será feito na oficina da escola se tiver ou num laboratorio fora da escola e emprestado por algumas
horas por semana.

Será constituido durante o curso um mostruário permanente dos materiais relativos
a decoraçaõ e amobiliamento: fazondas, tapetes, madeiras, vidros etc.

THEORY OF ARCHITECTURE 1 (PROPAEDEUTIC COURSE RELATED TO ART HISTORY)

Critical terminology. Properties of the critical language. Issues of method. Definitions. Critical analysis of buildings.

Reconstruction (using photography) of the architectural organisms and their spatial values, structural elements, and history.

Reconstruction of the process of historic-critical creation of a Brazilian architectural organism from the past (individual work). Design of the same organism in plan, elevation, sections, axonometric views. "Collective" critical discussion of each work.

Theory of Architecture 2

Characters of Buildings

Subdivision of the Architectural Organisms (for methodological purposes) into groups. Analysis of the diverse groups; freehand drawings, and global analytical study of the chosen examples (by "global" it should be understood that the study does not separate structural, urbanistic, historical and "tradition" components). The classes will have the character of seminars, with collective discussions, slide projections, drawings made on the blackboard and with colored pencil on large sheets of paper.

Particular character of the course Caracter of Buildings. Theory of Architecture 2 will emphasize the graphic–analytical application (freehand drawings of a large number of examples of architectural organisms, executed by each student, in plans, sections and spatial axonometrics, taken from books, photography, publications), material that will constitute the basis for a professional portfolio in the future.

Presentation (by each student) of a modern architectural organism, studied in all its spatial characteristics, diagrammatic, structural, technical functions and "historic" value. The work will be comprised of a critical written comparison and "linear" drawings (without shadows and light–dark or color effects) aiming for a perfect understanding, on the part of the students, of the chosen architectural example in its aesthetic expression, in its diagrammatic technical solution, in its urban integration and in its historical value.

A2.4 Course Syllabus: Theory of Architecture 1 (Propaedeutic Course Related to Art History) with handwritten notes and corrections by Lina Bo Bardi © Institute Lina Bo and P.M.Bardi

Teoria da Arquitetura 1º (Curso prepedeutico ligado a Historia da Arte).
Termine da critica. "Propriedade" da linguagem critica. Problemas de Metodo. Definições.
Analisi critica des edificios.
Restituição prospetida (de fotografias) des organismes arquitetexices nes valeres
espaciais, nes elementes estruturais, e nas ceerdfnadas histericas.
Reconstituição de precesse de criação historico-critica de um
organisme i arquitetexice brasileire de passade. (trabalho individual). Desenho de mesme organisme en planta,
elevação, certes, vistas assenemetricas. Discussãe critica "celetiva" de cada traba-
lhe.
                    Teoria da Arquitetura 2º
Caracteres des Edificies.
Subdivisãe des Organismes Arquitetexices (cem fins puramente metedelegices) en grupes.
Analisik des diverses grupes; cen desenhes a "mãe livre", e estude global analitico
des exemples escelhides, (cem "global" entendemes e estude nãe avulse das cempenentes
estruturais, urbanisticas, histericas e de costume. As aulas terãe caratere "seminari"
de seminarie, cem discussãe celetiva, prejecãe de slides, desenhes ae quadre
negre e en lapis de cer sebre grandes felhas de papel.
Carater peculiar de curse caraxteres des edificies 2º será a grande impertancia
dada à aplicaçãe grafice-analitica (desenhes a mãe livre de grande numere de ergantes
nismes arquitetexice, executades per cada alune, en plantas, certes e assenemetrias
espaciais, tirades de livres publicações), material que censtituirá ne future, a base
de ficharie de pesquisa da vida prefissienal.
Apresentaçãe (de cada alune) de um edificixexxx organisme arquitetexice mederne brasileire, (per causa de praxis imediate) estudade (en teda as carateristicas espaciais,
distributivas, estruturais, de funcienamente tecnice, e validade "histerica". O trabalhe
será censtituide de uma relaçãe escrita (critica) e de desenhes "lineares" (sem sembras
e sem efeites de clare-escure eu de cer) visande a perfeita per parte des
cenjunte arquitetexice na sua expressãe estetica, e na sua integraçãe urbanistica e na
sua validade histerica.

THEORY OF ARCHITECTURE 1 (PROPAEDEUTIC COURSE IN THE THEORY OF ARCHITECTURE): SUMMARY

1 Meaning and methodology of a historical analysis of the aesthetic theories.
2 Antiquity: Plato; Aristotle, old Neo-Platonism (Plotinus), Christianity (St. Augustine).
3 Middle Ages: The Scholastics and St. Thomas Aquinas.
4 Humanism and Renaissance (Neo-Platonism and Aristotelianism).
5 Rationalism of the seventeenth and eighteenth centuries (of Descartes and Diderot).
6 European Romanticism and its assumptions.
7 Hegel and Hegelianism.
8 Marxist aesthetics.
9 Critical panorama of contemporary currents (neo-positivism; Phenomenology, Existentialism).

Readings
Suggested texts (to be completed)

Excerpts:
 Plato (*Republic* and *Symposium*)
 Aristotle (*Poetics*) Cicero (*De oratore; Tusculunae Disputationes*)
 Plotinus (*Enneads*). Saint Augustine.
 St. Thomas Aquinas
 Leon Battista Alberti
 Marsilio Ficino (comments on Plato's *Symposium*)
 Giordano Bruno (*De Gli Eroici Furori*)
 Benvenuto Cellini (*La Vita*)
 Descartes (*Discourse on Method*)
 Lessing (*Laocoon*); Diderot (*Treatise on the Beautiful*)
 Shaftesbury (various Excerpts); Vico (*Scienza Nuova*)
Herder (on Poetry); Goethe (various Excerpts), Schiller (Writings on Aesthetics); Brothers Schlegel (Lessons. Characteristics and critiques).
Hegel (Aesthetics); Croce (*Breviario di estetica*)
Scott
Marx and Engels; Lukács; Gramsci
Readings on the latest aesthetic-critical currents.

A2.5 Course Syllabus: Theory of Architecture 1 (Propaedeutic Course in the Theory of Architecture) with handwritten notes and corrections by Lina Bo Bardi © Institute Lina Bo and P.M.Bardi

Teoria da Arquitetura 1°

SUMÁRIO DE ~~HISTÓRICA~~ (*Propedeutica à Teoria da arquitetura*)

1 – Sentido e metodologia de uma análise histórica das teorias estéticas.

2 – A Antiguidade: Platão, Aristóteles, Neo-platonismo antigo (~~Platão~~). *Plotino;*

2b – Cristianismo(Stº. Agostinho).

3 – Idade Média: A Escolástica e Stº. Tomás de Aquino.

4 – Humanismo e Renascença: (Neo-platonismo e Aristotelismo).

5 – O Racionalismo dos séculos XVII e XVIII (de Descartes e Diderot).

6 – O Romantismo europeu e seus pressupostos.

7 – Hegel e o hegelianismo.

8 – A Estética marxista.

9 – Panorama crítico das correntes contemporâneas(neo-positivismo; Fenomenologia; Existencialismo).

LEITURAS

França   Textos sugeridos (~~a completar~~) (*a completar*)

Trechos de: Platão(República e Banquete)

Aristóteles(Poética). Cícero (De oratore;)Tusculanae Disputationes).

Plotino ———— ~~Platão~~(Eneadas). Stº. Agostinho.

Stº Tomás de Aquino(Suma teológica).

Leon Battista Alberti;~~Moralia~~

(*Marsilio*)   Ficino(Comentário ao Banquete de Platão); *Eroici* Giordano Bruno (~~Eroci~~ Furori);

. Benvenuto Cellini(vita)

Descartes(Discurso sôbre o Método);

Lessing(Laocoonte); Diderot(Ensaio sôbre o Belo).

Shaftesbury; Vico(Scienza Nuova Seconda); (*Trechos várias*)

Herder (sôbre Poesia popular);Goethe; Schiller(Escritos sôbre Estética); *Irmãos* Schlegel(Lições Caracteristicas e críticas).

Hegel(Estética); Croce(Breviario de Estética);

Marx e Engels(~~~~); *Lukács; Gramsci –*

(*Trechos vários*);

UNIVERSITY EXTENSION COURSE CONTRIBUTION TO A TECHNICAL HUMANISM

The term "technical," adopted to describe the courses, was in a sense trying to make the problems of History, of Art (plastic arts, architecture, music) accessible to all serious professionals, according to a criterion not academic-abstract, but, as it were, vital and concrete. Hence the presence not only of experts but students and laureates of various faculties.

I History of Aesthetics

The term "aesthetics" adopted to characterize this course must not be understood in the traditional way, as "philosophy of art," but as a synthesis of theory and practice; that is why it includes not only the ideas that history, in its many periods, holds with reference to art, but also "Art History" and history, in general, in its many aspects, such as history of culture. Once Art History is separated from the theories that correspond to it, or these theories themselves have no historical concretization through artistic activity, they represent an abstraction outside of any historical continuity and are deprived of any actual interest.

I

1   Delimitation of the concept of aesthetics. Historical-critical methodology. "There is no present without the past, or past without the present."

2,3   The contemporary problematic and the issue with its origins. The historical process and the problem of its coherent development.

II

4   Plato and *mimesis*. The arts in *The Republic*.

5   Aristotle and *Poetics*. The function of the tragedy.

6   The neo-platonic concept of Beauty.

7   The Christian-medieval vision. General concepts.

8   Aesthetic ideas of the Patristics.

9,10   The scholastic aesthetics. St. Thomas Aquinas.

11   Italian Humanism.

12,13,14	From the Renaissance to the Baroque. The influence of the Aristotle's *Poetics*. Giordano Bruno and Poetry. Cartesian anti-aesthetics?
15	The meaning of the Counter-Reformation.
16	The baroque theories.
17,18,19,20	The eighteenth century and the Enlightenment. Diderot. Baumgarten. The doctrines about "beauty and the sublime." Shaftesbury. G.B. Vico. Lessing. Schiller and Goethe. Neo-classicism: Winckelmann.
21	Kant.
22	Schelling.
23,24	Hegel.
25,26	The romantic movement and its meaning. The ideal of "aesthetic man" and the moral and religious demands. Kierkegaard.
27,28	The second half of the nineteenth century. Positivism. Naturalistic aesthetics. Marxist aesthetics.
29,30	Neo-Kantian theories, psychologists, eclectics. Vischer, Groos and others. Wölfflin: "The pure visibility."
31,32,33	Contemporary historicism. De Sanctis. The aesthetics of B. Croce. The Gentilean Actual Idealism and the problem of feeling.
34	Aesthetics Today.

All the lectures will be accompanied by color slide projections and followed by debates.

Parallel to the course on the History of Aesthetics, the following items will be developed:

I Architecture and Industrial design course. (This course will be specifically dedicated to engineering, architecture, philosophy and linguistics students and laureates, but auditors from other schools will also be admitted)

II Special Lectures on subjects from other courses. For example, Greek Architecture, The Counter-Reformation (with examples taken from the colonial Portuguese–Brazilian architecture).

Guest lecturers will be invited, in exchange with national and foreign universities (such as the University of Bahia).

A didactic exhibition will be organized in connection with the courses.

A3.1 Course Syllabus for a University Extension Course: Contribution to a Technical Humanism, p.1 © Institute Lina Bo and P.M.Bardi

CURSOS DE EXTENSÃO UNIVERSITARIA :

Contribuição a um humanismo tecnico

O termo "tecnico" adotado para caracterizar êstes cursos corresponde em certo sentido á tentativa de colocar os problemas da Historia, da Arte (artes plasticas, arquitetura, música) ao alcance de todos os professionistas serios, segundo um criterio não acadêmico-abstrato,mas por assim dizer, vital e concreto. Daí a presença não só de"especialistas " mas de estudantes e laureados de varias faculdades.

I- Historia da Estética

O termo "estética" adotado para caracterizar êste curso, não deve ser entendido no sentido tradicional, como "filosofia da arte", mas como uma síntese de teoria e prática, incluindo, pois, não somente as ideias que , no decorrer da historia, em seus varios períodos, vigoraram com referência à arte, mas também a propria "Historia da arte" e evidentemente a historia em geral, em seus varios aspectos, como, digamos, historia da cultura, já que a historia da arte separada das teorias que lhe correspondem, ou estas teorias em si sem a concretização historica da atividade artistica, representariam uma abstração avulsa da continuidade historica e destituida de interesse atual.

I.

1. Delimitação do conceito de estética. Metodologia histórico -critica
   "Não há presente sem passado, nem passado sem presente".

2,3. A problematica contemporânea e o problema de suas origens. O sentido
   do processo histórico e o problema da coerencia de seu desenvolvimento.

II.

4. Platão e a mimesis. As artes na "República".

5. Aristóteles e a Poética . A função da ~~tragedia~~ tragedia.

6. O conceito neo-platonico de Beleza .

7. A visão cristã-medieval. Conceitos gerais.

8. As ideias estéticas da Patristica.

9, 10. A estética escolástica. Sto. Tomaz de Aquino.

11. O humanismo italiano.

12,13,14. Da Renascênça ao Barroco. A influência da Poética aristotélica.
   Giordano Bruno e a Poesia. Anti-estética cartesiana?

15. A significação da Contra-Reforma.

16. As teóricas barrocas.

17,18,19,20. O século XVIIIe o iluminismo. Diderot. Baumgarten.

A3.2 Course Syllabus for a University Extension Course: Contribution to a Technical Humanism, p.2 © Institute Lina Bo and P.M.Bardi

As doutrina acreca do "belo e do sublime". Shaftesbury. G.B.Vico. Lessing. Schiller e Goethe. O neo classicismo : Winckelmann.

     21. Kant.

     22. Schelling.

     23,24. Hegel

     25,26. O movimento romântico e seu sentido. O ideal do "homem estético" e as exigências morais e religiosas. ~~Kirkegaard~~ Kierkegaard.

     27,28. A segunda metade do século XIX. O Positivismo. As esteticas naturalisticas. A estética marxista .

  29,30. Teorias neo-kantianas, psicologistas, ecléticas . Vischer, Groos e outros. Wölfflin. A "pura visibilidade".

     31, 32,33. O historicismo contemporâneo. De Sanctis. A estetica de B. Croce. O atualismo gentiliano e o problema do sentimento.

       34. Algumas estéticas hodiernas.

Todas as palestras serão acompanhadas por projeções em cores e seguidas ~~pelos debates~~ debates.

A3.3 Course Syllabus for a University Extension Course: Contribution to a Technical Humanism, p.3 © Institute Lina Bo and P.M.Bardi

Paralelamente ao crso de Historia de Estética serão desenvolvidos:

II- Curso de arquitetura e industrial design. (x Este curso será especial-

mente dedicado a estudantes e laureados de engenharia, arquitetura,
Filosofia e letras , mas serão também admitidos ouvintes de xxx outras
escolas);

III. Conferências especiais, sôbre determinados assuntos tratados nos outros

cursos. Por exemplo; a arquitetura grega ,. a arquitetura da contra-reforma (com exemplos extraid s da arquitetura colonial luso-brasileira).

Serão convidados tambem conferencistas do Exterior , em interbambio
com universidades nacionais e estrangeiras (om por exemplo a Universidade da Bahia).
Serão organizadas mostras didáticas em conexão com os cursos.

Typewritten notes: "University Extension Course: Contribution to a Technical Humanism" Source: FAU/USP Architectural Library

INDEX

Page numbers in *italic* refer to illustrations, those followed by a letter n refer to notes.